# The desirable body

# THE DESIRABLE BODY

## Cultural fetishism
## and the erotics of consumption

Jon Stratton

Manchester University Press
Manchester and New York

distributed exclusively in the USA and Canada by St. Martin's Press

*Published by* Manchester University Press
Oxford Road, Manchester M13 9NR, UK
*and* Room 400, 175 Fifth Avenue, New York, NY 10010, USA

*Distributed exclusively in the USA and Canada*
*by* St. Martin's Press, Inc. 175 Fifth Avenue, New York, NY 10010, USA

*British Library Cataloguing-in-Publication Data*
A catalogue record is available from the British Library

*Library of Congress Cataloging-in-Publication Data applied for*

ISBN 0 7190 4701 3 *hardback*

First published 1996
00   99   98   97   96        10   9   8   7   6   5   4   3   2   1

Typeset in Aldus
by Koinonia, Manchester
Printed in Great Britain
by Bookcraft (Bath) Ltd

# Contents

# Acknowledgements

Many people have helped and supported me in many different ways during the period of this project. I would particularly like to thank Ien Ang, Ron Blaber, David Buchbinder, Rita Felski, Lynette Finch, Ann McGuire, Wendy Parkins, Grace Saw, Grant Stone, and Catherine Waldby, all of whom have read chapters – and in some cases the entire manuscript – making suggestions, providing emotional support, and being there when I needed to discuss ideas or, as I fear was all too often the case, complain about the difficulty of the task I had set myself. I would also like to thank Barbara Creed, who kindly sent me an unpublished copy of her paper 'From Doll to Dentata: Images of Women in Surrealist Art and the Cinema'.

I have greatly enjoyed working with Anita Roy at Manchester University Press; it would be difficult to surpass her editorial firmness and sensitivity when asking for the manuscript to be edited down by 30,000 words! Her readers must also be thanked for their sympathetic understanding of this project, particularly Jo Hodge, whose report on an early version was so suggestive but who, I am sure, will hardly recognise the published book. Thanks must also go to Terri-Ann White for the editing work she laboured so hard on whilst I was in Hawai'i. I would like to gratefully acknowledge the general support I have received from the School of Communication and Cultural Studies at Curtin University of Technology, in particular the helpfulness of the School Administrator, Sally Carter. I would like to thank the School and the University for enabling me substantially to edit the manuscript whilst on a semester's sabbatical, and the Program for Cultural Studies at the East–West Center in Honolulu, Hawai'i, where part of that sabbatical was taken. Geoff White, the Program's director, was an admirable host. The School of Humanities at Murdoch University generously funded the index. Thanks must also go to Andrew Wernick for sending me a transparency of the Braggi advertisement which he has analysed and which I have reanalysed in Chapter 6. Unfortunately, in the end, due to financial constraints the book had to be published without images.

Finally, I must give tremendous thanks to Helen Mumme, who keyed in this manuscript time and again in its various forms. Her patience, good humour, ability to read execrably scrawled notes and correct atrocious spelling, and her preparedness to work at awkward times have all been extraordinary.

It should go without saying that none of the people mentioned above are responsible in any way for the uses to which I have put their comments and suggestions. I, alone, am responsible for the final result.

# Introduction

This book is about the transformation in the experience of the body which occurs around the middle of the nineteenth century. What I am seeking an account for is the male eroticisation and spectacularisation of the female body that takes place in this period, at the same time that the male body is conscientiously hidden from view. In the late 1960s and 1970s the male body also becomes spectacularised – and, along with that spectacularisation, there has been the new experience of the male body as, from a male point of view, problematically eroticised. The book argues that the male eroticisation of the female body is one example of a more general structure founded on a culturally produced aspect of male desire which is the product of a male psychosexual fetishistic formation. I call this structure cultural fetishism. By now it should be clear that the ideas of psychoanalysis are important to my argument. In addition to outlining this fetishistic structure, I will examine how it has become allied with the capitalist requirement to increase consumption, something which has become paramount to capitalism since the spread of mass-production techniques in the early part of the twentieth century.

What I describe in this book is a phenomenon which, in the first instance, applies specifically to people living in 'Western' nation-states, by which I mean those nation-states in which the imbricated relation of the Enlightenment tradition of thought with capitalism, and with the accession to cultural power of the bourgeoisie, have been central. (This is the sense in which I shall use the term throughout the book.) I am, therefore, writing about the nation-states of western, central, and southern Europe and their settler colonies. It needs to be added that, whilst I write about the experience of cultural fetishism throughout these states in a manner which neither marks clearly the different historical trajectories of cultural fetishism in these different countries nor acknowledges the possibility of local inflections of the structure, both of these are important specificities which require recognition and further investigation. Furthermore, the spread of Euro-American practices is leading to complex inflections of the theme of this book in other parts of the world.

There are two more points that I need to establish clearly right at the beginning so that there can be no confusion. The first is that the main direction of this book is to outline the major parameters of a structure which overdetermines the experience, for both women and men, of living in the Western nation-state. To this end I am not so much concerned with the ways in which women and men make sense of this structure, position themselves in relation to it, express or resist it. In short, my interest is not, in the first place, in the subject as an active participant in the structure. Rather, I am concerned to outline the structure itself, and the main, general effects which it has had on those who have been interpellated by it. Following on from this, whilst the book is very much concerned with sexual difference – women and men, women's bodies and men's bodies – this is not an area that the book theorises. I am principally concerned with bodies, and I take the everyday distinctions between male bodies and female bodies – which have also been central to psychoanalysis – as my starting point, precisely because it is the cultural formation which overdetermines the everyday experience of the body that I am writing about. I must add that, whilst 'sex' is central to the argument of this book, 'race' is not. In the main, race is an unmarked category in this book. My typical male and female bodies are both 'white'. Whilst the question of how 'race' impacts on the structure I am describing is of very great importance, I simply have no room to discuss it here.

A bald assertion: the Freudian theorisation of the psychosexual development of the individual and of the effects of sexual desire are historically and culturally specific. Where psychoanalysis claims to provide a generalised understanding of desire and psychosexual development, in fact what it theorises is the focusing and enhancement of desire and the specifics of individual psychosexual development as they have been elaborated through the affective privatised patriarchal nuclear family and in societies where the discourse of this family form considers it to be foundational to social order or, we might say, to the very existence of society itself. This family form, which is a characteristic of the bourgeoisie, spread across Europe with the rise of the bourgeoisie to economic and cultural power during the sixteenth and seventeenth centuries.[1] In the following centuries the bourgeoisie set about 'moralising' the working class. One important component of this moralisation was the generalising of the bourgeois family form throughout the entire population. With this background in mind we must distinguish between the sexualisation of the body and the fetishisation of the body. The sexualisation of the body was a part of the circuit of enhanced male desire which was manifested in a new preoccupation with women's bodies and with sex generally which took place in Europe from around the sixteenth century. From a re-examination of the demographic data collected by E. A. Wrigley and R. S. Schofield, who were looking for ways of explaining the increase in England's population (from 4.93 million to 13.28 million) in the 150 years following the 1680s, Henry Abelove concludes 'that there was a remarkable increase in the incidence of cross-sex genital intercourse ... during the late eighteenth century in England'.[2] It appears that the increase took place in two stages, a lesser one during the late seventeenth and eighteenth centuries and a greater one during the nineteenth century. The lesser increase correlates with the enhancement of male desire that related to the new focus on sex and the new sexualisation of the (female) body.

Sigmund Freud's work and Jacques Lacan's work need to be understood as describing the psychosexual development of the individual at two different historical moments. And in Western capitalism these two different experiences are articulated with the two primary emphases in capitalism. Freud's work describes the experience of the individual in the nuclear family, which formed the cultural basis for a social order dominated by production capitalism. Abelove makes the further suggestive observation that 'the new popularity of intercourse so-called does correlate rather well with a dramatic rise in virtually all indices of production, a rise which the textbooks call the onset of the Industrial Revolution and which, as we know, distinguished late eighteenth-century England'.[3] In fact the period of the Industrial Revolution covers the time when the nuclear family form was being generally imposed throughout society and, also, when the supplementation of male desire through the effects of cultural fetishism was beginning to be established. This is the period of the greater increase in cross-sex genital intercourse.

Lacan's rewriting of Freud's ideas provides a shift of emphasis. His work may be understood as describing the psychosexual experience of the individual formed in the nuclear family, but living in a social order dominated by the modern state. This role of the state in, particularly male, psychosexual development begins towards the middle of the nineteenth century. In the early twentieth century the development of mass-production techniques led to a renewed emphasis on expanding and increasing consumption. In Western capitalism, though not necessarily in all forms of capitalism as it has spread around the world, the connection between, in the first place men's, experience and capitalism has been made through what I have called a supplementation of male sexual desire. Desire is central to both Freud's and Lacan's account of the individual, but each theorises it quite differently. Freud's theorisation expresses well the form of enhanced male desire founded on the privatised nuclear family. Lacan's theorisation describes the form of male sexual desire, based on lack, which is the result of the male experience of cultural fetishism, and which correlates with the increase in consumption in the West in the late nineteenth and twentieth centuries.

A major transformation in individual psychosexual experience began in the West around the turn of the nineteenth century but reached a critical mass around 1850. Freud started publishing his work on hysteria in the 1880s. He rapidly developed an image of the structure of the mind and coupled this structure with a model of the psychosexual development of the individual. In 1905 he brought together his work on psychosexual development in *Three Essays on the Theory of Sexuality*. Freud was describing the modern experience produced in the nuclear family. He was writing at the time when the experience he was describing was being supplemented by a different psychosexual experience. Broadly speaking, this is the experience outlined by Lacan.

Like other inheritors of the European Enlightenment tradition Freud, and to a large extent Lacan also, claimed to be providing an insight into the universal human condition. This is not the case. Freud's achievement lay in his ability to outline the historically – and psychosexually – prior system and to suggest its implications. As I will discuss in Chapter 1 the moment of crisis in Freud's intellectual work occurred around the question of whether the women he was analysing had really been sexually molested by their fathers or whether the daughters had desired their fathers and fantasised their fathers' approaches. As is well known, Freud opted for the latter view, opening the way for the conceptual elaboration of the Oedipus complex. I argue that both views were, in fact, correct. The Oedipal structure characterised the affective privatised patriarchal nuclear family – the family form of the bourgeoisie. However, from the early nineteenth century, male psychosexual development became subject to a supplementary desiring structure, one which, as we shall see, provoked – among other things – fathers' sexual desire for their daughters. Of course I am not suggesting that previously no fathers had sexually desired their daughters, nor, indeed, that from this time all fathers desired their daughters. Rather, from the early nineteenth century, a new desiring structure began to become important, one centred on the adult male desire for the phallicised female body. This structure had the effect of producing a male pre-occupation with pubescent girls and, within the family, compounded by the father's patriarchal fears which I will discuss below, a paternal desire for daughters, something which has continued to be strictly policed as being morally reprehensible.

For Freud adult desire is fundamentally sexual. It has, in the first place, a physical quality. It refers to the channelling of sexual energy. Freud describes desire as an instinct or drive. There are other drives but it is the sexual drive which he focuses on and which he identifies as an expression of the libido. He argues that the libido is shaped through a person's psychosexual development. Psycho-sexual development in the individual can be understood as a gradual focusing of desire until, in the post-Oedipal genital stage of the adult individual, most socially significant desire is, ultimately, an effect of sexual desire. Freud views desire as an active searching after sexual satisfaction: the lack of libidinal gratification produces anxiety; pleasure is an effect of achieving that gratification. Freud's theorisation of desire (unlike, for example, Plato's in *The Symposium*) does not construct it in relation to a human lack in the sense of an imperfection. Rather it is a lack in the sense of a distinction between what one has and what one wants. As the baby develops, its libidinal drive becomes narrowed and increasingly focused on genital sexual relations. The baby's generalised erotics – its poly-morphous perversity, in Freud's own term – is transformed into the adult's genital fixation. At the same time, Freud argues, whilst the male's desire develops as an active force, the female gives up her active desiring and inverts it into a need to be desired – and loved.

For Freud, then, desire – ultimately, adult male desire – is, in the first place, natural. It gets transformed through the specific cultural impact of the modern nuclear family. In Freud's work we can understand the enhancement of male desire as an effect of the focusing of sexual desire in the family. For Freud society is the effect of the limiting and sublimation of desire. We are now in a position to rewrite this.[4] Western capitalist society is powered by the focused and enhanced sexual desire which is formed through the individual's – in particular the male's – psychosexual development in the family. For Freud the Oedipus complex is the key feature in the organisation of the individual's desire, and in the individual's transition from being a child whose desire is turned inwards towards members of the family to being an adult whose desire is turned outwards towards other adults. The centrality of the Oedipus complex in the bourgeois nuclear family form was closely connected to the genital sexualising of desire, and its enhancement, especially in men. This new desire is, in a general sense, productive. What is lacked is itself produced as a lack through the effective dynamic of what is ultimately a sexual desire. If we understand Freud's theorisation of desire as describing a culturally specific phenomenon, then it becomes a description of how, within the bourgeois-originated nuclear family, the sexual aspect of desire is privileged and enhanced. Further, this form of desire also happens to be productive, especially for men. Since this desire operates in the space between what one has and what one wants, the person who is socially constructed to have an active desire, the male, will seek to reduce his anxiety by producing/acquiring what he wants.

Lacan's understanding of desire is quite different. Reworking Hegel's idea of desire, Lacan reconstructed Freud's theorisation. Lacan writes that 'man's desire is the *désir de l'Autre* (the desire of the Other) in which the *de* provides what grammarians call the 'subjective determination,' namely that it is *qua* Other that he desires (which is what provides the true compass of human passion)'.[5] What Lacan is claiming is that each individual's desire is, in fact, the desire to be desired by someone else. This is a fundamentally different kind of desire from the desire outlined by Freud. Lacan argues that 'Desire begins to take shape in the margin in which demand becomes separated from need'.[6] As Elizabeth Grosz outlines Lacan's understanding of desire: 'If need is a function of the Real and demand is a product of imaginary identifications, the third term in Lacan's libidinal trilogy is *desire*, the symbolic "equivalent or counterpart of need and demand".'[7] In Lacan's work, desire arises from a conception of the human being as always experiencing lack as a function of their constitution as a social adult. I am arguing that such an experience is historically and culturally specific and that what is actually being described is the form of desire which operates in cultural fetishism.

Ultimately, Lacan's theorisation of desire is determined by his notion of the phallus. The importance Lacan attributes to the phallus marks a major shift in the orientation of his work from that of Freud. For Lacan it is the castration complex, not the Oedipus complex, which drives the psychosexual development of the adult human being. Lacan writes that 'what is not a myth, and which [sic] Freud nevertheless formulated soon after the Oedipus complex, is the castration complex'.[8] Lacan makes the Oedipus complex a family drama dependent on the privileged existence of the experience of the castration complex. In Freud's work the castration complex was an important but secondary phenomenon which closed off the Oedipus complex in boys.

The change in emphasis reflects the novel importance of the phallus in Lacan's work. Here, the phallus is closely associated with both maleness and power. The phallus is not the penis. Rather, it is the mythic signifier, the bar and the column to use Lacan's terms, which marks the formation of society. Lacan puts it like this: 'The phallus is the privileged signifier of that mark in which the role of the logos is joined with the advent of desire.' The entry into language, a key moment in the individual's progress into the social, is simultaneously the entry into desire. However, precisely because the phallus is mythic, no-one, including the male who is marked as such by the physical presence of his penis, actually possesses the phallus. As Lacan writes: 'The fact that the phallus is a signifier means that it is in the place of the Other that the subject has access to it. But since this signifier is only veiled . . . it is this desire of the Other as such that the subject must recognize'.[9] Here we find the connection between the phallus and desire. In the end what is lacked, and what is desired, is the phallus. Lacan explains that this is as much the case for women, who 'lack' the penis, as for men:

> Clinical experience has shown us that this test of the desire of the Other is decisive not in the sense that the subject learns by it whether or not he has a real phallus, but in the sense that he learns that the mother does not have it. This is the moment of the experience without which no symptomatic consequence (phobia) or structural consequence (*Penisneid*) relating to the castration complex can take effect.[10]

The reference to a symptomatic consequence is to the male experience; that to structural consequence is a reference to women's experience. Lacan is here describing penis envy as a structural consequence of the foundational importance of the phallus. In the final analysis, however, it is not the penis women desire but the phallus and men too desire the phallus, having themselves only the penis.

At this point it is useful to examine Lacan's reformulation of Freud's version of the role of the father in the nuclear family. For Lacan it is not the actual father who is, ultimately, most important in the institutionalisation of the moral order of the family but, rather, the Name-of-the-Father. For the sake of brevity I will not quote Lacan's own prolix and circumlocutory prose from 'On the Possible Treatment of Psychosis'[11] but rather Grosz's succinct summary:

> In order for the dyadic structure [of mother/child] to give way to the plurality constituting the symbolic order, the narcissistic couple must be submitted to symbolic regulation. Within the confines of the nuclear family, this order is initiated by a third family member – the father – who most easily . . . can represent law, order, and authority for the child. It is not, however, the *real* or genetic father, but the *imaginary father* who acts as an incarnation or delegate of the *Symbolic Father*. In the case of his absence or failure to take up the Symbolic function, other authority figures – the teacher, headmaster, policeman, or ultimately, God, – may take his place in instilling in the child the sense of lawfulness and willing submission to social customs.'[12]

Grosz's examples of alternative patriarchal authority figures make clear that the symbolic Father – or the Name-of-the-Father – is to be found represented in the employees of the state. In Freud's work, which, as we have already noted, privileged the Oedipus complex, the nuclear family was reified into a cultural universal. This was necessary to sustain the universalist assumptions of human psychosexual development because the Oedipus complex, which took place within the confines of the family, marked a crucial stage in the individual's development. In Lacan's work, where it is the castration complex which occupies the crucial site for individual psychosexual development, the universalism in his theory is achieved by making the phallus the founding signifier of society. Freud's work can be reconstituted by recognising the historical and cultural particularity of the nuclear family. Lacan's work can be relativised not by understanding the privileging of the phallus as the founding signifier of some generalised society, but, rather, by understanding the experience of the privileging of the phallus as a consequence of the patriarchal articulation of the modern state. Before taking this argument further we need to look briefly at the role of Lacan's idea of the Law of the Father in his theory.

As we have seen, Lacan distinguishes between the actual father in the family – the man who only has a penis and who constantly feels he is standing in for someone else, the symbolic Father who has the phallus – and the primordial symbolic Father. For Lacan the basis of social life is the Law, which is proscriptive. Here he is following Freud's story of the origin of society. Taking up Charles Darwin's idea of an original primal horde, Freud constructs a mythical story in *Totem and Taboo* to account for the apparently universal existence of exogamy. In this story Freud begins by explaining that the primal horde is controlled by 'a violent and jealous father who keeps all the females for himself and drives away his sons as they grow up'.[13] He continues: 'One day the brothers who had been driven out came together, killed and devoured their father and so made an end to the patriarchal horde.'[14] However:

> After they had got rid of him, had satisfied their hatred and had put into effect their wish to identify themselves with him, the affection which had all this time been pushed under was bound to make itself felt. It did so in the form of remorse. A sense of guilt made its appearance . . . [15]

The upshot was that 'the dead father became stronger than the living one had been', with the effect that the sons instituted two taboos, one against eating the patriarchal totem and the other against having sexual relations with the women of the horde. The consequence of this latter taboo is the ban on incest, with the concomitant emphasis on exogamy. As Freud puts it in his recapitulation of the story in *Civilization and its Discontents*: 'The taboo-observances were the first "right" or "law".'[16] This, then, is the Law instated by the sons' communal guilt. For Freud society begins in their shared male guilt at the murder of their father, and is formed through the exchange of women which is an effect of this first proscriptive Law. In fact Freud describes the murder as 'this memorable and criminal deed, which was the beginning of so many things – of social organisation, of moral restrictions and of religion'.[17] If this is the founding moment of social order for Freud, then all other laws – and the assumption of their moral correctness – follow from it.

Lacan argues that it was the murder of the original Father which brought proscriptive Law into existence:

> '[Freud linked] the appearance of the signifier of the Father, as author of the Law, with death, even to the murder of the Father – thus showing that if this murder is the fruitful moment of debt through which the subject binds himself for life to the Law, the symbolic Father is, in so far as he signifies this Law, the dead Father.'[18]

It was not the original patriarch who laid down the Law of the Father; rather, the Law is the effect of the guilt and fear of the sons who murdered him. Thus, the Law of the Father is more powerful, and effective, precisely because it was a consequence of the putting-into-absence of the Father. I want to suggest that the literal expression of the Law of the Father is the experience of the law of the modern state. Or, to put it another way, Freud's and Lacan's descriptions of the origin of society are actually insightful extra-polations from the modern experience of the state.

The fully fledged modern state came into existence some time in the early nineteenth century – after the benchmark of the 1789 French Revolution. Anthony Giddens has usefully summed up the classical definition of the state as: '(a) centralized organs of govern-ment, associated with (b) claims to legitimate territorial control and (c) a distinct dominant elite or class, having definite modes of train-ing and status attributes'.[19] To this definition he has added: 'What is specifically late European is the fixing of very precise boundaries that actually do effectively mark the realm of the administration of the state.'[20] Within these boundaries:,

> control of the means of violence, as a monopoly or near-monopoly in the hands of the state, became possible only with the internal pacification of states. The differentiation between the police and standing army, or armed forces, has remained a fairly clear – although never wholly unambiguous – one in most European countries since the middle of the nineteenth century. This differentiation can be said to express the 'inward' and 'outward' stance of the state in respect of violence and its control.[21]

Within the nation-state, the state, through its institutions, monopolizes both legislation and violence. Moreover, as the state theorist Gianfranco Poggi puts it, the state '"speaks the law" in almost all aspects of its functioning'.[22]

Through the second half of the nineteenth century the experience of this new state structure became overwhelming. Eric Hobsbawm describes it like this:

> Seen from below, the state increasingly defined the largest stage on which the crucial activities determining human lives as subjects and citizens were played out. Indeed, it increasingly defined as well as registered their civil existence (*état civil*). It may not have been the only such stage, but its existence, frontiers and increasingly regular and probing interventions in the citizen's life were in the last analysis decisive.[23]

He explains how, at the same time, there was a 'mass-production' of invented traditions by nation-states seeking to legitimise their existence by laying claim to a mythic, apparently immemorial, past. Hobsbawm identifies this period as running from roughly 1870 to 1914.

In Freudian terms the state is experienced as being the institutional expression of the role of the primal father after his murder or, in Lacanian terms, as being in the situation of the symbolic Father. In political theory the equation of the state with the family has a venerable history which it is not my purpose to relate here. However, I will give just one example from Jean-Jacques Rousseau, whose work is often credited with providing some of the basic ideas of modern liberal democracy. Rousseau writes:

> The family may ... perhaps be seen as the first model of political societies: the head of state bears the image of the father, the people the image of his children, and all, being born free and equal, surrender their freedom only when they see advantage in doing so.[24]

Here we find Rousseau describing a family in which the mother has dropped from sight. The fundamental relations are between the father and his children. Rousseau's work should not be taken as uniquely innovative (it was Hegel, after all, who transcendentalised the state) but, rather, as a symptomatic expression of the (male) (bourgeois) experience of the modern state. The state is the institutional embodiment of the father of fathers – that is, the Father of the real fathers in the families which go to make up the state.

At this point we need to distinguish clearly the gendering of the state from the gendering of the nation – in that dual entity, the nation-state – within the psychic economy of modernity. Whilst the state is constructed as male, and in particular as the (symbolic) Father, the nation is constructed as female, and as the (virtuous and subordinate) Mother. As Andrew Parker, Mary Russo, Doris Sommer, and Patricia Yaeger point out in the Introduction to their edited collection *Nationalisms and Sexualities*, 'this trope of the nation-as-woman of course depends for its representational efficacy on a particular image of woman as chaste, dutiful, daughterly or maternal'.[25] The image of the nation-as-daughter is the effect of the subordination of the nation to the legislative and organisational determination of the state-as-symbolic-Father. In the patriarchal order of the state full membership is, mythically but with important historical effects, limited to men. The state is thought of as being composed of fraternal citizens (Freud's sons who murdered their f/Father), birthed by the nation-as-Mother but under the Law of the state-as-symbolic-Father. This mythic exclusion of women as citizens of the state is well explored by Carole Pateman in her book on the gendering of the social contract, *The Sexual Contract*.[26] We can extend this argument for an understanding of why the public domain of the state, civil society, has also been so relentlessly male-dominated. Here we should remember that, for Lacan, the symbolic force of the Law of the Father founds the realm of the symbolic order of culture which is fundamentally male. The emphasis on the sons/brothers has been investigated by Juliet Flower MacCannell in *The Regime of the Brother*.[27] A different emphasis on the privileging of relations between men in modernity has been taken by Eve Kosofsky Sedgwick in her book *Between Men*,[28] which describes the organisation of 'male homosocial desire', as she calls it in the book's subtitle, examining the distinction between male bonding and homosexuality through discussions of British and American literary texts.

The confusion in Freud's work, and in Lacan's also, lies in the conflation of society with the state. Freud's narrative may be read as combining a mythic account of the modern state as being an expression of phallic and patriarchal power with a story of the fetishistic consumption of the phallus and a further story about the commodification of women. The Lacanian Law of the Father can be understood as a way of thinking about the individual's experience of the proscriptive laws of the modern state. The symbolic Father has only ever existed as a signifier. This expresses the experience of the modern state. The state has no single site in which all proscriptive power is located. Even in totalitarian regimes the source of power is always to some extent dispersed. Everybody within the state, including the government, feels themselves to some extent subjected by the legislative power of the state. The more democratic the state, the more this is the case. The more totalitarian the state, the more the leader is felt to embody this phallic and patriarchal power. And yet the state, like Lacan's symbolic Father, has no physical existence. In terms of our experience as members of the state, the state exists in the first place through our experience of its proscriptive laws. If the state is experienced as the symbolic Father, then we need to remember that the symbolic Father bears the symbolic penis – that is, the phallus. It is the phallus which, finally, is the signifier of the symbolic Father's potency. It is no wonder that fathers – and, structurally, men in general – feel inadequate and fearful in the presence of the state. The potency of a man, expressed in his penis, can never be equal to the potency of the state, expressed in the phallus.

Lacan follows Freud in making society an effect of the inhibiting of demands. I have already discussed how, for Lacan, desire is produced in the space between need and demand. At the general, structural level the unassuageability of desire is a consequence of the experience of the existence of the Law. Lacan writes that 'it is this whim [of the Other] that introduces the phantom of the Omnipotence, not of the subject, but of the Other in which his demand is installed ... , and with this phantom the need for it to be checked by the Law'.[29] What all people, but in the first place men, are alienated from in this mythic order and at the same time finally barred from acquiring, is the phallus. What Lacan points out is that, in this phallic order, women will desire to be what men want them to be so that they will be desired and loved. What men want women to be is what men most desire. The fantasy is that this can be acquired in the act of possession. What men most desire is the phallus:

> I am saying that it is in order to be the phallus, that is to say, the signifier of the desire of the Other, that a woman will reject an essential part of femininity, namely all her attributes of masquerade. It is for that which she is not that she wishes to be desired as well as loved. But she finds the signifier of her own desire in the body of him to whom she addresses her demand for love. Perhaps it should not be forgotten that the organ that assumes this signifying function takes on the value of a fetish.[30]

Again, of course, Lacan has abstracted and universalised. This description of women's position in the phallic order can be more usefully understood in the light of the discussion of the state as the symbolic Father.

I have argued that Lacan's understanding of desire may be read as theorising the individual's, and in the first place the male's, experience of the state. I now want to suggest that the 'lack' which male citizens feel can be correlated with, and, indeed, provides the overdetermining context for, the 'lack' which drove the twentieth-century expansion of consumption. Stuart Ewen has described well how twentieth-century advertising encouraged people – especially, historically, women – to think of themselves as incomplete, as lacking certain qualities, from being plain (lacking beauty) to having bad breath (lacking sweet-smelling breath).[31] This social production of lack encouraged a constant consumption of new products in order to complement and erase the discovered and naturalised lack. In the first instance such an image of the female body as lacking derived from, and was legitimised by, the modern distinction between the 'perfect' (white) male body and the 'imperfect' female body. However, what the new advertising order – or, to use Andrew Wernick's term, the new promotional culture[32] – did was to reconstruct female 'imperfection' as lack and interpellate the lacking woman into a system of consumption in which purchasing commodities could be experienced as a profound attempt to mitigate her experience of her fundamental lack. In this reformation, consumption comes to be thought of as a complementary addition rather than a using-up of something.

The construction of the individual as lacking has become increasingly generalised. Men are now being interpellated in the same way. In addition, there has been a shift to 'lifestyle' advertising in which advertising places products as elements in a more general, image-based lifestyle. A person can buy into that lifestyle. In general the economic order has commodified not just everyday life, but the experience of everyday life. In an important insight Wernick has summed up this shift:

> In effect, during the course of advanced capitalist development the globalization and intensification of commodity production have led to a crucial economic modification in which (a) with mass production and mass marketing the moments of distribution, circulation, and exchange have become as strategic as technical improvements in production for profitability

and growth and (b) through commodity imaging the circulation and production processes have come to overlap. In which
context ... it has further come about that the (superstructural)
domain of expressive communication has been more and
more absorbed, not just in industry but as a direct aspect of
the sale of everything, into the integral working of the
commodified economic 'base'.[33]

The realm of ideas and fantasy has now been commodified and
integrated into a totalising capitalist system which is driven by consumption.

We must be clear here about the use of the term 'fetishism' in
this book. I distinguish the heightened male desire for the female
body which I describe as an aspect of cultural fetishism, and which
is a cultural effect, from the individual male's fear of the loss of his
penis which, in Freud's writings, provides the basic motivation for
the neurotic structure that he describes as fetishism. I will make use
of both these formulations. In recent years there have been many
fascinating accounts of fetishism which criticise, rework, or extend
Freud's idea. Here it will suffice to mention Emily Apter and
William Pietz's edited book *Fetishism as Cultural Discourse*,[34] the
issue of *New Formations* entitled *Perversity*,[35] and Lorraine
Gamman and Merja Makinen's book on *Female Fetishism*.[36] However, in this book I have, in the main, stuck with Freud's discussion
because it identifies a male pathology which is connected with a
particular cultural formation, namely the privileging of the penis as
the material correlative of the phallus and, therefore, as the marker
of social power. For Freud, fetishism was a male neurotic sexual
formation. In Chapter 1 I discuss the issues surrounding fetishism
in more detail. Here I will just note that, for Freud, fetishism is an
individual male solution to the fear caused by the sight of a
woman's 'lack' of a penis. What we have here is an aspect of the
castration complex. Cultural fetishism is rather different. First, cultural fetishism is an overdetermining general structure among men
in those modern nation-states where the state is experienced in the
way I have described. Second, cultural fetishism is neither a consequence of anything to do with women nor, more generally,
associated with a fear of castration. Rather, cultural fetishism is an
effect of a feeling of inadequacy, of relative impotence, provoked by
the experience of the power of the state. As a signifier of male
power, the penis is always inadequate when compared to the phallic
and patriarchal power of the modern state. The penis is never as big

– as powerful – as the phallus. In this circumstance the reaction is a desire to possess the phallus. We have here one way of appreciating the male urge for power in the public domain of the modern state. However, I do not want to pursue this general argument.

In Chapter 1 I provide an account of the historical establishment of cultural fetishism. I will focus on the effects of cultural fetishism on relations between the sexes. This is for three reasons. First, I want to show how cultural fetishism impacts on the organisation of male desire. Second, I want to show how it affects the male experience of the female body. Third, I want to suggest how cultural fetishism and the supplementary male desire associated with it drive the Western experience of commodity fetishism. I argue that, around 1850, the female body began to be fetishised as the phallus that men do not possess but wish they did. One symptom of this process is the male desire for 'male-looking, or, more generally, phallicised females – most obviously the pubescent girl.

Marx uses the term 'commodity fetishism' to describe the experience, in capitalism, of the commodity as an object without an origin. He argues that, because of the organisation of the capitalist exchange system, people do not experience commodities as the products of labour and they view social relations in terms of commodity ownership rather than class position in relation to the means of production. In Chapter 1 I argue that what I call active commodity fetishism is one effect of the new circulation of male desire put into play by cultural fetishism. The nub of this argument is that commodities become fetishes in the sense that they are experienced as phallic substitutes for the phallus that men do not have. Two objections will be immediately raised to this suggestion. The first is that such a formulation would only explain male consumption. The second is that, in the established gender division of labour, it is women who consume and men who produce the commodities. Both of these are valid points. However, the most immediate impact of cultural fetishism is that men fetishise women's bodies. Women are drawn into the circuit of male desire not on their own terms as women but as phallic substitutes. Using Lacanian ideas, Judith Butler has theorised this understanding – without, however, providing much of a sense of its historical and cultural specificity:

> 'Being' the Phallus and 'having' the Phallus denote divergent sexual positions, or nonpositions (impossible positions, really), within language. To 'be' the Phallus is to be the

'signifier' of the desire of the Other and to appear as this signifier. ... For women to 'be' the Phallus means, then, to reflect the power of the Phallus, to signify that power, to 'embody' the Phallus, to supply the site to which it penetrates, and to signify the Phallus through 'being' its Other, its absence, its lack, the dialectical confirmation of its identity.[37]

The internalisation of their positioning as phallic substitutes, combined with their own sense of their 'lack' of the phallus, provokes in women a drive to consume. Shopping has become a fetishistic experience in the sense that it serves to compensate women for their 'lack'.

A more focused way of understanding the cultural determination of cultural fetishism is by confronting again the vexed issue of penis envy. Freud considered it to be natural that a girl should desire to have a penis. We can reconstruct this culturally and historically by recognising that, in a patriarchal society, it is understandable that those who do not have the organ which is associated with power, and the opportunities in life allied to that power, should desire that organ. As Juliet Mitchell remarked some time ago in the first major culturalist reworking of Freud's ideas, 'in "penis-envy" we are talking not about an anatomical organ, but about the ideas of it that people hold and live by within the general culture, the order of human society.'[38] This theorisation can be used to explain some degree of female fetishistic consumption, particularly when allied to a discussion of narcissism. The structure of cultural fetishism overdetermines this more historically general structure. It adds a further neurotic drive based on male desire. In the modern state, it is no longer enough for women to want the penis; they now would need to have the phallus. Women are interpellated into a patriarchal structure where on the one hand, they are fetishistically constructed as phallic substitutes, whilst on the other hand, they consume in an attempt to satisfy a socially produced lack, not just of a penis but of the phallus.

The fetishism I am describing privileges sight. This is clearly so in the individual fetishism described by Freud, where it is the sight of a woman's 'lack' that generates the need for a fetishised substitute. It is also true of cultural fetishism, where the desire to appropriate the phallus is displaced on to a visible substitute. The changing experience of sight provides a secondary theme of this book. Lacan argues, following Jean-Paul Sartre, that our identities are partly produced in the gaze of the Other. Inevitably, given what has been said above, this gaze is an expression of the subject's experience of the desire which he or she has invested in the Other. Lacan notes that 'of all the objects in which the subject may recognise his dependence in the register of desire, the gaze is specified as unapprehensible'.[39] In line with his general attempt to develop a universal theory, Lacan wants to suggest that the gaze is a universal phenomenon arising out of the universal experience of the production of the subject. Again, however, we can usefully historicize his work. Where Lacan posits a universal subjectifying gaze of the Other, there is a history of the objectifying – and subjectifying – gaze which culminates in the panoptic gaze of the modern state. This is the history which Michel Foucault has outlined in the context of a discussion of the transformation of power and its relations to juridical practices, which serves as one defining aspect of the modern period. Taking as his exemplary model Jeremy Bentham's idea for a new kind of prison, the Panopticon, which he published in 1787, Foucault describes the spread of a new type of official gaze, one in which the 'seeing/being seen dyad'[40] is dissociated. Where previously power was exercised through the display of the powerful, and the scenes they chose to display, now power began to reside in the ability to gaze on the world without oneself being seen.

Within the closed system of the Panopticon, 'the panoptic schema makes any apparatus of power more intense: it assures its economy (in material, in personnel, in time); it assures its efficacity by its preventative character, its continuous functioning and its automatic mechanisms'.[41] Foucault comments further: 'The panoptic schema, without disappearing as such or losing any of its properties, was destined to spread through the social body; its vocation was to become a generalized function'.[42] Writing of pre-Revolutionary France, Foucault notes that 'the organization of a centralized police force had long been regarded, even by contemporaries, as the most direct expression of royal absolutism.'[43] However, he argues, 'in order to be exercised this [new schema of panoptic] power had to be given the instrument of permanent, exhaustive, omnipresent surveillance, capable of making all visible, as long as it could itself remain invisible. It had to be like a faceless gaze which transformed the whole social body into a field of perception'.[44] This instrument was the police force. It is therefore no surprise to discover that in both Britain and France the police force as the state-based institution executing the laws of the state – that is, the modern police force as we still have it – was set in place in the years around the turn of the nineteenth century. Stanley Palmer has argued that in Britain the modern police force took shape between 1780 and 1850.[45] The key date is usually taken to be 1829. It was in that year that Robert Peel, the Home Secretary, introduced into the House of Commons his Metropolis Police Improvement Bill. In France, by the time of the French Revolution, Paris had a 3,100-strong police force.[46] The Sûreté, the criminal investigation department, was set up in 1812. The police force, then, is the state institution which most provoked the experience of the modern state as the absent, symbolic Father. Louis Althusser's work, which provides a historical connection between the ideas of Lacan and Foucault, suggests this argument without developing it. In his important essay 'Ideology and Ideological State Apparatuses' it is the state, in the institutional form of a policeman, who hails the person and interpellates them as a subject.

At this point we should remember Lacan's idea of the subject's experience of an unapprehensible gaze. In Foucault's historical description, the subject – the citizen – lives within the powerful gaze, which is simultaneously an empowering gaze, of the unseen watcher. Not knowing if they are actually being gazed upon, the subject learns to act as if this is the case. Put forward to the British Parliament, Bentham's Panopticon outlined a new way of functioning for one part of the juridical order. Although Foucault rarely alludes to it in a clear-cut manner, what he describes in *Discipline and Punish* is the formation of the discursive regime of surveillance which is a central element in the expression of the modern state. Here, then, we have the point of connection with Lacan's description of the gaze. In the modern state the subject's experience is that they are being gazed upon. Given the understanding of the modern state as patriarchal, it is no wonder that the experience – in particular, the male experience – of that gaze is one of lack, the lack which gives rise, in turn, to the subject's own fetishising gaze. It is the general – again in the first place male – process, provoked by the recognition of phallic lack, to which I am giving the name 'cultural fetishism.' It is this development in the gaze which forms the subtext linking Chapters 2 and 3. Chapter 2 is concerned with the connections between the new visual media, cultural fetishism, and the two forms of surveillance, that of the state and the eroticising, fetishising gaze of the male, which, together, are elements in the formation of cultural fetishism. Chapter 3 describes how the sexualised female body is fetishised and transformed into a spectacle in a public domain which itself is eroticised as a consequence of the male fetishising gaze. It needs to be added that the changing situation of sight in the nineteenth century, its association with surveillance and its libidinization in the fetishistic gaze, provided a context for the new preoccupation with the image manifested in the inventions of photography, film, and, later, television and video. Since the beginning of the twentieth century, film has supplied visual images to a mass audience. For this reason examples drawn from films occupy an important place in this book.

As I have noted, cultural fetishism forms the basis for what I call active commodity fetishism. Again, as with the Freudian notion of fetishism, there have been a number of revisions of the Marxian idea of commodity fetishism in recent years, ranging from Kathy Myers's reworking of the theme in her discussion of the everyday practices involved in consumption capitalism,[47] to Slavoj Zizek's development of the idea in his reading of Marx through the prism of Lacan, *The Sublime Object of Ideology*.[48] I have chosen to return to Marx's original formulation because it is the kernel of his idea which is most important for my purposes. Like Freud, Marx must be read as a product of his time. His critical account of capitalism looks back over the period of industrial, production-oriented capitalism and his theory was shaped by the dominant discourses of his time. Whilst the activation of commodity fetishism began in the second half of the nineteenth century, it only became central with the new emphasis on consumption in the twentieth century. This book does not confront the problem of the Marxian legacy for our postmodern times; rather, I strategically appropriate the theme of commodity fetishism for my own explanatory purposes.

Chapter 4 examines the male fetishisation of the male body, a vexed process which acknowledges that, in a cultural order where cultural fetishism is an overdetermining structure, male-male desire becomes the dominant form of sexual attraction for men. Cultural fetishism is, therefore, closely associated with the cultural formation of the category of homosexuality.

Chapter 5 discusses the effects of cultural fetishism on the spectacular production of the female body. It begins by considering the relation between eating, consumption, and sexual desire. It goes on to look at the history of the shift in dominant female body image towards thinness and the historical construction of anorexia nervosa as a female illness. It also discusses the relationship between the male desire to consume the phallus, the capitalist concern with consumption, and the female body as a site of the cultural acting-out of these concerns. It is in this light that cannibalism became important as a late-twentieth-century theme.

Chapter 6 returns to the male body, looking at the spread of the emphasis on male personal consumption since the late 1960s and relating this to the new acceptability of homosexuality, the development of male-oriented style magazines, and a new cultural emphasis on two types of male body which, following Bram Dijkstra in *Idols of Perversity*,[49] I describe as the blond god and the ephebe. My examples in the latter part of this chapter are drawn from Hollywood films of the 1980s.

In the final chapter, Chapter 7, I examine one particular male fantasy about women and their bodies which draws its power from cultural fetishism. This is the idea of substituting gynoids, automata which look like women, for actual women. From roughly the middle of the nineteenth century onwards, there has been an increasing male interest in eroticised gynoids. My use of the term 'gynoid' follows that of Peter Wollen, who, in 'Cinema/Americanism/The Robot', argues that 'the dialectic between human and machine', which is central to the elaboration of Fordism, 'is mapped on to that between parent and child and also . . . that between male lover and female love-object'. Wollen goes on: 'Caught up in the circulation of desire, the automaton becomes both philosophical toy and sexual fetish or surrogate.'[50] It is the latter role of the gynoid with which I am concerned, but, whilst accepting Wollen's argument about machinery – an argument drawn from Andreas Huyssen's *After the Great Divide*[51] – I argue that the major source of the male preoccupation with the sexual fantasy of gynoids lies in their being male-produced figures which, as productions of male fantasy, can be shaped to accept passively the desire of men. In the light of this reworking of Huyssen's and Wollen's arguments, I extend the meaning of 'gynoid' from automata with a female appearance to non-mechanical models of women such as life-size dolls and shop mannequins. At the same time that the gynoid expresses the possibility of a fulfilment of male desire, its very phallicness presents it to men as a source of fear, fear that it will become active and threaten to destroy its male creators. It is in this context that I discuss the film *Eve of Destruction,* in which a gynoid – built as a war machine for the American state by the robotics engineer Eve, as her exact duplicate – takes on the active role that Eve herself has forsaken and threatens to blow up part of Manhattan with a tactical nuclear charge.

## NOTES

1   See, for example: E. Shorter, *The Making of the Modern Family* (New York, Basic Books, 1975); E. Zaretsky, *Capitalism, the Family and Personal Life* (New York, Harper and Row, 1976); L. Stone, *The Family, Sex and Marriage in England 1500-1800* (New York, Harper and Row, 1977).

2   Henry Abelove, 'Some Speculations on the History of "Sexual Intercourse" during the "Long Eighteenth Century" in England', in A. Parker, M. Russo, D. Sommer, and P. Yeager (eds), *Nationalisms and Sexualities* (New York, Routledge, 1992), p. 337.

3   *Ibid.*, p. 339.

4   At this point my argument has certain similarities with Foucault's as put forward in M. Foucault, *The History of Sexuality*, vol. 1, trans. Robert Hurley (New York, Pantheon, 1978).

5   J. Lacan, *Ecrits: A Selection*, trans. Alan Sheridan (New York, Norton, 1977), p. 312.

6   *Ibid.*, p. 311.

7   E. Grosz, *Jacques Lacan: A Feminist Introduction* (London, Routledge, 1990), p. 64.

8   Lacan, *Ecrits* p. 318.

9   *Ibid.*, p. 288.

10   *Ibid.*, p. 289.

11   *Ibid.*, esp. pp. 215–21.

12   Grosz, *Jacques Lacan* ,pp. 67–8.

13   S. Freud, *Totem and Taboo* in *The Standard Edition of the Complete Psychological Works of Sigmund Freud*, translated under the general editorship of james Strachey in collaboration with Anna Freud (London, The Hogarth Press/Institute of Psycho-Analysis, vol. 13, 1955), p. 141.

14   *Ibid* p. 141.

15   *Ibid.*, p. 143.

16   S. Freud, *Civilization and its Discontents* in *The Standard Edition*,vol. 21 (1958), p. 101.

17   *Totem and Taboo*, in *The Standard Edition*, vol. 13, p. 142.

18   Lacan, *Ecrits*, p. 199.

19   A. Giddens, *The Constitution of Society: Outline of the Theory of Structuration* (Cambridge, Polity Press, 1984), pp. 246–7.

20   A. Giddens, *Social Theory and Modern Sociology* (Cambridge, Polity Press, 1987), p. 172.

21   *Ibid.*, p. 172.

22   G. Poggi, *The State: Its Nature, Development and Prospects*

(Cambridge, Polity Press, 1990), p. 29.

23 E. Hobsbawm, 'Mass-producing Traditions: Europe, 1870-1914', in E. Hobsbawm and T. Ranger (eds), *The Invention of Tradition* (Cambridge, Cambridge University Press, 1983), p. 264.

24 J.-J. Rousseau, *The Social Contract*, trans. Maurice Cranston (Harmondsworth, Penguin, 1968), pp. 50–1.

25 Parker *et al.* (eds), *Nationalisms and Sexualities*, p. 6.

26 C. Pateman,*The Sexual Contract* (Cambridge, Polity Press, 1988).

27 J. F. MacCannell, *The Regime of the Brother: After the Patriarchy* (London, Routledge, 1991).

28 E. K. Sedgwick, *Between Men: English Literature and Male Homosocial Desire* (New York, Columbia University Press, 1985).

29 Lacan, *Ecrits*, p. 311.

30 *Ibid.*, p. 289–90.

31 S. Ewen, *Captains of Consciousness: Advertising and the Social Roots of the Consumer Culture* (New York, McGraw-Hill, 1976).

32 A. Wernick, *Promotional Culture: Advertising, Ideology, and Symbolic Expression* (London, Sage, 1991).

33 *Ibid.*, p. 185.

34 E. Apter and W. Pietz (eds.), *Fetishism as Cultural Discourse* (Ithaca, Cornell University Press, 1993).

35 *New Formations*, no. 19, (1993.)

36 L. Gamman and M. Makinen, *Female Fetishism: A New Look* (London, Lawrence and Wishart, 1994).

37 Judith Butler, *Gender Trouble: Feminism and the Subversion of Identity* (New York, Routledge, 1990), p. 44.

38 J. Mitchell, *Psychoanalysis and Feminism* (Harmondsworth, Penguin, 1974), p. xvi.

39 J. Lacan, *The Four Fundamental Concepts of Psychoanalysis*, ed. J.-A. Miller, trans. A. Sheridan (Harmondsworth, Penguin, 1991), p. 83.

40 M. Foucault, *Discipline and Punish: The Birth of the Prison*, trans. Alan Sheridan (New York, Vintage Books, 1979), p. 202.

41 *Ibid.*, p. 206.

42 *Ibid.*, p. 207.

43 *Ibid.*, p. 213.

44 *Ibid.*, p. 214.

45 S. Palmer, *Police and Protest in England and Ireland 1780-1850* (Cambridge, Cambridge University Press, 1988), p. 6.

46 *Ibid.*, p. 13.

47 K. Myers, *Understains* (London, Comedia, 1986).

48    S. Zizek, *The Sublime Object of Ideology* (London, Verso, 1989).

49    B. Dijkstra, *Idols of Perversity: Fantasies of the Feminine in Fin-de siècle Culture* (New York, Oxford University Press, 1986).

50    P. Wollen, 'Cinema/Americanism/The Robot', *New Formations*, no. 8 (1989), p. 16.

51    A. Huyssen, *After the Great Divide* (London, Macmillan, 1986).

# 1

# Commodity fetishism and cultural fetishism

The most important moment in the reconstruction of the modern experience of the body lies in a complex of changes that unfolded around the middle of the nineteenth century. It was during this period that the individual members of the modern nation-state began to experience the effects of the state's ability to reach into, and regulate, their daily lives. As we have already seen in the Introduction, this state was experienced as phallic, as the performance of a paternal and patriarchal power which was qualitatively greater than any actual father's power. It was this experience which formed the basis for what I have called cultural fetishism. The expression of male power lies in the penis, and no man's penis is ever as big as the mythic phallus of the state. Later in this chapter I will describe how this preoccupation with the penis and its mythic analogue was translated into a male fetishisation of the body of the pubescent girl. It was this fetishisation which began the general eroticisation of the life-world and led to a cultural, male-determined, reconstruction of the preferred female body as phallicised.

Although the individual fetishism outlined by Freud and based in the male's fear of castration inflects it, cultural fetishism refers to the effect of the institutionalisation of the difference between the individual man's penis and the cultural phallus which, in the light of his experience of the modern state, he comes to feel he should have. This effect is a fetishistically based supplementation of male desire, a supplementation based in the phallocentric preoccupation with the penis. The male experience of inadequacy is projected on to the female body which is produced as the key phallic fetish. At pubescence the girl's clothed body is beginning to be physically distinguishable from that of a boy. She is simultaneously sexualised as the object of male desire and fetishised as the phallus the man lacks. In an interaction between the neurotic fetishism described by Freud, which is located in a male fear of castration, and cultural fetishism, the male fear of castration, brought on by the knowledge that women 'lack' a penis, is transformed into a fetishisation of the female body as the expression of the male's experience of penile inadequacy in the face of the state's phallicism. Later in this chapter I will discuss the mid-nineteenth-century preoccupation with father–daughter incest. The father's fetishistic concern with his daughter is one of the most shocking – and yet discursively one of the most important – examples of the new order of cultural fetishism because of its location within the apparently asexual space of the nuclear family.

Where the fetishisation of the female body was, in the first place, bound up with the male experience of the state, the extension of that fetishisation to the male body was much more a consequence of the insistent spread of commodification and consumption. This brings me to the second major aspect of my argument in this chapter, which is the relation between cultural fetishism and consumption. The mass market developed in the second half of the nineteenth century. During this period there was a new emphasis on consumption. What this chapter will argue is that cultural fetishism underpinned the acceptance of consumption as a way of life, helping to revolutionise the experience of consumption and driving its association with spectacle. Central to this was the experience of a fetishistic desire which was focused on the assimilation of the phallic fetish.

Neil McKendrick has argued, with reference to England, that 'consumer behaviour was so rampant and the acceptance of commercial attitudes so pervasive that no one ... should doubt that the first of the world's consumer societies had unmistakably emerged by 1800'.[1] However, this was not a mass market. Hamish Fraser has outlined the putting into place of a mass market in Britain after 1850. He writes:

> In spite of problems and setbacks for many and the persistence of deep-seated poverty, for most people the late nineteenth century brought about a real improvement in living standards. The British people were able to concern themselves with more than mere subsistence; they had a surplus to spend on more and better food, on a wider range of clothing, on more elaborate furnishing for their homes and on a greater variety

of leisure pursuits. For the first time most people had a *choice* of how and where to spend their money.[2]

This choice was made possible by the mass market. Having a choice, though, is not the same as actually buying. The new relative prosperity among some sections of the population, and the new availability of a variety of commodities which could be bought, did not necessarily mean that there would be an increase in consumption. McKendrick writes of the 'unleashing of the acquisitive instincts',[3] whilst Fraser describes how 'growing demand [was] stimulated by advertising and modern sales techniques'.[4] Neither the essentialist claim for a human acquisitive instinct nor the sociological claim for the impact of advertising and modern sales techniques rings true. If there is an acquisitive instinct, how come the circumstances which enabled it to be set loose have never occurred in other societies? Moreover, the claim for an acquisitive instinct is a central feature of the bourgeois ideology of possessive individualism.[5] As for Fraser's argument, we will see that advertising did become very important in the configuration around consumption. However, advertising in the second half of the nineteenth century and beyond addressed a rather different human subject to earlier advertising. From the 1850s onwards, advertising, and its effectiveness, was bound up with the experience which was a consequence of the spread of cultural fetishism.

One of the first effects of the development of the mass market was a standardisation of consumption. For example, Rosalind Williams has described how, in France in the 1860s, there were still wide variations in whether or not bread was a part of the staple diet and, if so, what kind of bread. By 1900 everybody ate wheat bread. Similarly, in the 1860s there were significant differences in the quality and type of dress of peasant and working-class women. By the 1890s these differences were much less obvious: 'everyone wore shorter, simpler, more colorful clothes'.[6] This standardisation took place in the second half of the nineteenth century.

In France around the same time there was a transformation in shopping practices. Up until this period shops had tended to be small. They had no display windows, and commodities did not have prices marked on them. People decided before they went shopping what they wished to purchase. They went to the appropriate shop and bargained for what they wanted. There was an expectation that, if you entered a shop, you bought something. This was understandable given that, since you knew what you wanted, you would not have entered the shop if you did not intend to buy. This expectation was compounded by the lack of choice. Since there was no range of alternative commodities, and since prices were variable because of bargaining, there was little point in shopping around.

The nineteenth century saw all these shopping practices change. Display windows and fixed prices started to become commonplace, as did window shopping and impulse buying. Rachel Bowlby comments that this new form of shopping was known in France as *le nouveau commerce*.[7] The culmination of these changes is to be found in the department store. It brought together under one roof a very wide range of commodities. In addition, coupled with the expansion of industrial production, the store was able to offer a choice in particular types of commodity. Williams writes that the first department store was Bon Marché, which opened in Paris in 1852.[8] Bowlby has described how, in the first eight years, under the ownership of Aristide Boucicaut, turnover at the store increased tenfold, and continued to rise 'at a comparable rate through the subsequent decades'.[9] The instant success of Bon Marché led to the rapid spread of department stores both in Paris and in provincial French cities, and then in London and New York. In Sydney, Australia, Anthony Hordern and Sons opened their first Palace Emporium in 1881.[10] As Bowlby sums it up: 'People could now come and go, to look and dream, perchance to buy, and shopping became a new bourgeois leisure activity – a way of pleasantly passing the time, like going to a play or visiting a museum.'[11]

Display became of central importance. Williams has shown the close connection between the expositions which began with the one at Crystal Palace in London in 1851 and the first Paris exposition of 1855 (then 1867, 1878, 1889, and culminating in the one of 1900) and the new display techniques for commodities. Commodities were not simply shown. Williams writes that 'the purpose of all expositions was, in the popular phrase of the time, to teach a "lesson of things"'.[12] They were meant to be instructive celebrations of progress. The 1867 exposition had both a Palace of Industry and a History of Labour exhibit; that of 1889 had a Gallery of Machines, 'a long hall with a vault 400 feet across where sightseers could gaze from a suspended walkway at a sea of spinning wheels, clanking hammers, and whirring gears'.[13] In spite of this emphasis on machinery of production, the expositions came increasingly to display commodities as an aspect of their 'lesson of things' and, unlike the Crystal Palace exposition, the Paris one of 1855 'began the tradition of placing price tags on all objects, as well as of charging admission'.[14] Williams makes the point that exotic displays helped to give the commodities a desirability they had not previously had:

> Consumer goods, rather than other facets of culture, became focal points for desire. The seemingly contrary activities of hard-headed accounting and dreamy-eyed fantasizing merged as business appealed to consumers by inviting them into a fabulous world of pleasure, comfort, and amusement.[15]

The department stores' new preoccupation with display was epitomised in, and reinforced by, the displays of the great expositions. However, as we shall see, the production of desire by associating displayed commodities with exotic locations and other fantasy images tells only half the story.

Guy Debord has characterised the present-day experience of the commodified world in terms of spectacle. He argues that: 'In societies where modern conditions of production prevail, all of life presents itself as an immense accumulation of *spectacles*. Everything that was directly lived has moved away into a representation.'[16] He goes on to explain that: 'The spectacle is the moment when the commodity has attained the *total occupation* of social life. Not only is the relation to the commodity visible but it is all one sees: the world one sees is its world.'[17] Debord offers no history of this development. For this we can turn to Thomas Richards, who, in his book *The Commodity Culture of Victorian England*, argues that the establishment of the commodity as a spectacle began with the Great Exhibition in London in 1851.[18] For Richards what was so striking about the Great Exhibition was 'the use of the commodity as a semiotic medium – as icon, commemorative, utopia, language, phenomenology, annunciation; in a word, as spectacle'.[19] This was because the Exhibition was, above all else, a celebration of commodities. Put another and more succinct way, spectacle 'was the reorientation of representation around the economic dictates of capitalism'.[20]

Nevertheless, the Great Exhibition could not achieve the renovation of commodities all by itself. Richards notes that 'it was not until the 1880s that commodities were again able to achieve a monopoly of signification in the public sphere'.[21] The spectacle of the Great Exhibition, and subsequently the spectacularising impact of advertising, reconstituted the commodity as spectacle. However, in other circumstances, spectacularisation was capable of commodifying things which, previously, had not been commodities. Most importantly for our purposes here, Richards notes that 'the medium that transformed the self into a commodity was the same medium that had already transformed so much of culture into a commodity: spectacle'.[22] Richards outlines this process using Althusser's theorisation of the subject, in which the subject's identity as an individual is constituted through their being hailed by, in this case, spectacle.[23] In the Introduction we noted that Althusser's theorisation of subjectivity, which makes use of interpellation, is closely tied to the individual's experience in the modern state. Moreover, Althusser self-consciously built his theory of social subjectivity on Lacan's psychoanalytic understanding of the subject, which, as we also saw, describes the experience of the individual in the modern state. The commodification of the self through spectacle is secondary to the production of that self in the modern state.

Richards argues that in the years following the Great Exhibition advertising in England was transformed. Previously, 'despite all the stunts, tricks, and gimmicks that advertisers used to dress up their offerings, the representation of the commodities remained remarkably stable for the first half of the nineteenth century'.[24] He suggests that the Great Exhibition of 1851 'represents a pivotal moment in the history of advertising, for the particular style it created for the commodity ultimately transformed the advertising industry'.[25] This style was spectacle. Richards claims for advertising a foundational role in the spectacularisation of commodities. What the Great Exhibition started, advertising completed by bringing to bear on the representation of commodities a number of significant socio-cultural themes. In Richards's words: 'out of these four discrete exhibitions, macrocosmic and microcosmic, representing monarchy and empire, the healthy body and the female body, came all the familiar imperatives of modern commodity culture, with its emphasis on status, eroticism, health and female sexuality'.[26] Of these eroticism and female sexuality, both centred on the spectacle of the female body, are paramount.

Richards's history is a useful complement to Debord's work. However, it does not explain why spectacle took hold in the second half of the nineteenth century, or the relationship between spectacle and an increased desire to consume. We can make a start at understanding this by going back to Debord. Following Marxist theory, Debord considers that 'the principle of commodity fetishism [is] the domination of society by "intangible as well as tangible things", which reaches its absolute fulfilment in the spectacle, where the tangible world is replaced by a selection of images which exist above it, and which simultaneously impose themselves as the tangible *par excellence*'.[27] In order to understand Debord's point I want to turn, now, to Marx's own discussion of commodity fetishism, placing it within the change in the organisation of male desire already outlined in the Introduction and explaining the importance of this change for the formation of cultural fetishism.

Sixteen years after the Great Exhibition, fifteen after the landmark opening of the Bon Marché department store, and forty years before the American invention of the assembly line, Karl Marx developed the concept of commodity fetishism. Marx published *Capital* in German in 1867. The first English translation appeared in 1887. Marx's discussion of capitalism focused first on commodities and the experience of commodities in capitalism. However, his concern did not stay with consumption. The discussion of commodity fetishism provided a way for Marx to move past the spectacular deception of the commodity to the economic conditions of commodity production. For Marx commodity fetishism describes the experience in which the commodity hides the process of its own production. Here I will distinguish two different types of commodity fetishism. One I will describe as passive, the other as active. The commodity fetishism theorised by Marx is passive. Passive commodity fetishism disarticulates the experience of the commodity from the process of production so that the commodity seems to come into existence at the point of commercial exchange, the moment when it appears in a shop as an item to be sold and bought. Active commodity fetishism begins from the relations outlined by Marx but describes the energisation of the commodity, and of the commercial exchange, through its association with sexual desire. In the period when Marx was writing the mode of objectification of the commodity which he describes was being complemented by a new element, the supplementary phallic desire that operates in cultural fetishism. This energisation has been a major, though not the only, element in the post-1850s development of the society of the spectacle.

Over the second half of the nineteenth century there was an expansion in the range and quantity of commodities on the market. In the early decades of the twentieth century this expansion was compounded by the development of the assembly line and the corresponding leap in mass production. Credit for the first fundamental reorganisation is usually given to Henry Ford. The Ford Motor Company was founded in 1903. In the beginning Ford's factory was organised along craft lines. The Model T was introduced in 1908. By this time some changes had been made to the system, but the major changes were made in response to the demand for the Model T. By January 1914 the changes culminated in 'the inauguration of the first endless-chain conveyor for final assembly at Ford's Highland Park plant':

> Within three months, the assembly time for the Model T had been reduced to one-tenth the time formerly needed, and by 1925 an organisation had been created which produced almost as many cars in a single day as had been produced, early in the history of the Model T, in an entire year.[28]

At around the same time major changes were taking place in the management of workers. Frederick Winslow Taylor, who published his now classic book *The Principles of Scientific Management* in 1911, is usually described as the father of scientific management; but, as Marta Braun points out, his 'claim to paternity is based on his synthesizing and consolidating ideas already current in the United States and Great Britain'.[29] Such was the general nature of the changes in industrial production taking place that Taylor's book was translated into French in 1913 just at the time when time and motion studies, which it advocated, were provoking significant industrial unrest across France.

The effect of the introduction of new, assembly-line-based mass-production techniques was to increase the quantities of commodities available very considerably. Stuart Ewen remarks: 'In response to the exigencies of the productive system of the twentieth century, excessiveness replaced thrift as a social value. It became imperative to invest the laborer with a financial power and a psychic desire to consume.'[30] The cultural-fetishistic supplementation of male desire was the basis of this new psychic desire to consume. The desire to assimilate the phallic fetish became associated with the buying of commodities as those commodities became, themselves, constructed as fetishes. The process involved the libidinal energisation of the commodity, the key feature of active commodity fetishism.

The distinction between passive and active commodity fetishism is focused in particular on the relations between the commodity and the consumer. In passive commodity fetishism the commodity disguises from the consumer its origin in the process of capitalist production, appearing only as an object to the gaze of the consumer. The objectification of the commodity, its reification, is closely bound up with the commodity's apparently *sui generis* existence.

Active commodity fetishism describes a qualitatively more dynamic relation between the commodity and the consumer in which the commodity appears to entice the consumer into buying it. Passive commodity fetishism describes the objectification of the commodity in capitalism; active commodity fetishism describes a further process of incorporating the consumer in the process of commodification.

Quoting from his own *Contribution to the Critique of Political Economy*, Marx begins *Capital* by writing: 'The wealth of those societies in which the capitalist mode of production prevails, presents itself as "an immense accumulation of commodities", its unit being a single commodity.'[31] Wealth is not measured in money but in owned material goods. The commodity is the material expression of capitalist economic practice. Marx describes a commodity as 'an object outside us, a thing that by its properties satisfies human wants of some sort or another'.[32] He goes on to write that it makes no difference whether these wants 'spring from the stomach or from fancy'.[33] Sidestepping the debate over needs theory, what is important for Marx is the wanting, not its source.

Marx distinguishes between the use-value of a commodity and its exchange-value. Simply, use-value refers to the use to which a commodity may be put. Use-value is intrinsic to the commodity. Exchange-value, on the other hand, is determined by a commodity's relation to other commodities. Marx argues that 'the mystical character of commodities does not originate ... in their use-value'.[34] Rather, it is an effect on the commodity of the capitalist exchange system – that is, of the exchange system which constitutes the product of labour as a commodity. Wolfgang Fritz Haug has argued that, today, what has become important is not use-value itself but the appearance of use-value.[35] He goes on to suggest:

> Within the system of selling and buying, the aesthetic illusion – the commodity's promise of use-value – enters the arena as an independent function in selling. For economic reasons it is only natural and, under the pressures of competition, ultimately necessary to gain technological control over and independent production of this aesthetic process.[36]

It is the commodity's aesthetic appearance, its promise of use-value, which we have already discussed in terms of spectacle. What Haug's comment emphasises is that the spectacularization of the commodity serves to enhance its exchange-value.

Marx goes on to describe a commodity as 'a mysterious thing, simply because in it the social character of men's labour appears to them as an objective character stamped upon the product of that labour; because the relation of the producers to the sum total of their own labour is presented to them as a social relation, existing not between themselves, but between the products of their labour'.[37] The labour of the workers returns to them in the objectified form of commodities which are valued within the exchange system of capitalism. What Marx is outlining here is the objectifying effect of that system. In order to describe this experience Marx has recourse to a nineteenth-century anthropological analogy:

> In [the mist-enveloped regions of the religious world] the productions of the human brain appear as independent beings endowed with life, and entering into relation both with one another and the human race. So it is in the world of commodities with the products of men's hands. This I call the Fetishism which attaches itself to the products of labour, so soon as they are produced as commodities, and which is therefore inseparable from the production of commodities.[38]

For Marx the term 'fetishism' is an analogical description of the experience of commodities in relation to the labour process of production. Marx was not concerned with the relation between the commodity and the consumer other than as an extension of the mystification which is an effect of the capitalist exchange system. This relation is the one emphasised in the process of active commodity fetishism.

The capitalist system of exchange separates the commodity from the conditions of its production. The first consequence of this is that (passive) commodity fetishism, in disguising the origin of commodities in production, also hides the real capitalist relations of that production, namely that workers produce more value than what they receive in exchange for their labour. The second consequence, as Sut Jhally writes, is that, 'because the objectification of human labour in products is masked by the market system of generalised commodity production, the worker is unable to make the distinction between necessary and surplus labour-time, and thus cannot penetrate to the heart of capitalist exploitation'.[39] The effect is that 'the *real and full* meaning of production is hidden beneath the *empty appearance* in exchange'.[40] The exchange system of capitalism objectifies commodities.

Objectification is inherent in both passive and active commodity fetishism. The effect of the exchange relation at the point of sale for consumption is to reinforce the origin-less quality of the commodity. For example, milk is just there, on supermarket shelves, in cartons and bottles; cars are just there, in car showrooms, ready to be bought. It is at the point of sale for consumption that active commodity fetishism takes place. The historical context for its development lay in the establishment of the new shopping practices – for example, display, and particularly fantasy displays – as well as the more formalised cash-nexus structure of the fixed price which, coupled with the price being shown on the commodity, both increased the connection between commodity and purchaser and all but effaced the role of the shop assistant in the purchasing transaction. The most important component in the expression of active commodity fetishism was the development of the new, spectacularising advertising. As Jhally writes:

> Only once the real meaning has been systematically emptied out of commodities does advertising refill this void with its own symbols. Thus when products appear in the marketplace, although we may well be aware of them as products of human labour, because there is no specific social meaning accompanying this awareness, this symbolisation of advertising appears as more real and concrete.[41]

Jhally is explaining that, after passive commodity fetishism empties a commodity of the social meaning accruing from the relations of production of the commodity, it can then be refilled, making it desirable. This is the process of active commodity fetishism. The description is most appropriate for the new, spectacularising advertising.

The rise of modern advertising, which saw its task not as the disseminating of information but as the persuading of people to purchase the rapidly increasing number, and expanding array, of commodities, was coupled with the spread of mass production. As Stuart Ewen puts it, modern advertising 'must be seen as a direct response to the needs of mass industrial capitalism'.[42] Ewen dates its spread in the United States to the 1920s, when it 'played a role of growing significance in industry's attempt to develop a continually responsive consumer market'.[43] However, as we have seen, it has an earlier history in England in the second half of the nineteenth century. This form of advertising provided a new solution to a new problem.

Ewen has described the way the early mass advertising of the 1920s achieved its goal of increasing consumption. He writes that 'the functional goal of national advertising was the creation of desires and habits',[44] and adds a little later: 'It was recognised that in order to get people to consume and, more importantly, to keep them consuming, it was more efficient to endow them with a critical self-consciousness in tune with the "solutions" of the marketplace than to fragmentarily argue for products on their own merit.'[45] Advertising invests commodities with a particular kind of cultural meaning, one which aims to make the commodity desirable. In order to achieve this desirability advertising makes use of, and enhances, the desiring relation between commodity and consumer.

At this point we need to consider Freud's theory of fetishism in order to understand how individual fetishism connects with the social process of cultural fetishism and how both ultimately underpin active commodity fetishism. Freud's essay on fetishism was published in German in 1927. Like Marx, he took the idea of a fetish from the anthropological tradition, but Freud's emphasis was on the experience of the fetish as an emotionally charged object, exalted to a special status. Freud describes fetishism as an effect of desire. In his work fetishism is a peculiarly male experience. It is also an experience dependent on sight. We need to note here, though it will be discussed in more detail in the next chapter, that spectacle is, in the first place, a visual experience. For Freud fetishism relates to the male fear of castration. The boy's horror at seeing the apparently castrated woman leads to a substitution. As Freud writes, 'to put it plainly: the fetish is a substitute for the woman's (the mother's) penis that the little boy once believed in and ... does not want to give up'.[46] In Freud's work fetishism is a perversion, an effect of an incorrectly resolved Oedipus complex. Rather than accepting women's lack of a penis, men who are fetishists have come to terms with the knowledge that women do not have penises by a process of compensation. Whilst individual fetishism may be applicable to only a limited number of men, the castration complex which gives rise to it is generally applicable in our patriarchal culture and, in post-1850s society, is reinforced by the experience of phallic lack which drives cultural fetishism. This reinforcement suggests that all men develop a heightened fascination with women's bodies' phallic 'lack'.

Freud argues that psychosexual development through the Oedipus complex requires that at one point sons desire their mothers and daughters their fathers. In the female case it is among other things the recognition of her own lack of a penis, and the blame associated with her mother for this lack, that turns a girl towards her father. I have already argued that the preoccupation with the penis, and lack of it, articulates in individual experience with the phallocentric and phallocratic cultural ordering of Western capitalist society. It is also at this time that the girl's sexual desire is reconstructed from an active desiring to a passive desire to be desired. Gradually, and in the male case with the aid of the fear of castration by the father, a reorientation of sexual desire takes place. The effect of the acceptance that their object choices are prohibited leads boys – and girls, though the process is slower and does not have a psychosexual element – to direct their libidinous desire outside of the nuclear family.

In the Freudian model the little boy becomes a fetishist at the moment he denies what he sees, and he chooses as his complementary substitute something he has seen close to the moment of discovery of the woman's 'lack'. This is not, in the first place, what is going on when the pubescent girl's body becomes the fetishised object. Rather, this particular fetishisation is a consequence of the adult male's lived experience of his phallic inadequacy. In a cultural order dominated by the male body, the body of the pubescent girl is beginning to mark her as Other. Yet, as a pubescent girl, she is still experienced as safe because her body does not yet carry fully those mature female markers which signify her phallic 'lack'. She is, then, a not-boy who is not yet a woman either. At this moment the desire for her as a (potential) woman is reinforced by a fetishistic desire for her body as a phallic fetish. In the long run this fetishisation, and its associated desire, led to a reconstruction of what was considered to be the desirable female body, and a heightened male fascination with the female body – particularly its penile 'lack'.

The fetishisation of the female body constructed it as a site of fear as well as desire. This fear, the projection of men's repressed fear of their own phallic lack, was displaced on to women themselves, and especially on to 'active', and therefore phallic, women. Bram Dijkstra, in *Idols of Perversity*, has written a book which is a remarkable catalogue of artistic portrayals of the fear and aggression felt by bourgeois men towards women in the second half of the nineteenth century. He argues that 'the establishment of a fundamentally new, massively institutionalized, ritual-symbolic perception of the role of woman in society ... was ... the principal source of the pervasive antifeminine mood of the late nineteenth century –

and, by logical extension, of a number of elements of sexist mythology which still survive'.[47] Elsewhere in his book Dijkstra provides
some reasons for this male reaction to women:

> Born, for the most part, into middle-class households whose
> precepts about the nature of women had been taken from
> Michelet and his ilk, yet growing up in an age which saw
> women resist their marginalization, assert their sexual
> presence, and turn the conditions of their marginalization
> into an aggressive weapon, these men were often overcome by
> an antifeminine horror born of the disparity they observed
> between the idea of the perfect, sexless woman and the reality
> of healthy, assertive female bodies.[48]

Dijkstra's point is a good one, but it only tells one part of the story
of the construction of the bourgeois male experience of women
from the middle of the nineteenth century onwards.

Historically, the eroticisation of the body of the pubescent girl
developed in the context of the relatively new category of adolescence. Frank Musgrove claims Jean-Jacques Rousseau, whose views
on the family as a model for the state have already been discussed in
the Introduction, as the 'inventor' of adolescence in his book Emile,
first published in 1762.[49] Certainly, from the second half of the
eighteenth century, a new period of life was introduced between
childhood and adulthood. Meanwhile, the eroticisation of girls,
whilst focused on puberty, ranged back to pre-pubescence. Dijkstra
has described how, during the latter part of the nineteenth century,
paintings of children acquired a sexualised ambivalence whilst
painters searched for images of innocence: 'And so these innocents,
these children, began to take on, in the fantasies of painters, the
outlines of the female temptresses they were trying to escape.
Minds filled with the lustful shapes of worldly women soon discovered in children the lineaments of sin.'[50] However, this sin was only
incipient. Dijkstra quotes from Armand Silvestre's Le Nu au Salon:
Champ de Mars, published in 1892, in which, discussing a painting
by Armand Point entitled Puberty, Silvestre 'talked about how, in
Point's young girl "the disturbing unfolding of woman's essence",
would awaken "thoughts until now mysteriously slumbering in
deceptive serenity"'.[51] 'Thus', Dijkstra goes on, 'the appeal of puberty
was the prurient certainty of carnal knowledge, the shadow of evil
which, for instance, hovers threateningly behind the young girl in
Edvard Munch's familiar painting also called "Puberty"'.[52]

The sexual ambiguity around the male desire for the pubescent girl also led to an idealised feminisation of the male adolescent. As Dijkstra notes: 'The ephebe, the sensitive male adolescent, was the true ideal of aesthetic beauty.'[53] He goes on to describe how many artists 'found a sensuous purity in young male bodies which seemed to put the lusher contours of woman to shame'.[54] One solution to the problem posed by the male adolescent in the experience of cultural fetishism was to reconstitute the ideal adolescent as androgynous.

The culminating work in the discursive articulation of adolescence was G. Stanley Hall's two-volume *Adolescence: Its Psychology and Its Relations to Physiology, Anthropology, Sociology, Sex, Crime, Religion and Education*, published in the United States in 1904. Richards argues that, at the time Hall was writing, 'adolescence was becoming something more than a stage of life through which everyone passed'.[55] It was becoming closely associated with consumption. Briefly outlining Hall's book, Richards argues that his 'rendering of adolescence reads like an extended account of the modern consuming subject'.[56] That adolescent consuming subject became the teenager of the post-Second World War period.

I have already noted that Richards claims the exhibition of the female body as one of the building blocks of consumer culture. He traces the preoccupation with this sight to the development of what he describes as 'the seaside girl'.[57] Richards describes how, in Britain, the seaside resort was 'a site of fantasy and a primary locus of Victorian sexual politics,'[58] and goes on to suggest that 'at the beach the body of the adolescent or prepubescent girl became a cultural ideal'.[59] He sums up his claims thus: 'The space of leisure had become sexualised.'[60] In the next chapter we shall see that this (male) sexualisation of women was much more general than the leisure world of the seaside resort. Nevertheless, the seaside girl was an important British topos of the eroticisation of the pubescent girl. One reason for its importance was its respectability, or perhaps it would be better to say its public acceptance. Another reason, which depended on its acceptance, lies in the close association of the development of this topos with the spread of the commodity culture. Invented around the 1870s, the seaside girl soon became an advertising staple. As Richards notes: 'The seaside girl was the most modern form of spectacle devised by late-Victorian commodity culture, and it has proved to be the most lasting.'[61]

Attributing rather too much to this topos (after all, he never explains why it should be the *pubescent* girl who forms this key encouragement to consume), Richards describes how the seaside girl 'eulogized adolescence' and how 'at one and the same time she marked off the adolescent female body as an object of commodity culture and changed the shape of women's anatomy by making that body normative and compulsory'.[62] The seaside girl is, in fact, just one example of the effect of the fetishisation of the pubescent female body. Among other things the example shows how that fetishisation could have effects in everyday life. Where, in the nineteenth century, the concern with adolescence had centred on male youth and their transition to the public world, the seaside-girl topos heralds the public shift to a preoccupation with the pubescent/adolescent girl's body as a sexual object, a concern which provides one history for the post-Second-World-War teenage girl as both sexual object and consumer – things which, as we shall see, are literally embodied in Nabokov's Lolita character.

One socially unacceptable example of the new male bourgeois preoccupation with pubescent girls resulted in the campaigns in Great Britain during the late 1870s and 1880s against the white slave trade and child prostitution. A material outcome of these campaigns was the raising of the age of consent from thirteen to sixteen as a part of the Criminal Law Amendment Act of 1885. So great was the concern, Judith Walkowitz has argued, that 'the white-slavery and child-prostitution scandals had all the symptoms of a cultural paranoia overtaking Britain in the late nineteenth century'.[63] Deborah Gorham has described how 'organized protest against child prostitution manifested itself first as a protest against the traffic in English girls to state-regulated brothels in Belgium, Holland, and France'.[64] Alfred Dyer, a publisher of books and pamphlets on social purity, began the campaign in 1879. One peak in the campaign was the publication by the journalist W. T. Stead, in the summer of 1885, of a series of investigatory pieces under the general title of 'The Maiden Tribute of Modern Babylon' in the *Pall Mall Gazette*. Walkowitz describes 'The Maiden Tribute' as 'one of the most successful pieces of yellow journalism published in Britain during the nineteenth century'.[65] It would seem that there was, simultaneously, both an increase in child prostitution and a tremendous social preoccupation with the idea of it. Arguing for the raising of the age of consent, Stead himself claimed that 'the preventative operation of the law is much more effective than I anticipated, for it is almost the sole barrier against a constantly increasing appetite for the immature of both sexes'.[66] Walkowitz writes that after the publication of the series one public demonstration in London, held in Hyde Park, was estimated at 250,000 people.[67]

There was also a new concern with the seduction of girls. Where previously the seduction of working-class girls by bourgeois men 'had been of concern to the state only in so far as it deprived employers of the services of their servants and, of less concern, fathers of the marriage prospects of their daughters',[68] 'in the second half of the nineteenth century, seduction was repositioned, in popular perceptions if not in law, as a moral crime which threatened society'.[69] The age category of the girls described in this new discourse of seduction varied, but ran from young childhood to as old as twenty-one.[70]

The most emotive consequence of cultural fetishism has been the father's transgressive desire for his daughter's body. In his desire for his daughter the father seeks the phallus that will transform him from father to Father, a fantastic enterprise that would translate him from being a 'weak' individual father, patriarch of the family only to the extent of his subordination to the state, to being the patriarchal embodiment of the state, the possessor of the phallus. Possession of the daughter can be read, then, as an attempt both to gain the phallus and to secure the patriarchal role in the family in its contextual relation with the state, through an empirical demonstration of male sexual power. Because it is a case of such significance I want to turn to a discussion of the historicity of father–daughter incest, and to look at how Freud considered the issue.

Phallic desire is central to the cultural construction of the Oedipus complex. It is a desire constituted as both active and empowering. Within the classical, Oedipally structured, bourgeois nuclear family, two desiring relations are traditionally discounted. In the Oedipus-complex structure there is no concern with the sexual desire of mothers for sons or fathers for daughters. Now, if women give up their active sexual desire as a part of their recognition of their exclusion from the phallic order, we are left with the question of the relation of fathers and daughters.

From the middle of the nineteenth century there was an increasing discursive concern with father–daughter incest. In an important thesis (now a book) on the discursive construction of the working class in the nineteenth century, Lynette Finch, writing about Great Britain and Australia, argues that the period between 1850 and 1920 marks the first wave of modern reports which gave heavy emphasis to sexual behaviour in general, and incest in particular within working class families. During this period most major reports into the lives of the urban poor included direct or implied reference to incest. These surveys were, furthermore, specifically referring to a particular form of incest – sexual intercourse between father, or father-substitute and daughter, or (to a far lesser extent) brother–sister sexual relations.[71]

Finch points out that previously the concern over incest seems to have centred on the incestuous marriage of cousins, uncles and nieces.

Finch describes how the novel preoccupation with father–daughter incest became an important element in the bourgeois moralisation of the working class. She writes that, although incest was a crime in Scottish law and in some American states, it did not become a crime in other than ecclesiastical law in Britain until 1908.[72] The law in Britain was based on a law enacted in the Australian state of Victoria in 1891. Finch emphasises that 'the [Victorian] law that the legislative members debated covered only that aspect of incest which so worried middle class commentators – father–daughter incest'.[73]

Finch argues that the new bourgeois preoccupation with father–daughter incest 'signalled an attendant problem – the problem of the unnatural. *This* is how depraved these people are, the reports were designed to show. *This* is the level of sickness and irredeemability that is present among this class.'[74] Whilst this was the case, the historical problem would seem to be more complex. If the purpose of the new discourse was to exemplify the immoral behaviour of the working class, it would be expected that bourgeois concern with father–daughter incest would already be manifested in legislation – unless, possibly, such incest was thought to be so impossible that it did not need legislation. In fact the bourgeois reports documenting father–daughter incest predate the legislation criminalising this practice. What this suggests is that the reports on working-class behaviour exhibit a new bourgeois preoccupation.

It was not only in Britain and Australia that there was a new concern with father–daughter incest. In France in the second half of the nineteenth century there developed a medical literature on child abuse which focused particularly on sexual abuse. The beginning of this tradition seems to have been an article by Ambroise Auguste Tardieu entitled 'Etude médico-légale sur les sévices et mauvais traitements exercés sur des enfants' (A Medico-legal Study of Cruelty and Brutal Treatment Inflicted on Children), published in 1860.[75] Jeffrey Masson notes that in his slightly earlier book, *Etude médico-légale sur les attentats aux moeurs* (A Medico-legal Study of Assaults on Decency), published in 1857, 'Tardieu drew attention to the frequency of sexual assaults on children, especially young girls'.[76] Masson goes on to quote Tardieu from the final edition of his book (1878):

> What is even sadder is to see that ties of blood, far from con-stituting a barrier to these impardonable allurements, serve only too frequently to favor them. Fathers abuse their daughters, brothers abuse their sisters. These facts have been coming to my attention in increasing numbers. I can count twelve more cases since the last but one edition of this book.[77]

The types of incest which concerned Tardieu are the same as those discussed by Finch. What cannot be known is whether the increase in numbers coming to Tardieu's attention was the result of his publishing in this area, a discursive effect, or an actual increase in numbers. I would suggest all three. The discursive preoccupation with father–daughter incest in the late nineteenth century was fundamental to the new sexualisation of pubescent girls. Returning for a moment to Finch's work, it may well be that father–daughter incest was not uncommon in working-class households. However, it was not practised within a family structured through the Oedipus complex or, therefore, within the same eroticised order of proscrip-tion which was epitomised in the bourgeois discourse of incest.

The constant speaking about working-class father–daughter incest was matched by a total silence over incest within the bour-geois nuclear family. In the French literature the works by Tardieu were counterbalanced by writers such as Alfred Fournier and Paul Brouardel, who argued that children lie about being sexually inter-fered with. What is interesting in the cases they cite is the claim to moral probity of the men involved. Masson quotes an extract from Fournier's address to the Academy of Medicine in 1880 in which a rich, upper-class man (Masson's description) was accused of trying to rape a young girl from a poor, lower-class family: 'An excellent and perfectly honourable man, father of a family, justly honoured and absolutely incapable (I will gladly act as a guarantor) of any ignominious action, allowed himself to be caught in a trap of this kind.'[78] Bourgeois men, it would seem, would not engage in such sexual activity. In the British and Australian discourse on father–daughter incest, discussion always centred on the working class. It was the silence which surrounded even the possibility of father–daughter incest among the bourgeoisie, and the implicit rejection of the existence of any such incest, of which Freud ran foul.

In Freud's early work, as is well known, he claimed that hysteria was grounded in actual childhood sexual experience and he situated this back before pubescence, as early as early childhood. In 'The Aetiology of Hysteria', given first as an address to the Society for Psychiatry and Neurology in Vienna in 1896 and published the same year, Freud wrote:

> I therefore put forward the thesis that at the bottom of every case of hysteria there are one or more occurrences of premature sexual experience, occurrences which belong to the earliest years of childhood but which can be produced through the work of psycho-analysis in spite of the intervening decades. I believe that this is an important finding, the discovery of a *caput Nili* in neuropathology ...[79]

It has been traditionally argued that shortly after this Freud recognised his mistake and, in a letter to his friend and colleague Wilhelm Fleiss on 21 September 1897, recanted. In *An Autobiographical Study*, first published in German in 1925, Freud writes: 'When ... I was at last obliged to recognize that these scenes of seduction had never taken place, and that they were only phantasies which my patients had made up or which I myself had perhaps forced on them, I was for some time completely at a loss.' Freud's confusion continued until he realised 'that the neurotic symptoms were not related directly to actual events but to wishful phantasies'.[80]

In his book on Freud's seduction theory, Masson argues that Freud must have been familiar with the French literature on the sexual molestation of children. Masson makes clear the tremendous professional and social pressure placed on Freud by the psychiatric movement to recant. He also shows the extent to which Freud remained ambivalent for a long time over the importance of real sexual experiences as opposed to fantasies. In the light of this we need to recognise that there are two different arguments in Freud's work concerning incest. The first relates to traditional concerns with incest – that is to say, male incest with near female relatives but not father–daughter incest. In *Totem and Taboo*, for example, Freud writes:

a little more reflection will show that exogamy linked with the totem effects more (and therefore aims at more) than the prevention of incest with a man's mother and sisters. It makes sexual intercourse impossible for a man with all the women of his own clan (that is to say with a number of women who are not his blood-relatives) by treating them as though they were his blood-relatives.[81]

The focus here is on mother and sisters as well as those women identified by Finch as being of concern in ecclesiastical law, cousins and nieces. Father–daughter incest is mentioned only in a footnote, where it is reduced to a lineage problem associated with totemic proscription. This situation is accounted for in Freud's societal-origin myth, the story of the primal horde and the killing of the patriarch by the sons (discussed in the Introduction), where he makes it clear that what is at stake as a consequence of the patriarch's murder is incest between sons and mothers, and between the sons and their sisters. In his socially oriented work, then, Freud has a concern with incest that follows traditional lines.

Freud's second argument concerning incest is to be found in his theory of individual psychosexual development. This theory was developed in the context of Freud's rejection of his own seduction theory. So closely connected are these two things that Anna Freud wrote to Masson that: 'Keeping up the seduction theory would mean to abandon the Oedipus complex, and with it the whole importance of phantasy life, conscious or unconscious phantasy. In fact, I think there would have been no psychoanalysis afterwards.'[82] It is, as Anna Freud suggests, the Oedipus complex in its formulation for girls which legitimises the reconstruction of the seduction theory.

It should be noted first that Freud used the German term for seduction, *Verführung*. The consensus for translating the theory in English as the seduction theory echoes the late-nineteenth-century British discourse of seduction described by Finch and outlined above. The difference is that where the British discourse centres on bourgeois men and working-class girls, Freud's theory describes bourgeois fathers and daughters. In both cases the use of the term 'seduction' hides the power relation and force involved. As Masson notes, Freud uses words like 'rape', 'abuse', 'attack', 'assault', 'aggression' and 'trauma' to describe the parental action.[83]

Freud did rather more than simply transform the father–daughter scene from being real to being a fantasy. He also reversed the structure of desire. Rather than the father desiring the daughter, the daughter now desires the father. Her fantasy is that the father seduces her. It is this restructuring of desire that is legitimised by the female version of the Oedipus complex. In the *New Introductory Lectures on Psycho-Analysis*, first published in German in 1933, Freud puts it this way: 'in the Oedipus situation the girl's father has become her love-object, and we expect that in the normal course of development she will find her way from this paternal object to her final choice of an object'.[84] The 'normal course of development' refers to the resolution of the female version of the Oedipus complex. This involves not only the transfer of the girl's affections from her father to another man but, also, a shift in her erotogenic zone from the clitoris to the vagina. All in all the girl passes 'from her masculine phase to the feminine one to which she is biologically destined'.[85] As I have noted, what this means for Freud is that the girl gives up her active desire and becomes a passive object of desire, a situation where her desire is manifested in attempts to increase her desirability. The resolution of the Oedipus complex marks the girl's final loss of active desire and, with her positioning as a passive object, the possibility of her construction by the father (and other men) as a fetish.

This second argument of Freud's is not in the first place an argument about father–daughter incest but, rather, a claim about psychosexual relations within the family. The girl's desire for the father might lead to incest if the father does not have the proper moral probity; but, of course, all bourgeois fathers do. In the reformulation of the seduction theory the father has no desire for his daughter. However, as we have seen, bourgeois discourse spoke insistently about non-bourgeois fathers desiring their daughters and, indeed, about bourgeois men (fathers often) desiring the daughters of working-class fathers. Freud's acceptance of the dominant discourse about bourgeois fathers replicated in psychoanalytic theory the repression of bourgeois society over father–daughter incest. It is not the case, as Anna Freud claims, that the acceptance of the seduction theory would have entailed no development of psychoanalysis. That Anna Freud should suggest this signals the strength of the determination to continue to deny the bourgeois father's desire for his daughter. At the same time the preoccupation with father–daughter incest was displaced on to working–class fathers. At the moment when bourgeois society constructed father–daughter incest as *the* form of incest of concern, Freud was pressured into reconstructing his theory so that its presence was not apparent among the bourgeoisie.

In his celebrated letter to Fleiss, Freud comments to the effect that one consequence of accepting the seduction theory was 'the surprise that in all cases, the *father*, not excluding my own, had to be accused of being perverse – the realization of the unexpected frequency of hysteria, with precisely the same conditions prevailing in each, whereas surely such widespread perversions against children are not very probable'.[86] Freud was right both in the seduction theory and in his presentation of the daughter's Oedipal fantasy desire. They describe two quite different processes, the latter a function of the sexual organisation of the nuclear family, the former an aspect of the structure of cultural fetishism. Freud was working at the time when the father's desire for the daughter, and male desire for pubescent girls generally, was becoming common.

Freud made clear that fetishism is founded on the gaze. For the individual male it is the shock of the visual discovery that women do not have penises which provokes in some cases the fetishistic substitution. Cultural fetishism also operates in terms of sight. From the nineteenth century onwards, as will be discussed in the next two chapters, society has been dominated by spectacularisation. This spectacularity has been based in the spectacularisation of the female body. Frank Mort has noted that:

> Both written and visual pornography represented women for the male gaze across the virtue/vice, innocence/depravity oppositions. The clearest examples were in the photographic studies of child prostitutes dating from the 1860s and 1870s, where childhood innocence was erotically framed against visible signs of immoral sexuality, such as exposed genitalia or the depraved stare.[87]

The dichotomies Mort outlines are based on a primary sexualised/non-sexualised dichotomy. This, he writes, is most obvious in the photographs of child prostitutes. In these, the revelation of their genitalia, the focus of the fetishising stare, is set against the girls' discursively constructed childhood innocence. More generally, as in the example of advertising's use of the seaside girl, the fetishism attached to the pubescent girl is displaced on to commodities – though sometimes the pubescent girl, or rather her body, itself becomes commodified in prostitution.

Industrial capitalism articulated with the nuclear family in such a way that, as the family became the female haven of domesticity, so an ideological division of labour came into being in which men worked and women ran the home. As more and more goods were taken out of the home and produced as commodities in factories, so women became the shoppers for the home. William Leach has described how, in the United States, 'as early as the 1840s and 1850s, especially in the urban centers, shopping had become a woman's job, reflecting the gender differentiation of roles that resulted from the separation of workplace and home and that was supported by the rise of wage and salaried male labor'.[88] We can understand active commodity fetishism as a two-tier system: men consume women, and women consume manufactured commodities. In the Introduction I described how women's consumption may be understood as an attempt to compensate for the culturally constructed feeling of phallic lack.

Passive commodity fetishism is centred on the cash-nexus relation in which labour-power is sold and bought for the purpose of production. It was historically, ideologically, a male exchange. Active commodity fetishism is centred on the cash-nexus relation in which commodities are sold and bought. As shopping developed in importance in the mid-1800s it was, in the first place, a female practice. Leach argues that in the United States:

> After the Civil War the number of shopping women increased. In the late 1860s Alexander Turney Stewart, the first great department store prince, pioneered in institutionalizing shopping as a female activity. ... By 1915 women were doing between 80 and 85 percent of the consumer purchasing in the United States.[89]

The gendering of the economic division of labour between (male) production and (female) consumption attenuated even further the connection between the commodity in the shop and its production history. The department stores recognised the demonstrable fact that it was women who shopped and catered for women. They stocked, in the main, household items, women's clothes, and aids to 'feminine beauty'.

Commodities became feminised and eroticised. Display, fixed price, advertising, and desire combined to provoke one other aspect of the new shopping practice, impulse buying. Bowlby has pointed out that, for Marx, commodities were thought of in female terms. She quotes him from the beginning of the chapter on exchange in *Capital*. Here Marx described commodities as things which 'lack the power to resist man'. He went on: 'If they are unwilling, he can use force; in other words, he can take possession of them.'[90] Bowlby comments that 'the very imagery used of the relationship between commodities and buyers is one of seduction and rape'.[91] The same imagery, we should note, was used in the debates over the public safety of young girls, and by Freud in his discussions of father–daughter relations. Marx's metaphor expresses the close connection that was developing between women's bodies and commodities. Active sexual desire in modern Western culture, as we have already noted, is male. With the putting into place of cultural fetishism this male desire begins to be associated with appropriation. It is this reformation of desire in terms of appropriation which forms the connection between sexual desire and consumption. Both manufactured commodities and women's bodies became sites for appropriation and consumption. As we shall see in Chapter 5, the rise in recent years of the male cannibalistic eating of women in both life and fantasy acts out the appropriation/consumption of women.

In this system consumption takes place for phallic reassurance. Referring to the twentieth-century change in the dominant culturally acceptable body shape for women, Ewen points out that as the 'mania for thinness',[92] as he calls it, took hold, so also product design began to mimic the female body. To illustrate this point Ewen quotes from the premier American industrial designer Raymond Loewy, who, in redesigning the Studebaker car, gave the Starliner 'its hungry and slenderized look'.[93] Ewen goes on to note that the original Coca-Cola bottle, introduced in 1916, 'was a tribute in glass to the bounteous ideals of Victorian womanhood':

> Its indented waist separated a full bosom from broad hips. When, nearly fifty years later, Loewy was commissioned to bring the familiar trademark up to date, he merely drew upon the changed silhouette of femininity. Elongating the fluid glass, he put the bottle on a diet, achieving – once again – a 'slenderized look'.[94]

The Coca-Cola bottle, the phallic signifier in so many youth-oriented Coca-Cola advertisements, is, then, in the first place, the representation of an ideal female body. In a general comment Ewen writes that 'this association between product design and (particularly female) body ideal is, today, commonplace'.[95] And it is the feminised and phallicised commodity – its 'femininity' and phallicness being quite literally expressed in the Coca Cola bottle's form – which women as well as men consume.

In her description of the relation between desire and consumption, Bowlby does not make use of the idea of fetishism. Instead, arguing that Freud's work describes the cultural order of late-nineteenth and early-twentieth-century Western capitalist society, Bowlby makes use of Freud's elaboration of narcissism. She explains that, in this phallocentric order,

> girls must come to terms with the fact that they are already castrated, lacking the male organ and what it represents. If they do not, they are engaged in a futile attempt to take on the functions of a masculine subjectivity not their own. Hence the tendency of women to remain closer to the narcissism of childhood and outside the arenas of public achievement.[96]

From this point of view the female consumer is narcissistic. Making the point that Freud's description of the female psychosexual make-up can be read as a part of 'an interpretation of the implicit forms of gender relations in Europe at the turn of the century',[97] Bowlby suggests that women were constructed simultaneously as 'less active than men' and as 'more narcissistically absorbed in themselves, their beauty, their desirability as potential objects of male love'.[98] Marketers of consumer goods have appealed 'to [woman's] wish or need to adorn herself as an object of beauty'.[99] Bowlby goes on:

> The dominant ideology of feminine subjectivity in the late nineteenth century perfectly fitted woman to receive the advances of the seductive commodity offering to enhance her womanly attractions. Seducer and seduced, possessor and possessed of one another, women and commodities flaunt their images at one another in an amorous regard which both extends and reinforces the classical picture of the young girl gazing into the mirror in love with herself.[100]

We can understand now how narcissism complements the combination of active commodity fetishism and cultural fetishism as elements of the reconstruction of consumption. Emphasised as a female practice, it reinforces the female desire to purchase commodities. It also helps to make comprehensible the connection between the feminisation of commodities and their consumption by women. Narcissism, caught up in spectacle, operates within the overdetermining phallic economy.

Perhaps the best text to exemplify the coupling of the male fascination with pubescent girls and female consumption is Vladimir Nabokov's *Lolita*. Nabokov's best-known – and most notorious –

book was first published in an edition by Olympia Press in Paris in 1955. In a 1956 Afterword, Nabokov describes how the book was turned down by four American publishers, all of whom were shocked by its theme. Olympia Press have a reputation for publishing books with erotic themes that other publishers are wary of taking on. And yet the book's popularity was such that in 1962 *Lolita* was released as a major film. By this time the book had been reconstructed as comic. In 1980 that bastion of British publishing, Penguin, brought out an edition. On the back was an extract from a review by Philip Toynbee in the *Observer* which describes the book as 'pervasively and continuously funny'. Through this period the idea of a nymphet as propounded in the book, and the name Lolita itself, became associated with the idea of desirable pubescent girls, mature in the ways of the world well beyond their years, who flirted with – or even possibly seduced – older men. This reading, which represses the book's incestuous concerns and constructs Lolita as the one who desires and seduces, signifies the extent to which the story has come to voice the male fantasy articulated with the fetishisation of the pubescent girl.

*Lolita* is narrated by a man who was in his late thirties at the time the action begins. He gives himself the pseudonym of Humbert Humbert. He describes himself as a nympholept, a man preoccupied with nymphets. Nymphets are certain girls between the ages of nine and fourteen. This age spread actually fits within G. Stanley Hall's definition of adolescence in his 1904 book, *Adolescence*, already mentioned, which has it stretching from eight to eighteen.[101] In addition, we can note another reference of Dijkstra's:

> Paul Adam, in a very nasty article 'On Children' published in *La Revue Blanche* in 1895, saw the perverse erotic characteristics of woman as magnified in the behaviour of the female child. He contended that these female children, aged between eight and thirteen, 'found a perverse pleasure in watching sedentary middle-aged men expose themselves to them for a few pennies'.[102]

Humbert Humbert's lengthy description of the qualities of nymphets early on in the book details mostly what nymphets are not, though they should, he writes, have a 'fey grace' and an 'elusive, shifty, soul-shattering, insidious charm'.[103] As the book proceeds it is clear that this is not all. The nympholept must be constructed into a relation of sexual desire with the girl. She must have a pubescent body and express a combination of sexual innocence and naive experience. She must seem to the nympholept to be sexually enticing him whilst, at the same time, presenting an innocence which requires protection. Most important of all is the girl's age. Humbert remarks a number of times in the book that a girl gradually stops being a nymphet as she grows into a woman. Indeed, from time to time he considers this problem in relation to Lolita. As for the man, Humbert writes that 'there must be a gap of several years, never less than ten I should say, generally thirty or forty, and as many as ninety in a few known cases, between maiden and man to enable the latter to come under a nymphet's spell'.[104]

At the outset of the book Humbert tells a story from his own adolescence. When he was thirteen he met a girl a few months younger called Annabel Leigh. They were sexually attracted to each other but were never able to consummate their desire. Humbert suggests that it was the spell cast by Annabel which transformed him into a nympholept. So far as the book's narrative is concerned, the Annabel Leigh story serves as a distraction from the main issue. Humbert meets Lolita when he boards at her mother's house. Charlotte Haze is a widow. Humbert immediately recognises Lolita as a nymphet. Subsequently he plots to get closer to Lolita, and increase his control over her and access to her, by marrying Charlotte, who has fallen in love with him. Humbert Humbert in this way becomes Lolita's stepfather. Shortly after the marriage Charlotte dies, run over by a car after having discovered that Humbert has married her only because of his desire for her daughter. At this point Humbert puts round a story that he and Charlotte had had an affair some years earlier, implying that Lolita is really his natural daughter. Charlotte's death clears the way for Humbert's access to Lolita.

Humbert's relationship with Lolita is mediated by money and commodities. Before he picks her up from summer camp at Camp Q. to begin their sexual travels across the United States, Humbert buys her a wardrobe of clothes. Often he gives her money for sexual favours. In this relation there is an echo from another, earlier story when Humbert picked up a nymphet prostitute in Paris. Lolita is positioned both as a commodity – like a prostitute, she can be bought – and as a consumer. Throughout their time together Humbert is constantly buying her presents. At the end of the book Humbert is sought out by Lolita, now heavily pregnant and living in a parlous situation, who asks for a gift of money. Humbert gives her the money in exchange for the name of the man who stole her away from him. Lolita, as we know from the enclosing letter at the beginning of the book, dies in childbirth. None of this matters for the myth of Lolita which now circulates in Western culture. From the point of view of the general reception of the book, its ending is inconsequential. What is remembered is a very particular reading of the relationship between Lolita and Humbert.

The 1962 film works within the dominant reading. In the first place the film's construction as a comedy of manners undercuts the theme. The male leads, James Mason and Peter Sellers, both seek to highlight the comedy of the situation, as does Shelley Winters in the role of Charlotte Haze. Most importantly, however, Lolita herself is no longer twelve when Humbert meets her. Although her age is unspecified it is clear that she is meant to be about sixteen. She is already going to dances and parties where there are boys. This Lolita is a sexualised American teenager of the 1950s. The overall effect is a change of emphasis: Humbert is made more innocuous, becoming a relatively innocent fantasist almost unable to carry out his dreams in practice; Lolita becomes a 'fast' sixteen-year-old interested in seducing the lodger who married her mother.

*Lolita* was published into a United States – and a Western world more generally – in which the pubescent girl was being more and more obviously fetishised and, at the same time, discursively constructed as a consumer. In the book, Lolita consumed and Humbert Humbert consumed her, 'breaking her life' as he puts it. The book came to be read as the basis for a legitimating myth of the desiring nymphet; the film was made in such a way as to confirm this reading. The change in Lolita's age between the book and the film – that is, the reconstructing of Lolita as a teenager – is paralleled by the reconstruction of Lolita as the active seducer. The pubescent/adolescent girl has been transformed into a desiring and desirable teenager, and an active consumer.

## NOTES

1   N. McKendrick, 'Commercialization and the Economy', in N. McKendrick, J. Brewer, and J. H. Plumb (eds), *The Birth of a Consumer Society: The Commercialization of Eighteenth-century England* (London, Europa, 1982), p. 13.

2   W. H. Fraser, *The Coming of the Mass Market, 1850-1914* (London, Macmillan, 1981), p. ix.

3   McKendrick, 'Commercialization and the Economy', p. 16.

4   Fraser, *The Coming of the Mass Market*, p. ix.

5   See C. B. McPherson, *The Political Theory of Possessive Individual-ism* (Oxford, Clarendon Press, 1962).

6   R. Williams, *Dream Worlds: Mass Consumption in Late Nineteenth Century France* (Berkeley, University of California Press, 1982), p. 11.

7   R. Bowlby, *Just Looking: Consumer Culture in Dreiser, Gissing and Zola* (New York, Methuen, 1985), p. 3.

8   Williams, *Dream Worlds*, p. 66.

9   Bowlby, *Just Looking*, pp. 2–3.

10  On the Australian history of the department store see G. Reekie, *Temptations: Sex, Selling and the Department Store* (St Leonards, Allen and Unwin, 1993).

11  Bowlby, *Just Looking*, p. 4.

12  Williams, *Dream Worlds*, p. 58.

13  *Ibid.*, p. 59.

14  *Ibid.*, p. 59.

15  *Ibid.*, p. 66.

16  G. Debord, *The Society of the Spectacle* (Detroit, Black and Red, 1977), no. 1.

17  *Ibid.*, no. 42.

18  T. Richards, *The Commodity Culture of Victorian England: Advertising and Spectacle 1851–1914* (Stanford, Stanford University Press, 1990), Ch. 1.

19  *Ibid.*, p. 66.

20  *Ibid.*, p. 195.

21  *Ibid.*, p. 53.

22  *Ibid.*, p. 195.

23  L. Althusser, 'Ideology and Ideological State Apparatuses', in *Lenin and Philosophy* (London, Monthly Review Press, 1971).

24  Richards, *The Commodity Culture*, p. 49.

25  *Ibid.*, p. 53.

26  *Ibid.*, p. 71.

27  Debord, *The Society of the Spectacle*, no. 36.

28  H. Braverman, *Labor and Monopoly Capitalism: The Degradation of Work in the Twentieth Century* (New York, Monthly Review Press, 1974), p. 148.

29  M. Braun, *Picturing Time: The Work of Etienne-Jules Marey (1830-1904)* (Chicago, University of Chicago Press, 1974), p. 336.

30  S. Ewen, *Captains of Consciousness: Advertising and the Social Roots of Consumer Culture* (New York, McGraw-Hill, 1976), p. 25.

31  K. Marx, *Capital*, ed. F. Engels, vol. 1 (London, Lawrence and Wishart, 1954), p. 43.

32  *Ibid.*, p. 43.

33  *Ibid.*, p. 43.

34  *Ibid.*, p. 76.

35  W. F. Haug, *Critique of Commodity Aesthetics: Appearance, Sexuality and Advertising in Capitalist Society* (Cambridge, Polity Press, 1986), p. 16.

36  *Ibid.*, p. 17.

37  Marx, *Capital*, vol. 1 p. 77.

38  *Ibid.*, p. 77.

39  S. Jhally, *The Codes of Advertising: Fetishism and the Political Economy of Meaning in the Consumer Society* (New York, Routledge, 1990), p. 33.

40  *Ibid.*, p. 51.

41  *Ibid.*, p. 51.

42  Ewen, *Captains of Consciousness*, p. 31.

43  *Ibid.*, p. 32.

44  Ewen, *Captains of Consciousness*, p. 37.

45  *Ibid.*, pp. 38-9.

46  S. Freud, 'Fetishism', in *The Standard Edition of the Complete Psychological Works of Sigmund Freud*, translated under the general editorship of James Strachey in collaboration with Anna Freud (London, Hogarth Press/Institute of Psycho-Analysis), vol. 21 (1958), pp. 152–3.

47  B. Dijkstra, *Idols of Perversity: Fantasies of Feminine Evil in Fin-de-siècle Culture* (New York, Oxford University Press, 1986), pp. 5-6.

48  *Ibid.*, pp. 201–2.

49  F. Musgrove, *Youth and Society* (Indianopolis, Indiana University Press, 1965), p. 33.

50  Dijkstra, *Idols of Perversity*, p. 195.

51  *Ibid.*, p. 191.

52  *Ibid.*, p. 191.

53  *Ibid.*, p. 199.

54  *Ibid.*, p. 200.

55  Richards, *The Commodity Culture*, p. 243.

56  *Ibid.*, p. 243

57  *Ibid.*, Chapter 5, *passim*.

58  *Ibid.*, p. 227.

59    *Ibid.*, p. 228.

60    *Ibid.*, p. 228.

61    *Ibid.*, p. 240. In the celebrated July 1990 edition of *The Face*, Kate Moss is photographed in the guise of a seaside girl.

62    *Ibid.*, p. 241.

63    J. Walkowitz, *Prostitution and Victorian Society: Women, Class, and the State* (Cambridge, Cambridge University Press, 1980), p. 247.

64    D. Gorham, 'The "Maiden Tribute of Modern Babylon" Re-examined: Child Prostitution and the Idea of Childhood in Late-Victorian England', *Victorian Studies*, no. 21 (Spring 1978), p. 357.

65    Walkowitz, *Prostitution and Victorian Society*, p. 246.

66    W. T. Stead, 'The Maiden Tribute of Modern Babylon', *Pall Mall Gazette*, summer 1885.

67    Walkowitz, *Prostitution and Victorian Society*, p. 246.

68    L. Finch, 'Sexuality and the Working Class An Australian Case Study', doctoral thesis, University of Queensland, 1991, pp. 271–2. Now published in revised form as *The Classing Gaze: Sexuality, Class and Surveillance* (St Leonards, Allen and Unwin, 1993).

69    Finch, 'Sexuality and the Working Class', p. 272.

70    *Ibid.*, p. 265.

71    *Ibid.*, pp. 118–19.

72    *Ibid.*, p. 138.

73    *Ibid.*, p. 142.

74    *Ibid.*, p. 119.

75    This information comes from J. M. Masson, *Freud: The Assault on Truth* (London, Faber and Faber, 1984), p. 15.

76    *Ibid.*, p. 22.

77    Quoted in *ibid.*, p. 23.

78    Quoted in *ibid.*, p. 43.

79    S. Freud, 'The Aetiology of Hysteria', trans. J. Strachey, included as an appendix in *ibid.*, pp. 263–4.

80    S. Freud, *An Autobiographical Study*, in *The Standard Edition*, vol. 20 (1959), p. 34.

81    S. Freud, *Totem and Taboo*, in *The Standard Edition*, vol. 13 (1955), pp. 5–6.

82    Quoted in Masson, *Freud*, p. 113.

83    *Ibid.*, p. 3.

84    S. Freud, *New Introductory Lectures on Psycho-Analysis*, in *The Standard Edition*, vol. 22 (1959), pp. 118–19.

85    *Ibid.*, p. 119.

86   Quoted in Masson, *Freud*, p. 108.

87   F. Mort, *Dangerous Sexualities: Medico-moral Politics in England since 1830* (London, Routledge and Kegan Paul, 1987), p. 83.

88   W. Leach, 'Transformations in a Culture of Consumption: Women and the Department Store 1890-1925', *The Journal of American History*, 71: 2 (1984) p. 333.

89   *Ibid.*, p. 333.

90   Quoted in Bowlby, *Just Looking*, p. 27.

91   *Ibid.*, p. 27.

92   S. Ewen, *All Consuming Images: The Politics of Style in Contemporary Culture* (New York, Basic Books, 1988), p. 179.

93   R. Loewy, *Industrial Design* (1979), quoted in *ibid.*, p. 179.

94   Ewen, *All Consuming Images*, pp. 179-80.

95   *Ibid.*, p. 180.

96   Bowlby, *Just Looking*, p. 30.

97   *Ibid.*, p. 31.

98   *Ibid.*, p. 31.

99   *Ibid.*, p. 31.

100  *Ibid.*, p. 32.

101  Richards, *The Commodity Culture*, p. 244.

102  Dijkstra, *Idols of Perversity*, p. 196.

103  V. Nabokov, *Lolita* (Harmondsworth, Penguin, 1980), p. 17.

104  *Ibid.*, p. 17.

# 2

# Cultural fetishism, photography, and death

In this chapter I want to discuss the social aspects of the spread of cultural fetishism. As we saw in the previous chapter, according to Debord the rise of new media of communication, coupled with the capitalist emphasis on consumption and, therefore, on commodities, has led to a preoccupation with spectacle. Jean Baudrillard has taken on board this argument but placed it as a historical stage which is now past. He suggests that the preoccupation with the image, over any 'reality' that the image might be claimed to represent, signals a shift from an experience dominated by the logic of representation to an experience dominated by the logic of simulation, writing that:

> [Representation] starts from the principle that the sign and the real are equivalent (even if this equivalence is utopian, it is a fundamental axiom). Conversely, simulation starts from the utopia of this principle of equivalence, *from the radical negation of the sign as value*, from the sign as reversion and death sentence of every reference.[1]

Baudrillard describes simulation as 'the reigning scheme of the current phase' and asserts that it comes after the order of appearance, which he describes as 'the dominant scheme of the industrial era'.[2] For Baudrillard the shift to the order of simulation began in the immediate post-Second World War period. He distinguishes the society of the spectacle from the present order of simulation: 'We are no longer in the society of the spectacle which the situationists talked about, nor in the specific types of alienation and repression which this implied'.[3] With the coming of the new media and associated technologies, we are 'witnessing the end of perspective and panoptic space ... and hence the very *abolition of the spectacular*'.[4]

What this chapter suggests is that, rather than abolishing the spectacular, the experience of the logic of simulation is an effect of living in an increasingly spectacularised world. This new, hyperreal experience is staged when we are *within* the spectacle. I want to connect this development with cultural fetishism, showing how the fetishistic concern with the phallus has driven the acceptance of new visual technologies from the middle of the nineteenth century onwards. The history of the development of these technologies may be understood as a striving for 'better' representation, which, in effect, means a concern with the image quite different from any interest in the thing represented. The fascination with the image is driven by the scopophilia of fetishistic desire. It is this which produces the shift to an emphasis on simulacra, that is, here, a disregard of an 'original' reality in favour of a simulated one which has no origin. In the logic of fetishistic sight, the thing invested with the quality of the fetish is viewed as having the quality of the penis – or, in the case of cultural fetishism, the phallus. In an order dominated by the cultural-fetishistic gaze, that which is spectacularly presented is experienced in the context of a desire for the simulacrum as the 'real'. Here, it is the viewer's 'lack' which drives a consuming gaze. I am arguing that there is a continuum running from 'images' to 'commodities' that is determined by the fetishistic gaze. The key here is appearance, which, of course, underlies spectacle. Thus, to take the typifying example, an image of the female body and a gynoid are both experienced in the male fetishising gaze as worse or better simulacra, as is the female body itself. In this logic, which is the logic of simulation, it is the viewer's experience which is important.

Where the real was thought of in the order of representation as being 'alive,' the simulacrum – and the order of simulation in which it is privileged – is thought of as being, in the first place, 'dead'. Perhaps the most fundamental horror of Mary Shelley's *Frankenstein* (1818) is that the man-made male creature, the (failed) human simulacrum, is given life. And yet this is exactly what would make the desirable man-made women I discuss in Chapter 7 real. Here we might think of Deckard's desire for the most perfect of the replicants, Rachel, in *Blade Runner* (1982). From the point of view of the fetishist the fetish is always already not alive, and therefore must be 'dead'; it is the work of fetishism to bring it alive and, in doing so, to transform it from being that which the fetishist most desires and fears to being the thing itself, that which will complement the cultural fetishist's lack and end his nightmare.

Cultural fetishism takes the object and sexually energises it, transforming it from a passive recipient of desire into an, apparently, active but submissive agent of desire. It seems to ask to be consumed. The most important factor in the formation of this experience has been the spread of new technologies of (re)presentation, starting with photography. This chapter examines how the experience of the earliest of these technologies is implicated in the spread of cultural fetishism. In order to do this it is necessary to discuss briefly how the experience of sight as an aspect of the process of objectification was reconstituted in the articulation of cultural fetishism with active commodity fetishism.

I will develop a new history of modern visual technologies, arguing that, rather than being concerned with increasingly faithful representations of 'reality', they can be better understood as forming a trajectory towards greater simulation. This trajectory of media invention has emphasised the ability to (re)constitute the world in the image of fetishised experience – in other words, to produce the world we desire. This world would be full of objects which really do want us (the 'us' here speaks to men in the first instance) because they are already extensions of ourselves. In this fantastic, phallically dominated order, appearance is the basis of reality and simulation is appearance with depth. If photography was the first of the technologies to be developed in this cultural context, then the computer-generated possibilities of virtual reality are the most recent. The movement away from representation reached a watershed in the late 1960s. From this time on, those who live in the West have experienced the world increasingly in terms of simulation.

Over the fifteenth and sixteenth centuries two different forms of perspective developed, one in Italy and one in the Netherlands. Samuel Edgerton, Jr, argues that, in Italy, the painter and architect Brunelleschi discovered the vanishing point in 1425.[5] The theory of Italian perspective was laid out in Leon Battista Alberti's *Della pittura* in 1435. In Italian perspective, as put forward by Alberti, the viewer is positioned outside of the painting and the eye is led to a single vanishing point. Such a construction allows for the world of the painting to be arranged within a frame. The painting is, itself, of an objectified and delimited world.

Northern perspective, which was developed by the Dutch and outlined in the *Artificiali perspectiva* of Jean Pélerin, published in 1505, worked differently. Here, the position of the viewer was included in the painting. Hence, the experience of looking at paintings of the Dutch school is of being always already 'in' the world of the painting. One consequence of this is that, unlike paintings made according to the Italian system, these Dutch paintings often seem to 'just end' at the edge of the painting. These paintings are not of a neatly ordered and delimited world. Rather, they are of a slice of the same world of which the viewer is also a part.

As Svetlana Alpers has pointed out in her important book on seventeenth-century Dutch painting, the system of northern perspective produces an effect which is very similar to the effect produced in a photograph.[6] She writes:

> Many characteristics of photographs – those very characteristics that make them so real – are common also to the northern descriptive mode: fragmentariness; arbitrary frames; the immediacy that the first practitioners expressed by claiming that the photograph gave Nature the power to reproduce herself directly unaided by man. If we want historical precedence for the photographic image it is in the rich mixture of seeing, knowing, and picturing that manifested itself in seventeenth-century [Dutch] images.[7]

It is well known that the movement away from perspectival, realist painting began at about the same time that photography started to become an accessible and popular activity.[8] Both these developments started in France, which, after the Revolution of 1789, self-consciously constructed itself as a centralised, bureaucratised, bourgeois-dominated, modern state. It was in the United States, after France the most self-consciously modern nation-state, that the popularisation of photography reached its apogee. The shift in the dominant form of realist representational technology paralleled a shift in the dominant system of perspective. The surveillance system of the modern state effected a change in the individual's world-view such that they no longer felt that there was a possibility for them to surveil and dominate the world but, rather, felt themselves 'put into' the world, a part of the surveilled order.

Broadly speaking, the Italian system provides a fantasy of absolutist power, with a distanced spectator viewing an ordered world on her or his terms. In contrast, the Dutch system expresses the experience of the ordinary person living within the newly objectified and increasingly state-surveilled world. It is tempting to equate the difference with the importance of aristocratic ideology in Italy as compared to the rise and dominance of a burgher–bourgeois mentality in the Netherlands. This reading can be associated with

Foucault's historical argument about surveillance. On the one hand, as he says, 'in a society like that of the seventeenth century, the King's body wasn't a metaphor, but a political reality'. It centralised power. On the other hand, 'it's the body of society which becomes the new principle in the nineteenth century'.[9] With this shift there was a renewed sense of being always already within the order of vision – of the gaze, to use Lacan's word.

What became the modern understanding of sight was elaborated by Kepler, first in his *Ad Vitellionem* of 1604 and later in the *Dioptrice*, published in 1611. There are two key elements in Kepler's optical scheme and these form part of the general historical shift in the understanding of sight and its relation to the body. First, there was the claim for the intromission of light rather than its extramission – the claim, that is, that in vision light entered the eye, in contradistinction to the older idea that light exited the eye to illuminate the object seen. Second was his idea that the light entering the eye forms an inverted and reversed retinal image. David Lindberg writes:

> It is perhaps significant that Kepler employed the term *pictura* in discussing the inverted retinal image, for this is the first genuine instance in the history of visual theory of a real optical image within the eye – a picture – having an existence independent of the observer, formed by the focusing of all available rays on a surface. [10]

Kepler's metaphor of the viewed world as being a picture parallels the objectified construction of the world in perspectival paintings. His description of how human beings see coupled together the cultural experience implicit in both forms of perspective of an individual observer with the developing understanding of that individual as it was shortly to be outlined by Descartes.

In the second half of the nineteenth century, concurrent with the deployment of cultural fetishism, there was a further cultural change in the understanding of sight. The foundations for this change were laid in the early part of the century. Jonathan Crary argues that 'during the first few decades of the nineteenth century a new kind of observer took shape in Europe radically different from the type of observer dominant in the seventeenth and eighteenth centuries'.[11] There developed an experience of vision which Crary describes as 'subjective vision'.[12] In the formation of subjective vision, sight became disarticulated from touch. Crary argues that 'the same knowledge that allowed the increasing rationalization and control of the human subject in terms of new institutional and economic requirements was also a condition for new experiments in visual representation'.[13] The new emphasis on the subjective experience of vision was one aspect of the development of a new series of disciplines, the so-called human sciences, which took as their focus of concern the individual as the site for the production of knowledge. This new concentration of interest – which, as Crary notes (following Foucault), is one effect of the nineteenth-century practices of surveillance and discipline which produced the historical subject as an individual, and which are a function of the modern state – led to a new understanding of vision as actively constituted by the observer.

Discussing the deployment of the society of the spectacle, Crary writes that 'this autonomization of sight, occurring in many different domains, was a historical condition for the rebuilding of an observer fitted for the tasks of "spectacular" consumption'.[14] Subjective vision provided the basis for the experience of sight in terms of (male) desire which, as we discussed in the previous chapter, lies at the heart of the articulation of this society. The idea of the active construction of vision parallels the involvement of the viewer in the experience of fetishistic sight. It can be argued against Baudrillard that, instead of an actual end to perspectival and panoptic space, we are experiencing its apparent end as we become more and more caught up within it, and as all of us become a part of the mediated spectacle.

We need to distinguish two different historical forms of surveillance. There is, first, the kind of surveillance identified and outlined by Foucault. This form of surveillance is thoroughly imbricated with power. Furthermore, it cannot be attributed ultimately to any single individual. It is this form of surveillance which, historically, maps on to Lacan's psychosocial theorisation of the gaze. Foucault uses the image of the Panopticon to describe the surveillance form of modern, disciplinary society. In fact, this form of surveillance – and also the disciplinary system which Foucault describes – are characteristics of the modern state. It is, in an important sense, structural in that it is an organisational feature of the modern state and its institutions.

Bentham put forward his proposal for a new prison, the Panopticon or Inspection House, in 1787, two years before the French Revolution. Allan Sekula has provided a useful brief description: 'The operative principles of the Panopticon were isolation and perpetual surveillance. Inmates were to be held in a ring of individual cells. Unable to see into a central observation tower, they would be forced to assume that they were watched continually.'[15] Foucault comments:

> Furthermore, the arrangement of this machine is such that its enclosed nature does not preclude a permanent presence from the outside: ... anyone may come and exercise in the central tower the functions of surveillance, and this being the case, he can gain a clear idea of the way in which the surveillance is practised... . There is no risk, therefore, that the increase of power created by the panoptic machine may degenerate into tyranny; the disciplinary mechanism will be democratically controlled, since it will be constantly accessible 'to the great tribunal committee of the world.[16]

It would seem, then, that anybody might gain the right to observe. But, of course, this is not the case. As the modern democratic – and representational – state developed, so the citizens of the state were increasingly situated within a generalised panoptic regime and had little, if any, opportunity to become, themselves, observers. Where, in Italian perspective, the observer identifies with the position of the painter, and shares in the power of the painter who formed the perspectival view, in northern perspective the painter (like the later photographer) remains hidden from view whilst the observer is placed within the painted world. In this scheme the observer is removed from the site of power and, in the process, those who do occupy that site – who control the system – become even more invisible. The metaphor for this state power is the symbolic Father, the always already absent bearer of the phallus.

Foucault has described how, from the late eighteenth century onwards, there was a transformation in the relation between visibility and power. Previously it had been those exercising power who made themselves visible; now, on the other hand: 'Disciplinary power ... is exercised through its invisibility; at the same time it imposes on those whom it subjects a principle of compulsory visibility. In discipline it is the subjects who have to be seen'.[17] From about the time of the French Revolution panopticism became an ideal of the state. There was a correlation between the amount of power a person, group, or institution exercised and their visibility within the state. The more powerful, the less they were visible to the general population. The more visible a person was to the state, the more control the state could exercise over that person. Those with power could control their visibility and the flow of information that made them visible so that what was seen and known was what was wanted seen and known. The less powerful a person was, the less control they had over their visibility to the institutions of the state. As we saw in the Introduction, the combination of proscriptive power and surveillance is best expressed in the new police forces of, primarily, the nineteenth century. Foucault notes that 'the organization of the police apparatus [in eighteenth-century France] sanctioned a generalization of the disciplines that became co-extensive with the state itself'.[18] It should come as no surprise to discover that, in addition to outlining the Panoptic prison, Bentham advocated a Ministry of Police. However, centralised and hierarchised administrative bureaucracy is the most pervasive everyday form of this state-based disciplinary surveillance.

I have remarked that the expression of power manifested in the modern state – and that power, as Foucault described it, was effected in discipline – was experienced as that of the absent, because always already killed, symbolic Father. Here we are approaching a historicisation of Lacan's description of the gaze. Lacan makes the experience of being within the gaze a fundamental subjectifying moment: 'we are beings who are looked at, in the spectacle of the world. That which makes us conscious institutes us by the same token as *speculum mundi*'.[19] He argues that, 'the gaze is presented to us only in the form of a strange contingency, symbolic of what we find on the horizon, as the thrust of our experience, namely, the lack that constitutes castration anxiety'.[20] What is on the horizon, at the limit of vision, is, in perspectival terms, the vanishing point. The experience of the lack on the horizon, at the edge of the gaze, must be provoked by the phallus standing as a metonym for the symbolic Father. Through this historicising reconstruction of the gaze, we can see how it can be associated with Foucault's notion of surveillance as an expression of the individual's – and particularly the male's – experience of the modern state.

This contextualisation of the Lacanian theorisation of the gaze brings us back to cultural fetishism. 'Cultural fetishism' denotes the male subject's experience which is a consequence of the experiencing of the state's gaze as that of the symbolic phallic Father. It lays the basis for the second form of surveillance, the surveillance which, literally, energises spectacle, drives consumption, and leads to a preoccupation with simulation – that is, the fetishistic need to make the experience of the image more 'real'. This surveillance –

or, perhaps better, *gaze*, as it describes a fetishistically energised sight – is situated in the subject. As we saw in the previous chapter, there is a complex relation between cultural fetishism and the spectacularisation of commodities. Cultural fetishism is one factor in the production of spectacularisation, energising it.

The second form of surveillance articulates with power quite differently from the first. In the first system, to be surveilled was experienced as a loss of power; and surveillance and executive, disciplinary power were expected to run together. This is not the case in individual, spectacularising surveillance. This system was not, in the first place, concerned with power. The power effects of its psychosexual dynamics derive firstly from the fetish and have to be answered in terms of the empowerment or disempowerment of the person, object or commodity fetishised. In the second place, power, and remember we are here talking about individual power rather than state power, derives not only from the fetishistic relation but from an individual's, and by extension a group's, social position. In terms of surveillance the second regime has a complex and variegated relation to the first. Perhaps the most obvious conjuncture occurs when a group in power in the society fetishises another group. Here, the two forms of surveillance coincide. To take one example, white (middle-class) men occupy a privileged position within the state regime of surveillance, being more invisible than (all) women, whilst at the same time in the regime of individual surveillance, producing women's bodies as the site of spectacle.

The first form of surveillance does not have a libidinal component as such, but it is experienced as the expression of a patriarchal order. This form of surveillance derives from the specific historical and cultural conditions of the modern state. From an individual point of view it is experienced as tending towards the panoptic. The second regime of surveillance is a later development and occurs in relation to the spread of cultural fetishism, which, in turn, was a consequence of the individual's – and, in the first instance, the male's – psychosexual experience of the modern state. What connects cultural fetishism with surveillance is sight. Whereas in the first form of surveillance that surveillance primarily has to do with a monitoring, often involving the acquisition and storing of information, which need not necessarily privilege sight, in cultural fetishism, like the pathological fetishism described by Freud, sight is the libidinally energised sense. The (male) desire is always to find, appropriate, consume the (substitute for the) phallus.

The second regime of surveillance, to which we can give the name spectacularising surveillance, does not supplant the earlier, state-oriented form. Rather, the two operate in a complex relation with each other. However, what does happen at the level of day-to-day experience is that the second form of surveillance is experientially privileged. This is partly because state surveillance is mostly hidden or naturalised or both, and partly because spectacularising surveillance derives from the fetishistic concerns of the individual, both male and, by virtue of her cultural positioning, female. Moreover, as we also saw in the previous chapter, cultural fetishism (and the surveillance which derives from it and which is one aspect of it) comes into being as an attempt to negate the (male) experience of the modern (phallic) state. As a consequence it can appear as if the spectacularising system has supplanted the older surveillance system.

What I want to do now is to outline histories of these two surveillance regimes during the period that the second regime comes into being in the middle of the nineteenth century. Jean-Louis Comolli writes that:

> The second half of the nineteenth century lives in a sort of frenzy of the visible. It is, of course, the effect of the social multiplication of images: ever wider distribution of illustrated papers, waves of prints, caricatures etc. The effect also, however, of something of a geographical extension of the field of the visible and the representable: by journeys, explorations, colonisations, the whole world becomes visible at the same time that it becomes appropriatable. Similarly, there is a visibility of the expansion of industrialism, of the transformations of the landscape, of the production of towns and metropolises. There is, again, the development of the mechanical manufacture of objects which determines by a faultless force of repetition their ever identical reproduction, thus standardising the idea of the (artisanal) copy into that of the (industrial) series.[21]

What Comolli is describing is the concurrent increase in the importance of visual representation at the same time that there was a consolidation of industrial capitalism and the beginning of the spread of mass-produced commodities.

Comolli identifies two aspects of the frenzy of the visible. First, there is the spread of the field of vision. Western society had expanded to incorporate most of the geographical world through exploration and colonisation. Coupled with this there had been the development of new means of transport: railways, faster ships, and later, of course, cars and aeroplanes. People could travel more, and to further places, and more people could travel. There was more to see and people were able to see more of the things that were there because they travelled more but most importantly because there were more images available. People no longer primarily saw things; now they had come to see – and this is even more true today – an increasing number of representations. The most important source for the proliferation of images during this period was photography. The second half of the nineteenth century saw a tremendous rise in interest in both France and Britain – and in the United States – in the technology of image-making processes which culminated in what we know as photography. Photography was the first of the new visual media which subsequently included film, television, and video.

Crary has argued that photography occupies a different place from that of older visual technologies, such as painting, in the new order of commodified consumption:

> Photography is an element of a new and homogeneous terrain of consumption and circulation in which the observer becomes lodged. To understand the 'photography effect' in the nineteenth century, one must see it as a crucial component of a new cultural economy of value and exchange, not as part of a continuous history of visual representation.[22]

We can put this in terms already outlined in the previous chapter. Photography was deeply implicated in the spread of spectacularisation and its repositioning of the commodity. In order to understand this we need to examine in what ways the cultural positioning of photography marked a shift away from earlier representational concerns. The first thing to note about photography is that – unlike, for example, oil painting, which, like artisan production in general, only produced one image at a time – the kind of photographic technology which gained general acceptance was able to produce limitless copies from one photographic image. In this sense photography was an early example of the development of modern mass-production technology. We can begin to get a sense of how significant this development was by referring back to our earlier distinction between the two regimes of surveillance. Photography, like film and television, operates in both. That film and television developed in the way that they did – that is, as hierarchically organised media where ownership and control over the means of representation lay in the hands of a commercial, or state, elite, and which, as technologies, massified and passified their audiences –

reflects the extent to which their technological formation was conceptually overdetermined by the relation between the modern nation-state and its citizens. Of the two technologies, television is the better example of this. Photography developed differently. Whilst, as we shall see, it became an important adjunct to the surveillance methods of the state's institutions, nevertheless by the end of the nineteenth century photography had also become an individual, 'private' practice. In this context it was its fetishising aspect, its capacity for spectacularising surveillance, which was privileged. Film and television also spectacularly surveil, but they do so within the context of the formation of 'public' massified audiences, providing them with a common experience. In the case of television one of its ideals, epitomised in state-run national broadcasters, has often been quite explicitly described in terms of the production of a national audience. In this case what binds the national audience together is the shared experience of a particular spectacle. The typifying example is the broadcasting of the nation-state's celebrations of its own 'birth'.

Photography occupies a unique place among nineteenth- and twentieth-century visual technologies, up until the 1970s spread of home video, in developing as a demotic technology. Much of the confusion over the role of film and television in the society of the spectacle comes from a lack of recognition of the importance of their technological form. Film, television, and radio created their massified audiences as a consequence of their organisation as mass media. Newspapers utilised the print medium in the same way, and it is not at all coincidental that newspapers – which Benedict Anderson describes as, from this perspective, an 'extreme form' of the book – developed in tandem with the modern nation-state.[23] In this way they help to create the community of the nation-state in which disciplinary surveillance takes place. At times, sometimes in their news and current-affairs programmes, these media may also perform the function of disciplinary surveillance, representing individuals' activities, and often their relations with the state, as a public spectacle to the rest of the nation-state's imagined community. Film and television, particularly the latter, have not been important to the surveillence system of the state itself. Television has only been seriously used for surveillance in what is, interestingly, called closed-circuit television, and then on a small scale.

Far more than photography, film and television reinforced the massification of the individual cultural-fetishistic process. Film, but more obviously television, replicated the organisational structure of the state, making the state's citizens the audience and, as we have seen, helping to construct them as citizens in the process. The fantasy that the state can watch us through our television sets – an idea that first appears in George Orwell's novel *Nineteen Eighty-Four* – testifies to the structural congruence in the medium's social organisation between the construction of community and disciplinary surveillance. At the same time these media made a world visible to audiences for whom sight was becoming a part of a general fetishistic process. They spectacularised the world; but they did it, structurally speaking, on the state's terms rather than on the individual's terms.

In the libidinised economic order, driven by cultural fetishism, a further process – that of cultural repression – takes place. In Freud's work repression takes two forms, the second of which is an inflection of the first. He describes repression as a 'pathogenic process' in which impulses, issuing from the unconscious, are turned back from consciousness. In a well-known example Freud compares the unconscious to a large entrance hall and consciousness to a drawing room. Between the two there is a watchman. The watchman will not allow any impulses into consciousness that displease him.[24] Repression, then, describes the way in which certain wishes and memories are kept from an individual's consciousness. Further on Freud expresses the connection between latency and infantile amnesia in terms of 'the forgetting ... which veils our earliest youth from us and makes us strangers to it'.[25] He writes in this connection that:

> The task is set us in every psycho-analysis of bringing this forgotten period back into memory. It is impossible to avoid a suspicion that the beginnings of sexual life which are included in that period have provided a motive for its being forgotten – that this forgetting, in fact, is an outcome of repression.[26]

Latency sets in at the resolution of the Oedipus complex, repressing the awareness of childhood sexuality. Cultural repression refers to the process whereby the 'forgetting' of the production process and all that is entailed in it, which is an effect of the experience of exchange relations encapsulated as passive commodity fetishism, is reinforced by the eroticisation of commodities, the process I have called active commodity fetishism. Freud describes the watcher as male: he is an internalised version of the father. In the case of cultural repression it is, ultimately even though they are not directly linked, the fear of the symbolic Father and his phallic power which drives the 'forgetting' of the production process in the 'Western' consumption-driven capitalist order.

Cultural repression reinforces the impression that commodities have a *sui generis* existence by privileging the appearance of the commodity. Following on from this, it can be argued that the social experience of temporal flow in production capitalism was connected with the recognition, however slight, that commodities are produced. Cultural repression aids in the feeling of timelessness which many, including the Marxist cultural theorist Frederic Jameson, have claimed as a characteristic of postmodernity.[27] The effect of cultural repression, the social experience of active commodity fetishism, is that commodities are experienced as having no history. In addition, if the awareness of production helps to construct the modern experience of history, then a further effect of cultural repression is the experience of there being no history for commodities to have a place in. In a world experienced through cultural fetishism, pleasure is derived from consumption. The more desirable a commodity is experienced as being, the less its history of production will be recognised. The pleasure involved in consumption is closely associated with the appropriation of something which, because of the articulation of consumption with cultural fetishism, is desired ultimately in relation to a (phallic) lack.

One effect of spectacularising surveillance has been to alter the relation between invisibility and power. The fetishised object is made visible. Its appearance is spectacularised. Where the object was powerless, the fetish has power as an effect of the fear and desire which transform it into a fetish. In a fetishised world the spectacularised commodity, as appearance, draws power commensurate to its level of visibility. This applies as much to presidents as to commodities. This power, however, is a power given to the fetish by the viewer. It is a power dependent on appearance and determined by the structure of appropriation and consumption. In cultural fetishism the drive is always towards the internalisation of the fetish. Whilst the power relation with a fetishised commodity is always structured to enhance its desirability for consumption – this is what advertising does – the situation can be more complex. Highly visible people, for example, will often try to manipulate the power which comes from such fetishised visibility for their own purposes. The point which must be kept in mind is that the power of such visibility is always a power given by the viewer to the visible person – to their appearance, not to them as people – and is, therefore, dependent ultimately on the viewer. Being invested with people's desire in this way, the image can never correspond to the 'reality' of the commodity – or the person. One common experience of this kind of spectacular fame is a feeling that the image is larger than life, that it cannot be lived up to. The star may be taken as the typifying example here, including the Hollywood star system, rock stars, and sports stars.

In 1888, as the desiring structure of cultural fetishism was becoming pervasive in Western nation-states, Kodak put the first camera designed for popular use on the market. The Kodak Box Brownie was a key moment in the democratisation of photography. The production of images took a quantum leap. Photographs became ubiquitous. In 1895 H. G. Wells published *The Time Machine*. At one point in his travels through time, when he is under the earth with the Morlocks, the time traveller remarks: 'If only I had thought of a Kodak! I could have flashed that glimpse of the Underworld in a second, and examined it at leisure'.[28] The new technologies of image making were central to transforming the visible into spectacle. Rachel Bowlby has made the connection between the new preoccupation with commodities and these new technologies of visual presentation:

> The transformation of merchandise into a spectacle in fact suggests an analogy with an industry that developed fifty years after the first department stores: the cinema. In this case the pleasure of looking, just looking, is itself the commodity for which money is paid. The image is all ...[29]

She is describing the scopophilic fascination with appearance and connecting the spectacularisation of commodities with the development of the cinema. This is, really, the same point that I have already made about photography. The new visual technologies are staged within a spectacular regime to which the commodity is central. In the cinema, though, what one pays for is not the commodity itself but the pleasure of gazing (on it). In both the department store display and the cinema, what is gazed upon is the fetishised (image of the) commodity.

In order to understand the way in which the cultural positioning of photography was so radically different from that of earlier visual technologies, we can look briefly at oil painting. This technique developed in the fifteenth century in northern Europe but, John Berger tells us, 'did not fully establish its own norms, its own way of seeing, until the sixteenth century'.[30] He dates the period of the traditional oil painting as being roughly between 1500 and 1900. Berger has described how the context for oil painting was the representation of commodities: 'What distinguishes oil painting from other forms of painting is its ability to render the tangibility, the texture, the lustre, the solidity of what it depicts. It defines the real as that which you can put your hands on'.[31] The technical development of oil painting occurred in the context of a realist preoccupation with representation. Above all, the oil painting represents what it portrays as an object. Berger has outlined the connection between this kind of painting and capitalism: 'Oil painting did to appearances what capitalism did to social relations. It reduced everything to the equality of objects. Everything became exchangeable because everything became a commodity ... Oil painting conveyed a vision of total exteriority'.[32] What Berger is implying here is the connection between oil painting and passive commodity fetishism, how such realist painting prioritises the presence of the commodity over the past production which brought it into being.

Oil painting articulated with a capitalist system that emphasised the objectivity of the commodity in terms of its appearance. Berger argues that the basis for oil painting's 'traditional way of seeing was undermined by Impressionism and overthrown by Cubism. At about the same time the photograph took the place of the oil painting as the principal source of visual imagery'.[33] The reason for the shift away from oil-painting realism, we can now understand, was the impact of cultural fetishism and spectacle, which produced a new experience of the commodity. Both Impressionism and Cubism, and indeed the many other -isms of the period, were, in one way or another, preoccupied with a new emphasis on sight over and above what is seen. In these artistic developments we have another example of how the frenzy of the visible was, in the first place, a transformation of vision.

The traditional histories of photography view it as having a concern with realism which forms a continuity with the concerns of fine art. As Crary puts it: 'Overwhelmingly [the invention and dissemination of photography and other related forms of "realism" in the nineteenth century] have been presented as part of the continuous unfolding of a Renaissance-based mode of vision in which photography, and eventually cinema, are simply later instances of an ongoing deployment of perspectival space and perception'.[34] From this point of view photography takes on the representational concern of oil painting while fine art develops more subjective interests. Against this interpretation Crary argues that both the development of photography and the changes in the preoccupations of fine art are effects of the shift in the understanding of the experience of vision which begins in the early part of the century. He suggests that photography seemed to operate in the conventions of the older tradition:

> But photography had already abolished the inseparability of observer and camera obscura, bound together by a single point of view, and made the new camera an apparatus fundamentally independent of the spectator, yet which masqueraded as a transparent and incorporeal intermediary between observer and world. The prehistory of the spectacle and the 'pure perception' of modernism are lodged in the newly discovered territory of a fully embodied viewer ...[35]

The basis for both photography and Impressionism lay in the reconstruction of the individual as no longer (just) passive, to be gazed upon, but as actively gazing.

The construction of vision as subjective does not account, in and of itself, for the emphasis, from the middle of the nineteenth century, on the image – the frenzy of the visible. Where, for the previous four hundred years or so, the representational possibilities of oil painting had been, in general, sufficient for the objectification of commodities, the mechanical representation of the world was able to supply images which provided the possibility of experiencing the heightened sense of involvement with commodities which was a necessary concomitant of their fetishisation. Sight took on a libidinal charge which gave it an active quality. The discursive reconstruction of vision provided a context for this new experience of the sexualised gaze. Both the development of photography and the non-realist move in painting have the same source: not only the new experience of subjective vision but also the spread of the fetishising gaze, a gaze which is actively concerned with the production of appearance as real. As we have already seen, this was a crucial component in the establishment of the new scheme of simulation.

Photography has a history not in the realist, objectifying concerns of oil painting, but in the systematic hyper-illusory concerns of the *tableau vivant* and the panorama. Daguerre, the French inventor of the most successful mechanical forerunner of the photograph, the daguerreotype, in fact also developed his own version of the diorama, the popularity of which supported him whilst he searched for a mechanical means of representing the world. The popularity of photography was bound up with the spread of cultural fetishism and formed a part of the movement itself towards the establishment of the scheme of simulation. The *tableau vivant* and the panorama can be read in this history as forerunners in a history of technologies which increasingly approximate the simulatory experience. From around the middle of the nineteenth century the development of visual technologies takes on a new urgency. A lineage can be constructed which repositions those technologies usually thought of as communications media and which includes photography, film (including, of course, the regularly surfacing dream of readily accessible 3-D film), television, video, holography, and virtual reality. In virtual reality, and its precursor the late-eighteenth-century panorama, the individual does not relate to a reconstituted object but, rather, exists in an entirely constructed world and is 'within' the simulation.

The history of photography, and in particular the work of Louis Daguerre, can be read to illustrate the points I have been making. Daguerre began his career as an apprentice stage designer. After about three years he went to work for Pierre Prévost, who was a famous painter of panoramas. The technique of the panorama was patented by Robert Barker, an Irish portrait painter working in Edinburgh, in 1787. This was the same year that Bentham put forward his idea for the Panopticon. Foucault asks whether Bentham was aware of Barker's work and notes that in both constructions 'the visitors occupied exactly the place of the sovereign gaze'.[36] The point is that both inventions express the same discursive shift. Panoramas rapidly became extremely popular in both England and France. Helmut Gernsheim and Alison Gernsheim write:

> The general enthusiasm for panoramas in England, France, and other countries was caused by the astonishing illusion of reality of the depicted scene. Placed in the semi-darkness, and at the centre of a circular painting illuminated from above and embracing a continuous view of an entire region, the spectator lost all judgement of distance and space, for the different parts of the picture were painted so realistically and in such perfect perspective and scale that, in the absence of any means of comparison with real objects, a perfect illusion was given. [37]

After working for Prévost until 1816, Daguerre became a stage designer in his own right. In 1819 he was invited to become one of the chief designers at the Académie Royale de Musique.[38] During 1821 and 1822 Daguerre was busy developing the diorama. Gernsheim and Gernsheim suggest that Daguerre got his idea for the Diorama from König's Diaphanorama, which seems to have consisted, basically, of light on semi-transparent paper painted with landscapes and such like. My point here is not to emphasise the derivative nature of Daguerre's diorama but rather to demonstrate that, in addition to the panorama and the diorama, the early nineteenth century saw a massive upsurge in interest in ways of producing illusion effects. Thomas Richards notes that these became grander over time:

> The spectacles of the early Victorian stage conditioned their audiences always to expect more – and more and more. For example, the adoption of panoramas and dioramas as scenic backdrops did not satisfy audiences for long. Pretty soon technicians invented moving panoramas, painted on a single canvas and rolled between two large scrolls mounted vertically at each end of the stage'.[39]

He goes on to describe a moving panorama shown in 1848 which was 3,600 feet long and depicted a journey down the entire length of the Mississippi River. All these inventions did not attempt to construct what was depicted as distanced from the viewer, as in Italian perspective. Quite the opposite: they worked by including the viewer in the objectifying structure, as in the Dutch perspectival system.

Daguerre and his partner Bouton formed a joint-stock company and had a specially commissioned building built for the diorama which opened on 11 July 1822. Without going into detail, the diorama consisted of a large semi-transparent realist painting. It was back-lit from the windows of the building with the use of various stage-type devices to vary the light and to surround the painting so that its edges would not be seen and the illusion spoilt. What the crowds marvelled at, and it is clear that this was what they wanted, was the 'realistic' quality of the experience. Gernsheim and Gernsheim quote a reporter for *The Times* who wrote that, 'after a man has gazed to his heart's content, his eyes still half refuse to believe but the picture begins at the top of these steps, and that the steps themselves, and the planks, and other debris of apparatus, are part of the house in which he stands, and not of the show which he has paid to see'.[40] The show which this reporter and large numbers of other people were so desirous of seeing and so fascinated by was the 'realistic' appearance of an object (even if, as was often the case, it was a landscape) which was not present.

The diorama was so popular that Daguerre and Bouton opened another one in London and one in Liverpool; in addition a large number of similar institutions opened both in these cities and in other cities in Europe. All the time that Daguerre was running the diorama it would seem that he, like so many other people, particularly in France and Britain, was looking for a way of fixing visual images gained mechanically with a light-sensitive chemical. Rather than going into a technical history of photography, or even a history of Daguerre's collaboration with Niépce, father and son, I want to focus on one year and one event. By 1839 Daguerre had been more successful than anybody else in fixing images, so successfully that the daguerreotype had already been given its name. In January 1839, when Daguerre was trying to raise capital by public subscription, he published a broadsheet which ends: 'In conclusion, the DAGUERREOTYPE is not merely an instrument which serves to draw Nature; on the contrary it is a chemical and physical process which gives her the power to reproduce herself'.[41] Here Daguerre is making a hyperbolic claim to the simulatory ability of the daguerreotype. He asserts that it uses chemical and physical processes, which are natural, actually to reproduce nature. At this point modern claims to a distinction between the real and its representation are being set aside in favour of a simulatory claim. With the oil painting a clear distinction was always assumed between the object and its representation; indeed, following Berger, we might say that the purpose of the oil painting was to 'objectify' the object. However, Daguerre is claiming here that the new natural mechanical system produces a representation which is so perfect that it is, itself, 'Nature'; nature becomes, in effect, a simulacrum of itself operating within the logic of simulation.

Daguerre's concern with realistic illusion, which has been discussed in relation to his diorama, was matched only by his concern with the 'accurate' reproduction of the natural world. This is clearly demonstrated in the few of Daguerre's oil paintings which survive. For example – and, by the way, demonstrating an analogous assumption about photography and reality – Gernsheim and Gernsheim describe Daguerre's painting of Holyrood Chapel, Edinburgh, as 'so remarkably realistic that in a reproduction it may at

first sight be taken for a photograph'.[42] In the United States, Edgar
Allen Poe took up Daguerre's preoccupation with, and assumption
of, verisimilitude when he wrote:

> Perhaps, if we imagine the distinctness with which an object is
> reflected in a positively perfect mirror, we come as near to the
> reality as by any other means. For, in truth, the Daguerreo-
> typed plate is infinitely more accurate in its representation
> than any painting by human hands. If we examine a work of
> ordinary art, by means of a powerful microscope, all trace of
> resemblance to nature will disappear – but the closest scrutiny
> of the photogenic drawing discloses only a more absolute
> truth, a more perfect identity with the thing represented.[43]

In the context of the fetishisation of appearance an object is determined by what it appears to be; hence the fascination with kitsch
objects which look like one thing but 'are' something else – our
fascination, in fact, with masquerade. Poe here celebrates what he
claims is a technique which can give a perfect visual appearance, not
only beyond human sight but absolutely, and in this way exhibit an
absolute truth.

Operating within the unfolding logic of simulation, the claim
being made by Daguerre and Poe, and which was immediately
taken up as part of the realist debate in photography, was
supplemented by the use of negatives by Fox Talbot and Scott
Archer and others. Daguerre's technology produced a single positive picture. Talbot and Archer, who began to use collodion as a
developing agent, worked with negatives from which any number
of positive prints could be made. The same assumptions which
underlay the mechanical reproduction of commodities, a repetition
of the same – the defining quality of the simulacrum – here was
applied to images. From this point of view we can generate a
genealogy of photography in which the first concern was with the
ability to simulate the appearance of the world mechanically – that
is, there was an emphasis on spectacle – followed by the development of the ability to reproduce that appearance in multiple copies,
in this way literally increasing the visibility of (images of) the
world to everybody.

Unlike film and television, photography was rapidly taken up
by the state as a new and important component of the panoptic surveillance order. The outer limits of the panoptic state were mapped
by photographs. John Tagg describes it this way:

> A vast and repetitive archive of images is accumulated in which the smallest deviations may be noted, classified and filed. There are bodies and spaces. The bodies – workers, vagrants, criminals, patients, the insane, the poor, the colonised races – are taken one by one: isolated in a shallow, contained space; turned full face and subjected to an unreturnable gaze ... The spaces, too – uncharted territories, frontier lands, urban ghettoes, working-class slums, scenes of crime – are confronted with the same frontality and measured against an ideal space.[44]

The institutions of the state made most use of photography at the limits of state power. Here, where the naturalised performance of the state's power is weakest, disciplinary surveillance is most obvious and the state represents to itself those who are least interpellated, who require most to be made visible. Photography provides a permanent visible record of those who the state thinks are most in need of being surveilled and functions, here, within the Lacanian gaze of the state. In this patriarchally charged order it is not surprising to find that, like the police, official photographers (and, in fact, most private photographers) were male. The role of women, as we shall see in the next chapter, was to be photographed. At this point we find an understandable overlap between the state's use of photography and its 'individual' use within the fetishising scheme of spectacularising surveillance.

Sekula has more specifically delineated the connections between society as the newly constituted object of surveillance, the police force as the institutional apparatus of that surveillance, and the rapid taking-up by that police force of photography. He argues that the discursive construction of society constitutes the world as a terrain of individuals which requires mapping through surveillance. In France the Sûreté, newly formed in 1812, quickly made use of Daguerre's daguerreotype to accumulate a massive 80,000 images of criminals.[45] John Tagg has noted that, in England, 'the police employed civilian photographers from the 1840s onwards'.[46] Sekula shows how the use of photography differed between a concern to find the typical, and the typifying, criminal and, on the other hand, the need to identify the specific criminal. He explains how Alphonse Bertillon, in the 1880s, introduced the first truly systematic way of organising criminal identification records which made use of photographs:

His was a bipartite system, positioning a 'microscopic' individual record within a 'macroscopic' aggregate. First, he combined photographic portraiture, anthropometric description, and highly standardized and abbreviated written notes on a single fiche, or card. Second he organized these cards within a comprehensive, statistically based filing system.[47]

In this way, using photographs as records, Bertillon constructed a system for organising this archive of the surveilled world. Furthermore, Bertillon 'clearly saw the photograph as the final conclusive sign in the process of identification': 'Ultimately, it was the photographed face pulled from the file that had to match the rephotographed face of the suspect, even if this final "photographic" proof was dependent on a series of more abstract steps'.[48] Here the photograph provides the final moment of confirmation of the individual's identity in the surveillance system of the state.

The rapid spread, and popularity, of photography played an important part in the articulation of the new spectacular visibility. The social, where the object was constituted and mapped, was now beginning to be transformed into a spectacular space. What Tagg describes are the farthest reaches of this spectacular space, the edges where the state and the social meet. It is at this panoptic vanishing point that the state's surveillance becomes most obsessive. One feature of the frenzy of the visible lay in the new making-visible of the social, and the simulatory transformation of its contents into spectacle. The experience of this spectacular world, its powers, fear, and pleasures, is the consequence of what I have called cultural repression. This is indeed Debord's society of the spectacle.

In the late nineteenth century death began to operate as a metaphor for the experience of the appropriation of 'real life' into the simulatory world constructed by active commodity fetishism. The metaphor of death describes the cultural experience of spectacle, specifically the spectacle energised by the fetishism of cultural fetishism. In 'What is Enlightenment?' Foucault describes what modernity in painting meant to the French poet and essayist Baudelaire (1821-67), who thought of the modern artist in terms of spectacle, as a combination of the *flâneur* and the dandy. Paraphrasing and elaborating on Baudelaire, Foucault writes: 'The modern painter is the one who can show the dark frock-coat as "the necessary costume of our time", the one who knows how to make manifest, in the fashion of the day, the essential, permanent, obsessive relation that our age entertains with death'.[49] Where the 'real', nature, is associated with life, so the spectacle, and simulation in general, is thought of as being the region of death. In terms of this binary structure, the always already 'dead' fetish is brought to 'life' by the libidinal energy of the fetishist. Freud himself uses this metaphor, writing about what happens 'when the fetish comes to life, so to speak'.[50] It is within this general context that the fetishistic experience of spectacularising surveillance by the photograph came to be associated with death.

Pornographic photographs and photographs of dead people mark the limits of the fetishistic relation between photography and the body. In fact, photography has always been closely associated with death. In the last half of the nineteenth century it was not uncommon to take photographs of dead loved ones. Writing about the United States, Stanley Burns writes that 'postmortem photography, photographing a dead person, was a common practice in the nineteenth and early twentieth centuries'.[51] He goes on to note that 'postmortem photographs make up the largest group of nineteenth-century American genre photographs'.[52] In many countries the police would often take photographs of criminals they had killed in the line of duty – in Australia, for example, there are many photographs of the bodies of bush rangers killed whilst resisting arrest. In a slightly different register, the French criminologist Charles Marie Debierre's book *Le Crâne des criminels* (1895), which argued that criminals were degenerate, contained a chapter which included 'photographs of the severed heads of convicts, "taken one quarter of an hour after decapitation"'.[53] More common today, as Christian Metz notes, is 'the social practice of keeping photographs in memory of loved ones who are no longer alive'.[54] He goes on to argue that, because of the stillness of the photograph, it 'maintains the memory of the dead *as being dead*'.[55]

Roland Barthes describes the experience of being photographed as one of objectification, and goes on to associate it with death. He puts it like this:

> In terms of image-repertoire, the Photograph (the one I intend) represents the very subtle moment when, to tell the truth, I am neither subject nor object but a subject who feels he is becoming an object: I then experience a micro-version of death (of parenthesis): I am truly becoming a specter.[56]

The intimate relation between Barthes and his photographic image is constructed through Barthes's gaze – and through the general gaze produced by cultural fetishism. Barthes's experience of becoming a spectre is an effect of his spectatorial gaze on his image. It is the power invested in the photographic image which transforms Barthes into his own spectre.[57]

A little later Barthes is more explicit about the relation between photography and death. He writes: 'Ultimately, what I am seeking in the photograph taken of me (the "intention" with which I look at it) is Death: Death is the *eidos* of that Photograph'.[58] Berkeley Kaite has summed up a part of Metz's argument about the relation of photography and the fetish:

> Like photography, the fetish overlays with death and loss in the way it captures and ossifies a moment that is highly condensed and ultimately mis-represented or misquoted and 'cut' out of its referent. Of equal importance here is what the fetish does not say (or cannot say), in other words what it summons in absence or the absence – loss – that it evokes. What Phillipe Dubois calls 'thanatography', or photography's affiliation with death, is the subversive phantasy/fiction that challenges, or gives new meaning to, the 'presumed real'.[59]

For the photograph to be experienced in terms of a loss, a death, it must be fetishised. Metz writes that 'the fetish is related to death through the terms of castration and fear, to the off-frame in terms of the look, glance, or gaze'.[60] For Metz what concentrates the gaze on the photograph is the fetishistic fear of what is beyond the photographic frame – as he puts it – what has been 'cut off' by the photograph. Here, he is arguing that death provides the experiential counterpart to the fear of castration in the individual's fetishistic experience. In the experience of cultural fetishism the idea of death has a different source. Death, in the form of capital punishment, is the final disciplinary sanction of the state, the presence of the already dead social, symbolic Father. The lack of the phallus places men (and women) in a situation where this ultimate sanction is always a possibility. In this sense death, and fear of death, pervades the modern state. The surveillance photographs of the state carry the resonance of death.

Underlying the spectacle, then, is a more general fetishistic preoccupation with death. Barthes's seeking of his own death in his photograph reworks a connection that was made in *La Poste de Paris* in 1895 by a commentator on the first public showing of the Lumière brothers' moving films:

The beauty of the invention resides in the novelty and ingenuity of the apparatus. When these apparatuses are made available to the public, everybody will be able to photograph those dear to them, no longer as static forms but with their movements, their actions, familiar gestures, capturing the speech on their very lips. Then, death will no longer be absolute.[61]

In this fantasy, film will be able to keep alive as a spectacle those dear to us, those we love. Death will be overcome by spectacle.

As Mary Ann Doane points out, early film ( like photography) was deeply implicated with death. She describes three films with self-explanatory titles, *Execution of a Spy* (1902), *Reading the Death Sentence* (1903), and *An Execution by Hanging* (1905), and goes on: 'This fascination with death or the brink of death is also sustained in films like *Beheading the Chinese Prisoner* (1900), where the prisoner's head is displayed directly to the spectator and *Electrocuting An Elephant* (1903), in which smoke rising from the elephant's feet and the elephant's collapse assure the spectator of the authenticity of this depiction of death'.[62]

In this chapter I have wanted to show how the historical movement towards the logic of simulation is, at least partly, driven by the putting into place of the structure of cultural fetishism. In this development spectacularisation plays an important part. As the fetishistic aspect of the spread of spectacularisation, it is also what underpins the emphasis on the importance of simulation. I have also wanted to show that surveillance needs to be understood as having two different forms: one which came to be located in the state and which is experienced in terms of the patriarchal understanding of the state (Foucault's and Lacan's theorisations respectively), and one located in the individual and a function of the fetishistic gaze. It is this form of the gaze, which is a part of active commodity fetishism and is connected to spectacularisation, which provokes the association of the new visual media with death, whilst, more generally, the state is experienced as the territorial space of (the fear of) death. Baudrillard has argued that the social is '*the accumulation of death*'.[63] It is this experience that I am describing.

## NOTES

1   J. Baudrillard, *Simulations* (New York, Semiotext(e), 1983), p. 11.

2   *Ibid.*, p. 83.

3   *Ibid.*, p. 54

4   *Ibid.*, p. 54

5   S. Edgerton, Jr,. *The Renaissance Rediscovery of Linear Perspective* (New York, Basic Books, 1975), pp. 124–42.

6   S. Alpers, *The Art of Describing: Dutch Art in the Seventeenth Century* (Chicago, University of Chicago Press, 1984), pp. 243-4.

7   *Ibid.*, p. 43.

8   With a lack of historical contextualisation Alpers suggests that 'one might say that the photographic image, the Dutch art of describing and ... Impressionist painting are all examples of a constant artistic option in the art of the West'( *The Art of Describing*, p. 244).

9   M. Foucault, 'Body/Power', in C. Gordon (ed. and trans.), *Power/Knowledge: Selected Interviews and Other Writings 1972-1977 by Michel Foucault* (Brighton, Harvester Press, 1980), p. 55.

10  D. C. Lindberg, *Theories of Vision from al-Kindi to Kepler* (Chicago, University of Chicago Press, 1976), p. 202.

11  J. Crary, *Techniques of the Observer: On Vision and Modernity in the Nineteenth Century* (Cambridge, Mass, MIT Press, 1990), p. 6.

12  *Ibid.*, p. 9.

13  *Ibid.*, p. 9.

14  *Ibid.*, p. 19.

15  A. Sekula, 'The Body and the Archive', *October*, no. 39 (Winter 1986), p. 9.

16  M. Foucault, *Discipline and Punish: The Birth of the Prison*, trans. A. Sheridan (New York, Vintage Books, 1979), p. 207.

17  *Ibid.*, p. 187.

18  *Ibid.*, p. 215.

19  J. Lacan, 'The Split between the Eye and the Gaze', in *The Four Fundamental Concepts of Psychoanalysis*, ed. J.-A. Miller, trans. A. Sheridan (Harmondsworth, Penguin, 1979), p. 75.

20  *Ibid.*, pp. 72–3.

21  J.-L. Comolli, 'Machines of the Visible', in T. de Lauretis and S. Heath (eds), *The Cinematic Apparatus* (London, Macmillan, 1980), pp. 122–3.

22  Crary, *Techniques of the Observer*, p. 13.

23  On this relation and its implications see B. Anderson, *Imagined Communities: Reflections on the Origin and Spread of Nationalism*, revised edn (London, Verso, 1991), ch. 2.

24 S. Freud, 'Resistance and Repression', in *The Standard Edition of the Complete Psychological Works of Sigmund Freud*, translated under the general editorship of James Strachey in collaboration with Anna Freud (London, Hogarth Press/Institute of Psycho-Analysis, vol. 16 (1958), pp. 295–6.

25 *Ibid.*, p. 326.

26 *Ibid.*, p. 326.

27 F. Jameson, 'Postmodernism, or The Cultural Logic of Late Capitalism', *New Left Review*, no. 146 (1984), pp. 53–92.

28 *Three Prophetic Novels of H. G. Wells*, selected and introduced by E. F. Bleiler (New York, Dover, 1960), p. 305.

29 R. Bowlby, *Just Looking: Consumer Culture in Dreiser, Gissing and Zola* (New York, Methuen, 1985), p. 6.

30 J. Berger, *Ways of Seeing* (London, BBC, 1972), p. 84.

31 *Ibid.*, p. 88.

32 *Ibid.*, p. 87.

33 *Ibid.*, p. 84.

34 Crary, *Techniques of the Observer*, p. 4.

35 *Ibid.*, p. 136.

36 Foucault, *Discipline and Punish*, p. 317 n. 4.

37 H. Gernsheim and A. Gernsheim, *L. J. M. Daguerre: The History of the Diorama and the Daguerreotype* (New York, Dover, 1968), p. 6.

38 *Ibid.*, p. 11. All the following details of Daguerre's life come from this book.

39 T. Richards, *The Commodity Culture of Victorian England: Advertising and Spectacle 1851–1914* (Stanford, Stanford University Press, 1990), pp. 56–7.

40 Quoted in Gernsheim and Gernsheim, *L. J. M. Daguerre*, p. 17.

41 *Ibid.*, p. 81.

42 *Ibid.*, p. 27.

43 Edgar Allen Poe, 'The Daguerreotype', in A. Trachtenberg (ed.), *Classic Essays on Photography* (New Haven, Leete's Island Books, 1980), p. 38. Here, again, we have the idea of the photograph as like a mirror image – this time a positive one.

44 J. Tagg, *The Burden of Representation: Essays on Photographies and Histories* (Basingstoke, Macmillan, 1988), p. 64.

45 P. Paul, *Murder Under the Microscope: The Story of Scotland Yard's Forensic Science Laboratory* (London, Futura, 1990), p. 43.

46 J. Tagg, 'Power and Photography: Part One. A Means of Surveillance: The Photograph as Evidence in Law', *Screen Education*, no. 36 (Autumn 1980), p. 23.

47   Sekula, 'The Body and the Archive', p. 18.

48   *Ibid.*, p. 29.

49   M. Foucault, 'What is Enlightenment?', in P. Rabinow, *The Foucault Reader* (New York, Pantheon, 1984), p. 40. Foucault is quoting from Baudelaire's *The Mirror of Art: Critical Studies* (ed. and trans. J. Mayne: London, Phaidon, 1955).

50   S. Freud, 'Fetishism', in *The Standard Edition*, vol. 21 (1958), p. 149.

51   S. Burns, *Sleeping Beauty: Memorial Photography in America* (Altadena, Calif., Twelvetrees Press, 1990), Preface, no pagination.

52   *Ibid.*, Preface, no pagination.

53   Sekula, 'The Body and the Archive', p. 40.

54   C. Metz, 'Photography and Fetish', *October*, no. 34 (Fall 1985), p. 84.

55   *Ibid.*, p. 84.

56   R. Barthes, *Camera Lucida: Reflections on Photography* (New York, Hill and Wang, 1981), pp. 13–14.

57   Taking a photograph is often likened to shooting. In 1899 Etienne-Jules Marey, the celebrated French physiologist who used photo-graphy to study animate movement, invented a special camera which looked like a gun and which he called an electric gun camera (M. Braun *Picturing Time: The World of Etienne-Jules Marey (1830–1904)* (Chicago, University of Chicago Press, 1992), p. 195). More generally, Susan Sontag has written about the way photography is talked about using the metaphor of the gun. She argues that 'to photograph some-one is a sublimated murder' (S. Sontag, *On Photography* (New York, Farrar, Straus and Giroux, 1977), p. 15). Implicitly recognising the sexual desire associated with photography and its cultural fetishistic form, Sontag also writes that 'the act of taking pictures is a semblance of appropriation, a semblance of rape' (Ibid., p. 24). In Michael Powell's 1959 film *Peeping Tom*, Mark, the murderer, kills his female victims with the sharpened end of one leg of his film camera's tripod stand as he is filming them.

58   Barthes, *Camera Lucida*, p. 15.

59   B. Kaite, 'The Fetish in *Sex, Lies and Videotape*: Whither the Phal-lus?', in Arthur and Marilouise Kroker (ed.), *The Hysterical Male: New Feminist Theory* (Basingstoke, Macmillan, 1991), p. 177.

60   Metz, 'Photography and Fetish', p. 85.

61   Quoted from D. Cook, *A History of Narrative Film*, revised edn (New York, Norton, rev. ed. 1990), p. 13.

62   M. A. Doane, 'Technology's Body: Cinematic Vision in Modernity', *Differences: A Journal of Feminist Cultural Studies* (1993), pp. 6–7.

63   J. Baudrillard, *In the Shadow of the Silent Majorities, The End of the Social and Other Essays* (New York, Semiotext(e), 1983), p. 73.

# 3

# The spectacularisation
# of the female body

In Chapter 1, I argued that from around the middle of the nine-teenth century the female body began to be fetishised. The male experience of that fetishisation was that the female body was, in itself, desirable. It became a spectacle. In the previous chapter I argued that the social effect of the fetishistic structure of cultural fetishism was the spread of spectacularising surveillance. In this chapter I want to develop this argument, showing how the female body – which I have argued has been the paramount fetish in the phallic economy of cultural fetishism – became spectacularly surveilled. The greater presence of women in the public world out-side of the home provided one site for spectacularising surveillance. In the first part of this chapter I will examine how this new visibility was experienced by men – in particular by the *flâneur*, whose prac-tices were transformed as a consequence of the spread of the fetishisation of the female body.

In the second part of this chapter I will examine the increasing preoccupation among men with viewing the naked female body, something exemplified in the historical transformation of the *tableau vivant* into the striptease. The new spectacularising surveil-lance of the female body had a very particular effect on women themselves. In the second half of the nineteenth century a new ill-ness began to be diagnosed. Hysteria took many forms but most of them were, in some way, expressed through the female body. I examine these developments in the context of the new male sur-veillance of the female body and, in the final section of this chapter, set this spectacularising surveillance of women's bodies in the broader context of photography and film, which, as visual media, have become central to the circulation of images of the female body.

Denise Riley argues for a close connection between the nineteenth-century deployment of the social and a reconstruction of the discourse of 'women':

> What did change the concept of 'women' by furnishing it with a new terrain was not so much class, which multiplied the old ambiguities as it refurbished them, but 'the social'. ... This new production of 'the social' offered a magnificent occasion for the rehabilitation of 'women'. In its very founding conceptions, it was feminised; in its detail, it provided the chances for some women to enter upon the work of restoring other, more damaged, women to a newly conceived sphere of grace.[1]

Riley describes the relation between the discursive construction of women and the social in terms of a double feminisation:

> In so far as the concerns of the social *are* familial standards – health, education, hygiene, fertility, demography, chastity and fecundity – and the heart of the family is inexorably the woman, then the woman is also solidly inside of that which has to some degree already been feminised.[2]

And she goes on to note that one effect of the construction of women as the core of the social was a new visibility in the public gaze.

This new visibility was not only the effect of a new analytic concern with those areas of life previously regarded as private, and therefore not for gazing upon. Women on their own were entering the public street-life of cities. City streets had, historically, been a male preserve, like the public domain more generally. Women's presence on the streets was, therefore, on male terms. Up to this period in the middle of the nineteenth century respectable women had, in general, appeared on the street in the company of a man. Referring to the writers of mid-century Australian etiquette books, Lynette Finch notes that:

> Lingering on the streets was viewed by these authors, but also by a range of middle class reformers, as inherently dangerous and immoral. The streets were to be used only as a thoroughfare and not as meeting places. For some philanthropic groups the street socialisation of working class youth lowered the moral character of females so much that they were inseparable from prostitutes.[3]

We have seen how women took on the role of the buyers of the increasing numbers of commodities becoming available in the shops and the new department stores. This required their greater presence, increasingly without a male escort, outside of the home, in the streets to and from the shops and, partly as a corollary of this, in the new places of relaxation such as, in Britain, the new tearooms which, Hamish Fraser tells us, 'burgeoned in the later decades of the [nineteenth] century'.[4] In 1887 Lyons's first tearoom was opened. By 1910 the company had ninety-eight in London.[5] Moreover, working-class women had to pass through the streets going to and from their places of work. Throughout the second half of the nineteenth century women of all classes were to be found in increasing numbers outside of the home, and on the streets of the cities. The presence of so many unaccompanied women was a novelty, and proved to be very confusing to men.

The bourgeois (male) concern with women on the streets centred on a preoccupation with prostitution and, specifically, streetwalkers. Judith Walkowitz has described how, in Britain:

> By the 1850s prostitution had become 'the Great Social Evil', not simply an affront to morality, but a vital aspect of the social economy as well. Commentaries on prostitution took a variety of forms: novels, manifestos, letters to the editor, and police reports. Embedded in bluebooks on overcrowding, workhouse children, factory conditions, and women's employment were obligatory references to the immorality consequent upon deleterious social conditions.[6]

She goes on to note that, judging from their diaries, prostitution was also 'a private obsession for some respectable Victorians'.[7] In France in 1836 Alexandre Parent-Duchâtelet published his pioneering survey on prostitution in Paris. Parent-Duchâtelet's work was an early model of social investigation. He 'prepared a demographic study of 12,000 prostitutes who had been inscribed [in the police register] over a fifteen year period (1816-1831)'.[8] In Britain, the 1840s saw a new style of scientific social investigation 'formally proceeding from an examination of causes to results, extent, and remedies for prostitution'.[9] These new studies culminated in William Acton's *Prostitution Considered in Its Moral, Social and Sanitary Aspects in London and Other Large Cities; with Proposals for the Mitigation and Prevention of Its Attendant Evils*, which was published in 1857. Acton was an important campaigner for the regulation of prostitution:

> he argued for the recognition of a social evil already tacitly sanctioned by English society. His analysis was also shaped by

a sense of the perils of male sexual license as well as its inevitability. He looked to regulation to establish some boundaries for this dangerous natural impulse. The need to legitimize a regulation system informed his social portrait of prostitutes as well.[10]

It was Acton's study, among others, which prepared the way for the debates over the Contagious Diseases Acts later in the century. Elizabeth Wilson has summed up this (male) preoccupation with prostitution in the second half of the nineteenth century by suggesting that 'prostitution was the great fear of the age'.[11]

The theme of the streetwalker combines the economic connotations of the street as part of the 'male' economic order of the public domain – which is where most wage-labour-based productive work takes place – with the presence of women on the streets. From a male point of view all these women were commodified. In contrast the courtesan represented, particularly in Paris, an older and relatively acceptable face of prostitution. She was not paid directly for sex, and she did not solicit in a direct way. To the extent that she foregrounded the economic transaction, the streetwalker was a worker. Classified by Marx as a member of the lumpenproletariat because she did not engage in organised productive labour and did not sell her labour-power, nevertheless the association of the streetwalker was with the manual labourer. Selling her time and the use of her body, things the manual labourer also sells, a part of the threat of the streetwalker was the opportunity she provided for deconstructing the moral order of wage labour.

Usually poor women forced, through economic necessity, on to the streets, streetwalkers sold sex in a direct transaction. In order to get customers the streetwalker made herself as sexually desirable as she could. Walkowitz notes that, 'in their dress, prostitutes emulated the conspicuous display of Victorian ladies'.[12] She describes how, 'bonnetless, without shawls, they presented themselves "in their figure" to passersby'.[13] In other words, in order to make themselves desirable they displayed the outline of their bodies in their clothes and, in doing so, helped to eroticise the display of the bourgeois women they emulated. The streetwalker was a woman who had made access to her body a commodity, and who attempted to increase her sexual desirability by showing her body off. We have already noticed in Chapter 1 that Marx made a connection between women's bodies and commodities. The streetwalker makes clear, as a limit case, the male associations of the street, the economic, and women who frequented the street. In addition, the streetwalker literalised the new libidinised spectacularisation of commodities.

The concern with the streetwalker, or the woman constructed in male eyes as a streetwalker, provides one context for the fetishisation of the female body in the public domain. As Wilson argues:

> The prostitute was a 'public woman', but the problem in nineteenth century urban life was whether every woman in the new, disordered world of the city – the public sphere of pavements, cafés and theatres – was a public woman and thus a prostitute. The very presence of unattended – unowned – women constituted a threat both to male power and to male frailty. Yet although the male ruling class did all it could to restrict the movement of women in cities, it proved impossible to banish them from public spaces. Women continued to crowd into city centres and the factory districts.[14]

There are two reasons why it proved impossible to banish women from the public domain. The first was that large numbers of working-class women worked in the factories. The second was that, with shopping becoming women's business, more women, and certainly more middle-class women, were going out to the shops. In Australia this shift took place a little later:

> By 1907, the heaviest trading day was not Pay Friday but the following Monday. The reason, according to the local Newcastle [New South Wales] factories and shops inspector, was that Saturday was increasingly devoted to family leisure pursuits such as picnics and visits to the seaside.[15]

Reekie explains: 'The inspector's observation suggests that working-class women and their families were redefining shopping, not as a family activity to be carried out at leisure, but as domestic labour most properly performed by women during the breadwinner's working hours.'[16] The woman was being constructed through division of labour as a consumer at the same time that she was being fetishised and spectacularised as an object of visual consumption.

In *Just Looking*, Rachel Bowlby has a cartoon taken from *La Vie de Londres*, published in Paris in 1890.[17] It shows the bustle of Regent Street, one of the major shopping streets in London. The caption reads: 'Shopping, *c'est courre les magasins: voilà pour les dames; mais pour les messieurs, c'est courre les shoppingeuses! Shop qui peut!*' Bowlby translates this as '*Shopping* is checking out the stores – for ladies; for gentlemen, it's checking out the *lady*

shoppers! *Shop qui peut!'* The final sentence – 'Shop who can!' –
signifies the celebration of shopping. Shopping is for both women
and men. The caption highlights the importance of sight, and its
association with commodification. While the women look (the new
practice of window shopping), and maybe buy commodities, the
men look at the women. But can they buy the women? At this point
we have made clear the problem described by Wilson. Are all
women in the public domain public women – streetwalkers?
Certainly they walk the streets. Does every woman have her price?
The cartoon implies the end consequence of the conjunctures under
discussion. Women on the streets are associated with prostitution;
as the fetishistic viewing of commodities spreads, so the streetwalker, whose body is commodified and who attracts the gaze of
men, is associated with the middle-class women who are shopping.
As the fetishistic order spreads, so all women become eroticised –
not only those who set out to attract men but also those whose concern is shopping, for whom there develops the preoccupation with
'looking good' (for whom?) when they go out.

   In order to understand how this aspect of the new desiring structure comes about, we need to look at the nineteenth-century history of
the *flâneur*. We have seen now how women were transformed in
the sight of men. On the streets of the cities, going shopping,
women became eroticised and commodified. They were, in a word,
fetishised. The history of the reconstruction of men as voyeurs lies
in the history of the *flâneur*. The first important critical discussion
of the *flâneur* is that of Walter Benjamin in *Charles Baudelaire: A
Lyric Poet in the Era of High Capitalism* (trans. 1973). The *flâneur*
is male. For Benjamin he is a mid-century product of the new city
life where people entirely unacquainted with each other jostle
together on the streets. Following the title of a short story by Edgar
Allen Poe, Benjamin describes the *flâneur* as the man of the crowd.
He strolls the streets at a leisurely pace; observation is the key to his
lifestyle. He watches and deduces an understanding of people from
their dress and their behaviour. Benjamin describes the *flâneur* as
one 'who goes botanizing on the asphalt'.[18]

   Benjamin gives material reasons for the spread of the *flâneur*.
He notes: 'Before Haussmann wide pavements were rare, and the
narrow ones afforded little protection from vehicles. Strolling could
hardly have assumed the importance it did without the arcades.'[19]
He goes on to provide a description of the arcades, drawn from an
1852 illustrated guide to Paris:

The arcades, a rather recent invention of industrial luxury, ...
are glass-covered, marble-panelled passageways through
entire complexes of houses whose proprietors have combined
for such speculations. Both sides of these passageways, which
are lighted from above, are lined with the most elegant shops,
so that such an arcade is a city, even a world, in miniature.[20]

Benjamin is suggesting that what enabled the *flâneur* to flourish
were broad pavements and an absence of vehicles. The arcades provided just such an environment. At this point we should note that
the arcades were full of shops. The visitors to the arcades would
have been mainly women shoppers.

The history of the *flâneur* can be traced back to the early part of
the nineteenth century. Wilson discusses a pamphlet from 1806
entitled *Le Flâneur au Salon, ou M. Bonhomme, Examen Joyeux des
Tableaux, Mêlé de Vaudevilles* which describes the life of a M. Bonhomme as he observes society. As Wilson describes it, M.
Bonhomme 'spends most of his day simply looking at the urban
spectacle'.[21] When not doing this he passes the time in cafés and
restaurants: 'he chooses establishments frequented by actors,
writers, journalists and painters – that is, his interests are primarily
aesthetic'.[22] He also watches 'the lower ranks of society – for
example he watches soldiers, workers and "grisettes" at an open-air
dance'.[23] Here we find the expression of the relation between power,
one's position in the social hierarchy, and surveillance. Unlike the
later *flâneurs*, who shop mainly for women, Wilson notes that for
M. Bonhomme 'women play but a minor role in his life'.[24]
However, he does window-shop, 'looking at books, new fashions,
hats, combs, jewellery and novelties of all kinds'.[25] By the 1840s
M. Bonhomme's lifestyle had become more common. Now,
though, one of the *flâneur's* first concerns was looking at the
women on the street. Benjamin's *flâneur*, fascinated by the unknown members of the crowd, occupies a transitional position,
though of course this form of *flânerie* continues after the
libidinizing of the male gaze. From the 1830s on, the streetwalker
provided a libidinal focus for the connections between the woman
(shopper) on the streets, the economic order, and the commodity.
For the mid-century *flâneur* this focus was becoming generalised to
all the women on the streets regardless of their class or their purpose there. The later *flâneur* mediated his window shopping
through his surveilling, desiring, and commodifying gaze on the
women in the streets.

Janet Wolff has discussed how there were no, and could be no, *flâneuses*. When, in 1831, George Sand wanted to travel around Paris she disguised herself as a man.[26] As we have noted, the public streets were a male domain. Men gazed; women were gazed upon. Starting from suggestive comments by Marx and Baudelaire, Wilson has argued that the *flâneur* was equatable with the prostitute; and 'just as the *flâneur* was a prostitute, perhaps also the prostitute could be said to be the female *flâneur'*.[27] This is a problematic equation for a number of reasons. I want to concentrate on just one here. Wilson uses the image of the prostitute to emphasise women's active engagement with the city. She criticises a generally held feminist view which suggests that

> the urban scene was at all times represented from the point of view of the male gaze: in paintings and photographs men voyeuristically stare, women are passively subjected to the gaze. The public arena – cafés and places of entertainment such as the Folies Bergères – offered a *'mise en scène'*, or setting where men of the bourgeoisie could meet and seduce or purchase working-class women. Middle-class women were restricted to certain limited public spaces designated as respectable: parks and the opera, for example.[28]

Wilson's examples are drawn from Paris, but she is illustrating a more general point. Her criticism of this position is that it over-states the case:

> Women did participate actively as well as passively in the spectacle, and the whole Parisian atmosphere of pleasure and excess, both sexual and political, did create an environment in which women were able to gain certain freedoms – even if the price of this was their over-sexualisation and their participation in what was often a voyeuristic spectacle.[29]

In her equation of the *flâneur* with the prostitute, Wilson seems to mistake a most important difference. Whilst the *flâneur* was some-times also a dandy, the key to *flânerie* was the activity of gazing, which we can understand as being spectacularising surveillance, rather than being gazed upon. In contrast the streetwalker, who may, of course, also have gazed on the city during her time on the streets, set herself up to be gazed upon in order to pursue her trade. It is here that the analogy between the prostitute and the commod-ity is most powerful. The prostitute makes her commodity, her body, desirable just as manufactured commodities are made to look desirable. The cultural fetishism which underlies active commodity fetishism complements, and ultimately overdetermines, this spectacular move.

In describing the prostitute as a female *flâneur*, Wilson seems to be thinking most of her sheer presence on the streets and her ability to go anywhere, since she did not abide by the moral norms which dictated where a woman was allowed to go. It is this, perhaps, as well as the tendency for these women to dress up, which leads Wilson to suggest that women more generally participated in the Parisian spectacle. Women, as she says, gained certain freedoms. This is indisputable, but it is the other side of Wilson's argument which concerns me here – what she describes as the 'over-sexualisation' of women and their participation in 'what was often a voyeuristic spectacle'. My point is a simple one: this over-sexualisation – which I am describing as eroticisation – and the male voyeurism associated with it, are consequences of the new fetishisation of women's bodies.

In her article on the *flâneur* Susan Buck-Morss discusses the situation of the prostitute:

> Benjamin wrote: 'The love of the prostitute is apotheosis of *Einfühlung* [empathic identity] onto the commodity.' In the 19th century this is what was new about the 'oldest profession'. The prostitute's natural body resembled the lifeless mannequin used for the display of the latest fashion; the more expensive her outfit, the greater her appeal.[30]

In the newly emerging world of active commodity fetishism the position of the prostitute in the culture of the street altered. Previously her body had just been an object for sale; now it became itself a spectacular commodity. For Cesare Lombroso, the celebrated Italian criminologist and one of the founders of the discipline, 'the female adheres to normality more so than the male. Woman makes even a lesser criminal. Ultimately only the prostitute reaches the level of deviance of the male.'[31] We have already seen Riley describe the social as based on familial standards which are claimed as those of women. For Lombroso the prostitute seems to be the most removed from those standards. Commenting on his claim, Guiliana Bruno notes that streetwalking 'incorporates the ultimate "criminal" pleasure – that of *flânerie*'.[32] Here we are returned to Wilson's argument. The context for the male spectacularising gaze was men's position in the social hierarchy. In the surveillance order organised by the modern state, in which the patriarchal state itself was at the pinnacle, men could watch women – and bourgeois men could surveil working-class men. This class/gender system led to complexities. For example, it is more acceptable for middle-class women to watch working-class men than the other way round. Nevertheless, in the terms set by this hierarchical system, the streetwalker, occupying one of its lowest places, was to be gazed upon; she was not supposed to gaze. As the streetwalker's body, in common with those of women more generally, became fetishised, so she was constructed as a passive object of male desire. The streetwalker who gazed upon the cityscape was occupying what was, in the first place, a male role, regardless of the degree of libidinization of that gaze. In this way the streetwalker's gaze was transgressive – deviant, as Lombroso would say.

Benjamin discusses a poem of Baudelaire's about prostitution in which he writes:

> Against the lamplight, whose shivering is the wind's,
> Prostitution spreads its light and life in the streets:
> Like an anthill opening its issue it penetrates
> Mysteriously everywhere by its own occult route;
> Like an enemy mining the foundations of a fort,
> Or a worm in an apple, eating what all should eat,
> It circulates securely in the city's clogged heart.
> ('Le crépuscule du soir', lines 14-20)

Benjamin argues that commodities 'derive [a charm] from the crowd that surges around and intoxicates them',[33] and comments on Baudelaire's poem: 'Only the mass of inhabitants permits prostitution to spread over large parts of the city. And only the mass makes it possible for the sexual object to become intoxicated with the hundred stimuli which it produces.'[34] Rather than the mass of inhabitants as such, it was the new, female mass on the street which enabled prostitution to spread. This is because, with increased numbers of women on the streets, it became less possible to identify the streetwalker. However, that such a spread did take place depended on the reformation of male sexual desire. What the idea of the spread of prostitution over the city really describes is the movement of streetwalkers out of the working-class areas where they lived and into other areas, the middle-class suburbs and, more likely, the new shopping areas. Finally, the spread of prostitution serves as a metaphor for the spread of the male fetishisation of women's bodies in the everyday public life of the street. I have already described the effect of this: every woman on the street was commodified and became – from the point of view of the male observer, the *flâneur*, and regardless of her own intentions – a (potential) prostitute.

Another theme runs through Benjamin's discussion of the *flâneur*. This is the importance of the interior. The arcades through which he strolled were enclosed. Benjamin writes:

> If the arcade is the classical form of the *intérieur*, which is how the *flâneur* sees the street, the department store is the form of the *intérieur*'s decay. The bazaar is the last hangout of the *flâneur*. If in the beginning the street had become an *intérieur* for him, now this *intérieur* turned into a street, and he roamed through the labyrinth of the city.[35]

For Benjamin one of the most important premises of the practice of *flânerie* was that the *flâneur* should experience the space in which he strolled and observed as being enclosed.

The theoretical basis for this idea comes at the beginning of Benjamin's chapter on the *flâneur*. Here he describes the situation of the writer in the marketplace. The similarity with the *flâneur* is that both observe, and Benjamin makes the connection through the brief vogue for the genre of physiologies in France which, he writes, declined in the 1840s. He provides a description of the genre:

> It is a panorama literature. It was not by chance that *Le Livre des cent-et-un, Les François peints par eux-mêmes, Le Diable à Paris, La Grande Ville* enjoyed the favour of the capital city at the same time as the dioramas. These books consist of individual sketches which, as it were, reproduce the plastic foreground of those panoramas with their anecdotal form and the extensive background of the panoramas with their store of information.[36]

At the heart of Benjamin's argument is the idea that 'once a writer had entered the marketplace, he looked around as in a diorama'.[37] In the previous chapter I discussed the tremendous vogue for panoramas and dioramas during this period. Benjamin is arguing that the experience of the capitalist marketplace – that is, the system of exchange – is of a closed system. The *flâneur* experiences the street, indeed the public domain generally, as a marketplace. It is, however, a marketplace in which the recognition of commodification – what we are really talking about here is active commodity fetishism, the recognition of *fetishised* commodification – is suppressed. The department store represents the decay of the *intérieur* not from the point of view of the female consumer but from that of the male observer, the man who consumes fetishised female bodies. It is a decayed form of *intérieur* because it makes so obvious the interwoven connections of economic exchange and desire which articulate the new situation of women in the public domain.

Benjamin argues that the *flâneur* declined with the passing of the arcades. We can now see, on the contrary, that the whole of the public domain was becoming eroticized and every man was becoming a *flâneur*. Crucial to this development was the fetishisation of the female body itself. With the spread of cultural fetishism the female body – and in particular the naked female body – became the obsessive site for the male gaze. This gaze quite literally staged the female body as the voyeuristic object of spectacularising surveillance. It is to this development that I now want to turn.

At the historical moment of the coming-into-being of the modern state – the French Revolution – the Marquis de Sade put forward an image of the female body which would become a part of everyday life during the ensuing century. As Barthes puts it:

> the Sadian body is in fact a body seen from a distance in the full light of the stage; it is merely a *very well lit* body the very illumination of which, even, distant, effaces individuality ... but allows the pure charm to come through; totally desirable and absolutely inaccessible, the lit body has as its natural arena the intimate theater, the nightclub, the fantasy, or the Sadian presentation ...[38]

The very well lit, and of course female and naked, Sadian body, seen from a distance – the body as spectacularisingly surveilled fetish – is an inflection of the idea of the painter's *tableau*, the posed scene, discussed as an aesthetic concept by Diderot.[39] During the nineteenth century the *tableau* was reconstituted in the bourgeois entertainment of the *tableau vivant*. This, in turn, provided one historical context for the development of striptease – the most obvious connection is that form of striptease where the performer acts a part. And so we are returned to Sade's desirable well lit body; desirable because it is fetishised.[40]

In the United States the *tableau vivant* became a source of commercial enterprise. Robert Allen describes how 'throughout the 1830s New York theaters and museums offered "personifications" of famous paintings and statues "performed" by individuals or companies at entr'acte entertainments or as a part of dramatic vehicles'.[41] By the late 1840s it had gone down-market to become a working-class entertainment. At the same time, Allen writes, the paintings depicted came increasingly to include naked or near-naked women – the women who represented these figures in the *tableaux* wore skin-coloured tights.

Striptease can be defined as a gradual revelation of, tradition-ally, the female body for a male audience Whilst the uncovering of the female body may always carry a sexual charge in a society where it is usually covered up, the advent of striptease reflects the new fetishisation of the female body. In this practice the female body is eroticised as a spectacle in the male gaze. The transformation of the *tableau vivant* into the striptease took place towards the end of the nineteenth century. Whilst the *tableau vivant* provides a gen-eral historical source, Allen provides an American history which focuses on the introduction of a new form of burlesque. This was a consequence of the American discovery of belly dancing during the Chicago World's Columbian Exhibition of 1893. In the puritan United States, belly dancing became known as cooch dancing and it was used as an excuse for baring parts of the female anatomy. Mark Gabor, in his history of the pin-up, provides a context here:

> Actresses and dancing girls, as well as burlesque queens, 'show girls', chorus girls, and movie starlets, came to repre-sent the promiscuous image of women, relished in the main by men of lower socio-economic standing. One recalls pin-ups like Lillie Langtry and Lillian Russell and Little Egypt, who, at the 1893 Chicago World's Fair, drove crowds of men mad by gyrating in a new dance called the cooch.[42]

From 1893 onwards, the American adaptation of belly dancing trans-formed it into an increasingly explicit sexual routine performed by increasingly naked women. Allen writes:

> The inclusion of the cooch dance as a standard feature of bur-lesque after the 1890s centered the form once and for all around undisguised sexual exhibitionism. The cooch dance linked sexual display of the female performer and the scopic desire of the male patron in a more direct and intimate fashion than any previous feature of burlesque.[43]

Here we have the new importance of the fetishising gaze. By the early 1910s burlesque shows were including dramatic excuses for women to take their clothes off, though still only as far as flesh-coloured tights. These strips were done in low lighting. The shift to female nakedness in full light occurred, it is claimed, in 1917 at the Minsky brothers' burlesque theatre – the National Winter Garden Theater on New York's lower East Side.[44] Another history of strip-tease constructs it as a French development. In this narrative, on 9 February 1893, at the Moulin Rouge in Paris, an artist's model named Mona entertained the students at the Four Arts Ball by gradually taking her clothes off. She was fined a hundred francs, but within a year a professional striptease was taking place at an-other Parisian music hall with the title 'Le Coucher d'Yvette'. Both these origin stories locate the key moment in striptease's history in the period between 1890 and 1920. Doubtless, there are many other origin stories. In his history of striptease, for example, Richard Wortley claims that 'one landmark [in its French development] was the appearance in 1907 at the Moulin Rouge of an actress called Germaine Aymos, who entered dressed only in three small shells'.[45] She was prosecuted for this act of indecency. The important point is that cultural changes taking place throughout the West were pro-viding a context in which the slow disrobing of the female body before an audience of men became erotically meaningful.

In the first half of the twentieth century, striptease seems to have been most popular in the United States. Paralleling the spread of consumerism, it increased in popularity in Europe during the 1950s. Reflecting the American influence, the French use the English term developed in the United States, *le striptease*. By 1960 the increase in so-called strip clubs in London was drawing comment. The strip clubs were edging out the English erotic vaudeville shows epitomised by those at the Windmill Theatre. These included staged nudity in *tableaux vivants*. One of the jobs of the Lord Chamber-lain, the theatre censor, was to police the rule that nudes could not move. Wortley notes that the strip clubs 'emerged out of the nude revues of the 1950s, with the most notable difference that the girls now moved'.[46] The best known of the new strip clubs was Raymond's Revuebar, opened by Paul Raymond in 1959. Epitomis-ing the shift in male interest, the Windmill closed in 1964.

In his American history, Allen notes that by the late 1920s 'the narrative context had been eliminated from striptease; it needed no narrative to support its spectacle'.[47] Given the title of the French entertainment we can see how that, too, had a narrative legitima-tion which, subsequently, decreased in importance. Summing up this shift, Allen writes: 'In the place of that larger narrative is the self-evident rationale provided by spectacle: the stripper is what she does, and she does what she does because of who she is.'[48] What the stripper is, is a fetish. She is no longer an actor performing in a narrative. She is a person whose purpose on the stage is to display her body as a spectacle for the watching men. If we ask why it is that men want to watch a woman disrobing, we are really asking two questions. First, why do they want to look at the naked female body? And, second, why do they want to see its gradual revelation? We find our answer to both questions in the cultural-fetishistic concern with the female body. The trajectory from the 1840s commercial *tableau vivant* to the 1920s striptease was one of increasing focus on that body. In striptease the woman is literally selling the visibility of her body. Unlike the streetwalker who, ultimately, sells the physical sex act, striptease commodifies the scopophilic concern with the sight of the female body. In striptease the female body is consumed by men as a spectacle. The act climaxes in the revelation of what is not there – that is, the absence of the penis – whilst the body itself is eroticised as a phallic substitute. The history of the transformation of the *tableau vivant* and burlesque into the striptease parallels the establishment of the modern state. The eroticisation of the world couples the sight of the female body – in this case as a commodity – and manufactured commodities in a fetishistic structure of desire expressed through the male gaze.

Ken Russell's film *Salome's Last Dance* (1987) contains within it Oscar Wilde's play *Salome* (French 1893, English 1894). Like the myth of Lolita, as distinct from Nabokov's novel, the play concerns a sexually precocious pubescent daughter who entices and manipulates her stepfather. Herod is, in addition, a king, as well as being a subject of Rome. He embodies the position of the symbolic Father in the state – though, of course, lacking the phallus, the fantastic 'real' power of disposal that he craves. And this even more so given his subjection to Rome. Salome is both androgynous in her puberty and sexually alluring. Herod demands that she dance for him, offering her anything she wants. She dances a striptease. Herod's focus is on the moment of revelation and display of her vagina. At this moment in the film a substitution is made and a boy resembling Salome reveals a penis. Herod looks shocked. After a very brief shot, the boy is replaced by Salome, now naked. Herod is satisfied and reassured. Salome goes on to ask for the head of John the Baptist, which Herod is loath to give her. In Freudian terms decapitation is a metaphor for castration, and killing John – whom he does not want

to kill anyway – at Salome's behest evidences Herod's own emas-
culation as king. The pubescent Salome embodies the male fantasy
of the fetish that is both desired and feared. The revelation of the
penis at the end of the dance can also be read in terms of the Freudian castration complex. Here, the penis is the reassuring sign that
Herod wants to see, whilst at the same time seeing it on his object of
desire disturbs him. The action takes place within the context of
Salome's youthful androgyny and Herod's paternal – and, given his
gubernatorial situation, patriarchal – position. His desire for her is a
desire for the phallic fetish which will secure his power. On this
reading Herod unsettles his own power through his (incestuous)
desire – whilst, on a structural level, this desire is itself a consequence of his desire to secure that power.

From around the 1850s a new kind of illness began to make its
appearance among, especially, the women of the bourgeoisie.
Richard Gordon writes that:

> suddenly, in the second half of the nineteenth century, it
> seemed to burst onto the scene, into the forefront of medical
> controversy and public discussion. Although solid statistics
> are clearly lacking, available evidence does suggest that in fact
> the prevalence of hysteria during the nineteenth century
> actually increased, and that its visibility was not simply a con-
> sequence of the increased attention that was being paid to it.[49]

Hysteria's symptoms were visibly manifested through the body.
These symptoms included, in Gordon's list, 'paralyses, sensory dis-
turbances such as blindness, fainting spells, even seizures'.[50] As its
name suggests, it was thought for some time to have a physical
origin in women's reproductive organs. Outwardly displayed in a
bewildering variety of bodily symptoms, hysteria was thought to be
traceable back to something essentially female rather than being a
cultural phenomenon. As such, it could only be an illness of women.

In the 1880s William Playfair, the celebrated English doctor and,
among other positions he held, Professor of Obstetric Medicine at
King's College, published a series of articles popularising the American Weir Mitchell's treatment for hysteria. Mitchell argued for a
psychological reading of hysteria and developed a treatment which,
in part, included the removal of the patient from her usual sur-
roundings, a special diet, massage, and electrical stimulation of the
muscles. In an article entitled 'Notes on the Systematic Treatment
of Nerve Prostration and Hysteria connected with Uterine Disease',

first published in the *Lancet* in 1881, Playfair describes hysteria as having 'protean symptoms'. He writes: 'Now, in a large number of these cases there is, or has been, very real uterine mischief. I shall not be accused, I am sure, of any disposition to minimise the influence of local uterine disorder on the general health.'[51] He goes on to argue that 'the pain, the backache, the leucorrhea, the difficulty in progression, the disordered menstruation, which are attendants on the local troubles, have ended in producing a state of general disturbance in which all the bodily functions become implicated'.[52] Here we can see how the claim that hysteria was a psychological illness was still being backed up by a claimed physiological origin in the (female) body.

In France during this same period Jean-Martin Charcot was working at the Salpêtrière women's hospital for nervous diseases in Paris. Between October 1885 and February 1886 Freud went to Paris to work with Charcot. Charcot's neuropathological orientation meant that he tended to view hysteria as a form of nervous illness. Nevertheless, Thomas Szasz sums up his discussion of Charcot's work by suggesting that 'Charcot's orientation to the problem of hysteria was neither organic nor psychological'. He goes on: 'Although Charcot did not overthrow a narrowly medical conceptualization of hysteria, he did not really fully accept this view. He recognized and clearly stated that problems in human relationships may be expressed by hysterical symptoms.'[53] Josef Breuer and Freud, but particularly Freud, were to increase the emphasis on the mental and the social in their discussions of hysteria.

In their paper 'On the Psychical Mechanism of Hysterical Phenomena: Preliminary Communication', first published in 1893, Breuer and Freud make the claim that '*Hysterics suffer mainly from reminiscences.*'[54] Later they argue that 'the motor phenomena of hysterical attacks can be interpreted partly as universal forms of reaction appropriate to the affect accompanying the memory ... , partly as a direct expression of these memories'.[55] Breuer and Freud's point is that if a person is unable to experience the affect associated with a particular event then, even when consciously they have 'forgotten' that event, the affect will appear – in a visible disturbance of the body's functioning – at a later date.

Usually this argument is taken to be a first working-out of Freud's idea of an unconscious, and the notion of repression which goes along with it. There is, though, another way into Breuer and Freud's discussion. This is to see it as an argument concerned with emotion, the body, and display. In commentaries on Freud's under-standing of individual development it is common to emphasise infantile sexuality and adult sexuality and to place between them the Oedipus complex. Most outlines of Freud's work tend to centre on the effects of the Oedipus complex. However, the period of infantile sexuality is ended not by the Oedipus complex but by the period which Freud calls latency. In *Three Essays on the Theory of Sexuality* he argues: 'One gets an impression from civilized children that the construction of these dams [disgust, feelings of shame, and the claims of aesthetic and moral ideals] is a product of education, and no doubt education has much to do with it. But in reality this development is organically determined and fixed by heredity.'[56] Again, we have Freud's universalistic reductionism. In fact, as Freud almost acknowledges, the prime mover in the onset of latency is the modern cultural attitude towards the body. In *The Introductory Lectures on Psycho-Analysis* Freud describes latency as beginning 'from about the sixth to eighth year of life onwards'.[57] Freud's description of latency in relation to the sexual drive is actu-ally a description of a cultural mechanism for the alienation of the individual from the experience of their body. Latency may be understood as the production in everyday life of what Descartes argued as the distinction between the mind and the body. Nabokov's nympholept, Humbert Humbert, placed the desirable nymphet between the ages of nine and fourteen – that is, at the time of pubescence right on the border of latency and adolescence. The now objectified (female) body is here being reconstituted as a site that provokes desire.

The Oedipus complex having been resolved before latency, at puberty sexual desire is directed outside the family. This is the moment when the person, with a mind and body now clearly separated, enters the social. The period of latency sets in place the objectification of the individual's body to themselves as well as to others. We need to understand this psychosexual period in the development of the individual within the context of the modern construction of the body-as-object. From the fifteenth century onwards, and associated with the rise of the bourgeoisie, there was a shift towards an understanding of the body as an objectified entity, closed off from the world in which it exists. Norbert Elias has described this new ideology of the body as that of *homo clausus*.[58] Ideally, this new body would have no orifices, and no flows such as those of food and excreta, to connect it with the world. The

privileged body was the male body. It was claimed to be the perfect
body, the body to which women, with their flawed bodies and
'medical problems' such as menstruation and birth, could only
aspire. Peter Stallybrass and Allon White describe the latency period
of Freud's patient the Wolf Man like this: 'His process of "forgetting" the body produced its own symptoms: anorexia (which lasted
until he was told "about one of his uncles who had refused to eat in
the same way and had wasted away to death while he was still
young"); constipation.'[59] The Wolf Man was refusing the flows
through mouth and anus. He was objectifying his body by cutting it
off from the world. The most unusual aspect of this story is that the
Wolf Man was male. He wanted a body more perfect even than the
relatively holeless male body he already had. In the nineteenth century the Wolf Man's hysterical symptoms were rarely found in
men. It was for women that latency was most profound, ideally
separating them from all carnal desires and pleasures. Indeed in
some ways we might equate the cultural roles of the castration
complex for men with latency for women. Hysteria may then be
understood as the symptomatic presentation on the surface of the
alienated and objectified body, where in the case of women sexual
desire had also been constructed into a passive form, a body now
also fetishised and spectacularised, of forms of mental distress.

In the previous chapter we saw that spectacularising surveillance (one factor in the experience of the frenzy of the visible) provided a very important context for the development of the new
visual media. Photography and, later, film were central in the
scopophilic fetishisation of the female body from their inception.
The first photographs of naked women were taken around the
1840s. These were, Susan Sontag asserts, of prostitutes – that is to
say, women whose bodies were already established as commodified
and spectacularised. Gisèle Freund notes that in France, 'as early as
1850, a law had been passed prohibiting the sale of obscene photographs as an act offensive to both morality and tradition'.[60] By the
1890s, in the United States at least, magazines were being published
which included photographs and other pictures of naked and near-
naked women. *Munsey's*, for example, a general-interest magazine
which ran from 1889 to 1929, in addition to its other features,
'specialized in nude and semi-nude pictures'.[61] The seaside girl, a
theme discussed in Chapter 1, was also picked up by these new
magazines. *Truth Magazine* (1886–1902) 'featured "bathing girls"
but refused to print photographs actually taken at the beach. It

preferred to idealize the bathing beauty through studio photography, because "in the water she is a fright"'.[62] In Britain this shift took place somewhat later – as was to be the case with striptease. Gabor tells us that 'the only significant turn-of-the-century British publication that followed the American magazines in carrying a wide selection of girlie pictures was *Photo Bits*, which was started in 1898'.[63] He also argues that picture postcards were important in helping to develop the generic form of the pin-up which is the basis of the posed photographs in men's magazines, writing that 'the earliest postcards of bathing beauties [the seaside girl again] came from France around 1900 and soon thereafter such cards were also made available in England'.[64]

In 1856 Dr Hugh Diamond, who was both a founder member of the Royal Photographic Society and resident superintendent of the Female Department of the Surrey County Lunatic Asylum, read a paper to the Royal Society entitled 'On the Application of Photography to the Physiognomic and Mental Phenomena of Insanity'. Versions of this paper were twice published in 1856, in the *Saturday Review* and the *Photographic Journal*. In 1859 the editors of the *Lancet* argued that 'Photography is so essentially the Art of Truth – and the representative of Truth in Art – that it would seem to be the essential means of reproducing all forms and structures of which Science seeks for delineation'.[65] One of Diamond's points was that 'the Photographer secures with unerring accuracy the external phenomena of each passion, as the really certain indication of internal derangement, and exhibits to the eye the well known sympathy which exists between the diseased brain and the organs and features of the body'.[66] Following on from the claims about photographic verisimilitude discussed in the previous chapter, the claim here was that photography accurately represents the truth which is displayed on the visible surface of the body. It cannot be coincidental that Diamond was in charge of the Female Department of the asylum. Although he made the traditional connection between the diseased brain and the physical symptoms, his work operated in terms of, and reinforced, the spectacular fetishisation of the female body.

A little before Freud's visit to the Salpêtrière, Charcot and Paul Richer set up a photographic department at the hospital to take photographs of the patients.[67] Ilza Veith writes that the Salpêtrière 'usually housed some five thousand neurotic indigents, epileptics, and insane patients'.[68] Between 1888 and 1904 seventeen volumes of the illustrated journal *La Nouvelle Iconographie de la Salpêtrière* appeared.[69] It may well be that, at least in part, the importance of sight in Freud's work stemmed from his time working with Charcot. Although Charcot seems to have had some male patients, these photographs were all of women.[70] Braun notes that, 'in a fascinating study, *Invention de l'hystérie, Charcot et l'icono-graphie photographique de la Salpêtrière* (Paris: Macula, 1982), Georges Didi-Huberman describes how photography was endorsed by Charcot to give scientific validity to the staged gestures and tab-leaux that were used to invent a visual model for hysteria'.[71] Often hysterical symptoms came and went without warning. What is implied here is another spectacular staging of the female body, to set beside the *tableau vivant*. Here, photography gave an authen-ticity to the symptoms photographed which, in turn, provided a codified inventory of visual hysterical manifestations. This can be taken a step further. Following Stephen Heath in *The Sexual Fix*, Linda Williams writes that 'Charcot's running commentary on the "passionate attitudes" recorded in the photographic record of the hysterical attack is arranged in narrative succession: "'threat', 'appeal', 'amorous supplication', 'eroticism', 'ecstasy'"'. The very terms suggest nothing so much as the standard hard-core depiction of the progres-sion to climax ending in male orgasm.'[72] The male progress is here an effect of the organisation of the sequence of the female hysteric's gestures.

These photographs form a surveillance of the female body. The photographer was male. As we saw more generally in the previous chapter, here also the photograph established the power relation and mapped the gender relation. One of the most popular photo-graphic devices of the latter part of the nineteenth century was the stereoscope. As Jonathan Crary describes it, it provided the viewer with a kind of three-dimensional effect: 'Our eyes follow a choppy and erratic path into its depth: it is an assemblage of local zones of three-dimensionality, zones imbued with a hallucinatory clarity, but which when taken together never coalesce into a homogeneous field.'[73] The stereoscope can be fitted into the simulatory lineage, outlined in the previous chapter, which included the panorama and the diorama. In this case also the spectator gazed on a three-dimen-sional illusion from the outside. Crary goes on: 'It is no coincidence that the stereoscope became increasingly synonymous with erotic and pornographic imagery in the course of the nineteenth century. The very effects of tangibility that Wheatstone had sought from the beginning were quickly turned into a mass form of ocular

possession.'[74] The stereoscope became so associated with pornography that, Crary observes, some commentators have even linked
its demise to its connection with such subject matter.

In 1887 Eadweard Muybridge published *Animal Locomotion*
in eleven volumes. He used an apparatus of his own design, which
he called a zoopraxiscope, to take a rapid sequence of photographs to
show how animals move. Among his photographs were many
sequences of men, women, and children. This project of Muybridge
was funded by the University of Pennsylvania. In most of the
photographs the people are naked. According to Robert Taft's introduction to a 1955 edition of the human photographs, among the
men used were the 'professor of physical culture', the 'champion
runner', and 'instructors at the Fencing and Sparring Club'.[75] The
women, on the other hand, were professional artists' models – in
other words, women paid to display their bodies naked. Commenting on the artist–model relationship, Lynda Nead writes 'According
to the mythology, the artist's female model is also his mistress and
the intensity of the artistic process is mirrored only by the intensity
of their sexual relationship.'[76] There is also a myth that many, if not
most, artists' nude models were prostitutes. In these associations
we find a libidinal structure which is transferred to photography (as
in Sontag's claim that the early photographs of nudes used prostitutes as models) and to film. Braun argues that many of
Muybridge's sequences of women show them engaged in 'particularly awkward and ungainly actions and what were, at that time,
certainly forbidden activities'.[77] She goes on: 'The photographs
objectify erotic impulses and extend voyeuristic curiosity in a
language we now recognise as taken from the standard pornographic vocabulary.'[78] This vocabulary was, of course, just in the
process of formation at this time.

Williams has also noted this difference between the men and
the women in Muybridge's photographs:

> While naked and semi-naked women perform many of [the]
> same tasks [as the men], in their activities and gestures we see
> how the greater sexuality already encoded in the woman's
> body feeds into a new cinematic power exerted over her whole
> physical being. We see, in other words, how an unprecedented
> conjunction of pleasure and power 'implants' a cinematic per-
> version of fetishism in the prototypical cinema's first halting
> steps towards narrative.[79]

The naked female body is not just visible; it is experienced by Muybridge, the male photographer, and by his audience, as displayed – as a spectacle. In some of the photographs of the men they wear brief underpants or jockstraps to conceal their genitalia. When the women wear clothes they are putting them on or taking them off or else wearing lengthy diaphanous skirts. Where the male garments simply conceal, the female garments reinforce the nakedness of the women's bodies.

In a celebrated article on Hollywood cinema, Laura Mulvey discussed the way it worked within, and reinforced, a psychoanalytic structuring of desire and the gaze. She argued that there are 'two contradictory aspects of the pleasurable structures of looking in the conventional cinematic situation': 'The first, scopophilic, arises from pleasure in using another person as an object of sexual stimulation through sight. The second, developed through narcissism and the constitution of the ego, comes from identification with the image seen.'[80] Mulvey goes on: 'In a world ordered by sexual imbalance, pleasure in looking has been split between active/male and passive/female.'[81] It is within this overarching structural context that Hollywood films are, in the main, organised. Thus, within the films, men tend to carry the action of the narrative whilst women tend to be displayed as spectacle. Mulvey writes that 'the function of woman in forming the patriarchal unconscious is twofold, she first symbolises the castration threat by her real absence of a penis and second thereby raises her child into the symbolic'.[82] The world described by Mulvey is, in fact, the world of the mid nineteenth century onwards. Her psychoanalytic description of Hollywood film shows well how these films operate within the cultural-fetishistic ordering of society to articulate and reinforce the respective positions of women and men. What Mulvey outlines is, ultimately, the situating of the male viewer in relation to films which are constructed from the point of view of the male gaze. In this reworked form Mulvey's argument allows us to understand better the concerns in photography with photographing women and the different circumstances in which Muybridge, among many others, photographed and filmed women and men.

In her book on hard-core film pornography Williams has described the earliest stag films in the Kinsey collection. These films include the ten-minute German film *Am Abend* (*c.* 1910), the Argentinian *El satario* (*c.* 1907-12), and the American *A Free Ride* (probably *c.* 1917-19). One of the points she makes is that even though the early stag films begin with a rudimentary narrative, this narrative dissipates as soon as the hard-core scenes of genital sex begin. Furthermore, she writes, 'most stag films do, in their hard-core sequences, use some form of address to a camera whose point of view is aligned more with the front-row (male) spectator brought momentarily closer for a better look than with the free-floating, shifting points of internal identification that operate in the linear cause–effect of cinematic narration'.[83] Here, then, we have another example of the development of spectacularising surveillance. In this case the narrative ordering of the films gives way to the spectacle of the sexual act. In a general way this 'problem' of pornographic films – the constant move away from narrative to atemporal spectacle – parallels the historical shift of emphasis in striptease from narrative to spectacle. At the same time, in these films the male viewer is interpellated as a voyeur, his sight libidinally energised both by, and in relation to, the performers. Just as the spectator in a strip-tease show is reminded that he must not touch – he can only look – so here, in these early hard-core films, the spectator finds himself positioned as the voyeur of the spectacle.

Photography and film were invented and popularised within a developing scopophilic order. They articulated within this order with the established power relations. These media also provided one means by which women in everyday life came to be experienced as eroticised. Bruno has discussed the close connection between the early concerns of the cinema and anatomical investigation. She has summed up this connection by suggesting that 'studies on the genesis of cinema have revealed an impulse to reenact transformations, mutilations, and reconstructions upon the female body that are not dissimilar to the anatomy lesson'.[84] She argues that:

> On the basis of anatomy and its perceptual model of the body, we may establish an epistemological relation between the cinematic eye and the anatomist's eye. The anatomical-analytical gaze provides a model of perception, proleptically pointing toward film's visuality. Film articulates anatomies of the visible.[85]

Here, she is suggesting that the connection between film and ana-tomical investigation is an effect of the inherent quality of film: its concern with the visible. We can make the different point that, in the circumstances in which film was invented and popularised, film's emphasis on the visible was able to reproduce and reinforce the

spectacularity which was an effect of the instatement of cultural fetishism. In these circumstances the connection between film and anatomical investigation becomes clearer. Bruno quotes Walter Benjamin
from 'The Work of Art in the Age of Mechanical Reproduction':

> Magician and surgeon compare to painter and cameraman.
> The painter maintains in his work a natural distance from
> reality, the cameraman penetrates deeply into its web. There
> is a tremendous difference between the pictures they obtain
> ... That of the cameraman consists of multiple fragments
> which are assembled under a new law.[86]

He distinguishes the cameraman from the painter. Here again,
whilst Benjamin is describing a difference based on the properties of
painting and film, we can better appreciate the point in the context
of the discussion in the previous chapter about the new concerns
associated with photography and film – the frenzy of the visible.

Constance Balides has described a number of very early films
which help to train and reinforce the male gaze on women's bodies
in everyday life:

> In *What Happened on Twenty-Third Street, New York City*
> (Edison, 1901) a man and a woman walk down a busy city
> street. As the woman passes over a grated vent in the sidewalk
> escaping air blows her skirt up around her knees. In *What
> Demoralized the Barber Shop* (Edison, 1901) two women (or
> men dressed as women) stand at the top of the stairs that lead
> to a basement barber shop and lift their skirts to reveal their
> legs and stockings. Pandemonium ensues as the men in the
> shop below attempt to get a better look.[87]

Balides goes on to describe a number of other films of the same type
in which women, apparently going about their everyday lives, are
subject to an eroticising gaze from the camera.

These films are quite different from those in the developing
genre of pornographic films in which the preoccupation is with
female nakedness as such. The films described by Balides construct
the male viewer into an everyday life in which he focuses his sight
on possible glimpses of a part of the female body as a woman goes
about her everyday life on the streets. In *What Demoralized the
Barber Shop*, and in other films of this type, men's concerns and
responses are built into the film. In case the male viewer's gaze is
not yet eroticised enough in everyday life, he need only learn from
the excited reactions of the clientele in the barber's shop to know

what he should be feeling. Here we are brought back to the recon-struction of the *flâneur*.

Balides sums up a part of her argument in this way: 'By making the space of the everyday the place of display of women's bodies or some unexpected sexual intimacy, the films produce everyday life as something other, something else besides a location for the practice of everyday life.'[88] This is not quite the case. The films described by Balides do not produce everyday life as something other. Rather, they produce and reconstruct everyday life as eroticised, and therefore as the site of libidinized spectacle. In this way they operate in the context of the general eroticisation of everyday life that took place from the second half of the nineteenth century onwards, an eroticisation driven by male desire and focused on the spectacle of the female body.

## NOTES

1   D. Riley, *'Am I that Name?': Feminism and the Category of Woman in History* (Basingstoke, Macmillan, 1988) p. 48.

2   *Ibid.*, p. 50.

3   L. Finch, *The Classing Gaze: Sexuality, Class and Surveillence* (St Leonards, Allen and Unwin, 1993), p. 95.

4   W. H. Fraser, *The Coming of the Mass Market, 1850-1914* (Hamden, Conn., Archon Books, 1981), p. 21.

5   *Ibid.*, p. 213.

6   J. Walkowitz, *Prostitution and Victorian Society: Women, Class and the State* (Cambridge, Cambridge University Press, 1980), p. 32.

7   *Ibid.*, p. 32.

8   *Ibid.*, p. 36.

9   *Ibid.*, p. 32.

10  *Ibid.*, p. 44.

11  E. Wilson, 'The Invisible *Flâneur*', *New Left Review*, 191 (1992), p. 92.

12  Walkowitz, *Prostitution and Victorian Society*, p. 26.

13  *Ibid.*, p. 26.

14  Wilson, 'The Invisible *Flâneur*', p. 93.

15  G. Reekie, *Temptations: Sex, Selling and the Department Store* (St Leonards, Allen and Unwin, 1993), p. 36.

16  *Ibid.*, p. 36.

17  R. Bowlby, *Just Looking: Consumer Culture in the Age of Dreiser, Gissing and Zola* (New York, Methuen, 1985), p. 81.

18  W. Benjamin, *Charles Baudelaire: A Lyric Poet in the Era of High Capitalism*, trans. H. Zohn (London, Verso, 1983), p. 36.

19  *Ibid.*, p. 36.

20  Quoted in *ibid.*, pp. 36-7.

21  Wilson, 'The Invisible *Flâneur*', p. 94.

22  *Ibid.*, p. 94.

23  *Ibid.*, p. 94.

24  *Ibid.*, p. 94.

25  *Ibid.*, p. 94.

26  J. Wolff, 'The Invisible *Flâneuse*', in J. Wolff, *Feminine Sentences: Essays on Women and Culture* (Cambridge, Polity Press, 1990).

27  E. Wilson, *The Sphinx in the City: Urban Life, the Control of Disorder, and Women* (London, Virago, 1991), p. 55.

28  *Ibid.*, p. 56.

29  *Ibid.*, p. 56.

30  S. Buck-Morss, 'The Flaneur, the Sandwichman and the Whore: The Politics of Loitering', *New German Critique*, no. 39 (1986), pp. 120–1.

31  G. Bruno, 'Spectatorial Embodiments: Anatomies of the Visible and the Female Bodyscape', *Camera Obscura*, no. 28 (1992), p. 252.

32  *Ibid.*, p. 252.

33  Benjamin, *Charles Baudelaire*, p. 56.

34  *Ibid.*, p. 57.

35  *Ibid.*, p. 54.

36  *Ibid.*, p. 35.

37  *Ibid.*, p. 35.

38  R. Barthes, *Sade, Fourier, Loyola*, trans. R. Miller (Berkeley, University of California Press, 1989), p. 128.

39  R. Barthes, 'Diderot, Brecht, Eisenstein', in S. Heath (ed. and trans.), *Image–Music–Text* (London, Fontana, 1977).

40  In 'Diderot, Barthes, *Vertigo*' (in V. Burgin *et al* (eds), *Formations of Fantasy* (London, Methuen, 1986)) Victor Burgin provides a history for the idea of the *tableau*, tracing it back to the beginning of the eighteenth century. He focuses on Lord Shaftesbury and Diderot as key theorists of the idea. Peter Brooks, in *The Melodramatic Imagination: Balzac, Henry James, Melodrama, and the Mode of Excess* (New Haven, Yale University Press, 1976), provides one history of the development of the *tableau vivant* in the French melodramas of the early nineteenth century.

41  R. Allen, *Horrible Prettiness: Burlesque and American Culture* (Chapel Hill, University of North Carolina Press, 1991), p. 92.

42   M. Gabor, *The Pin-up*: *A Modest History* (New York, Universe Books, 1972), p. 58.

43   Allen, *Horrible Prettiness*, p. 231.

44   *Ibid.*, p. 248.

45   R. Wortley, *A Pictorial History of Striptease*: *100 Years of Undressing to Music* (London, Treasury Press, 1976), p. 30.

46   *Ibid.*, p. 83.

47   Allen, *Horrible Prettiness*, p. 264.

48   *Ibid.*, p. 264.

49   R. Gordon, *Anorexia and Bulimia: Anatomy of a Social Epidemic* (Oxford, Basil Blackwell, 1990), p. 1.

50   *Ibid.*, p. 1.

51   W. Playfair, *The Systematic Treatment of Nerve Prostration and Hysteria* (London, Smith, Elder and Co., 1883), p. 12.

52   *Ibid.*, p. 12.

53   T. Szasz, *The Myth of Mental Illness* (New York, Harper and Row, 1961), p. 34.

54   J. Breuer and S. Freud, *Studies on Hysteria*, ed. Angela Richards, The Pelican Freud Library (Harmondsworth, Penguin, 1974), vol. 3, p. 58.

55   *Ibid.*, p. 66.

56   S. Freud, *Three Essays on the Theory of Sexuality*, in *The Standard Edition of the Complete Psychological Works of Sigmund Freud*, translated under the general editorship of J. Strachey in collaboration with A. Freud (London, The Hogarth Press/Institute for Psychoanalysis), vol. 7 (1953), p. 177.

57   S. Freud, *The Introductory Lectures on Psycho-Analysis*, in *The Standard Edition*, vol. 16 (1958), p. 326.

58   N. Elias, *The Civilizing Process*, vol. 1: *The History of Manners* (Oxford, Basil Blackwell, 1983).

59   P. Stallybrass and A. White, *The Politics and Poetics of Transgression* (London, Methuen, 1986), p. 166.

60   G. Freund, *Photography and Society* (Boston, D. R. Godine, 1980), p. 85.

61   Gabor, *The Pin-up*, p. 41.

62   *Ibid.*, p. 43.

63   *Ibid.*, p. 49.

64   *Ibid.*, p. 52.

65   All this information, including the quotation from Diamond, is from J. Tagg, *The Burden of Representation: Essays on Photographies and Histories* (Basingstoke, Macmillan, 1988), p. 77–8.

66   Diamond, quoted in *ibid.*, p. 78.

67   *Ibid.*, p. 81.

68   I. Veith, *Hysteria: The History of a Disease* (Chicago, University of Chicago Press, 1965), p. 229.

69   M. Braun, *Picturing Time: The Work of Etienne Jules-Marey (1830–1904)* (Chicago, University of Chicago Press, 1992), p. 85.

70   S. Heath, *The Sexual Fix* (London, Macmillan, 1982), p. 36.

71   Braun, *Picturing Time*, p. 398, n. 84.

72   L. Williams, *Hard Core: Power, Pleasure and the 'Frenzy of the Visible'* (Berkeley, University of California Press, 1989), pp. 50–51.

73   J. Crary, *Techniques of the Observer: On Vision and Modernity in the Nineteenth Century* (Cambridge, Mass., MIT Press, 1990), p. 126.

74   *Ibid.*, p. 127.

75   R. Taft, Introduction to Eadweard Muybridge, *The Human Figure in Motion* (New York, Dover Publications, 1955), p. x.

76   L. Nead, *The Female Nude: Art, Obscenity, and Sexuality* (London, Routledge, 1992), p. 50.

77   Braun, *Picturing Time*, p. 249.

78   *Ibid.*, p. 249.

79   Williams, *Hard Core*, p. 39.

80   L. Mulvey, 'Visual Pleasure and Narrative Cinema', *Screen*, 16:3 (1975), p. 10.

81   *Ibid.*, p. 11.

82   *Ibid.*, p. 6.

83   Williams, *Hard Core*, p. 71.

84   Bruno, 'Spectatorial Embodiments', p. 245.

85   *Ibid.*, p. 242.

86   Quoted in *ibid.*, p. 243.

87   C. Balides, 'Scenes of Exposure in the Practice of Everyday Life: Women in the Cinema of Attractions', *Screen*, 34:1 (1992), pp. 19-20.

88   Balides, 'Scenes of Exposure', p. 25.

# The fetishisation
# of the male body

I have explained that the key experience of cultural fetishism is a male preoccupation with his perceived phallic lack. This produces a circuit of male desire which is supplementary to the male sex drive. The desire for women becomes secondary in this supplementary circuit in the sense that they are desired not for what they are but for what they are constructed as – namely, the phallus which men lack. As was discussed in the Introduction, the phallus is the cultural version of the penis, in everyday life a defining part of the male anatomy. The desire for the phallus translates into a complex form of male–male desire which excludes women as women, their bodies marked by the 'lack', even, of the penis, including those bodies remade as phallic fetishes. After all, other men at least have the penis, obviating the problem of the castration complex. As we shall see, this male–male desire takes two forms. One is a scheme of narcissistic identification with a man considered to have the phallic, patriarchal quality. The other constructs certain males as phallic substitutes who may, then, be 'consumed' in the hope that they will provide the missing phallus.

There are many contingent reasons for the suppression of male–male desire in modern Western culture, but one reason which is central to my argument is that this supplementary circuit of desire comes too close to expressing men's insecurity in the modern state. It is repressed. In the Introduction I have already discussed the way that in theories of the modern state, from the social contract to Freud, women are absent. Here, we also have a cultural contextualisation for the particularity of modern male bonding, and for homosociality. In addition, the fetishistic preoccupation with male–male desire has been a major component in the formation of a new discursive category, the homosexual. Historically, this category also came into being in the second half of the nineteenth century. This is not to say that before this there were no men who sexually desired other men, or that all homosexual desire is an effect of cultural fetishism. Of course neither of these things is the case. Rather, it is to suggest that, since the second half of the nineteenth century, male–male desire has been discursively constructed as the site for a previously non-existent category, the homosexual. What we also need to recognise is that, if, culturally speaking, male–male desire dominates over male–female desire as a result of men's fear caused by their experience of phallic lack, the straight male fear of the homosexual develops out of an acknowledgement that, to the extent that all men are implicated in cultural fetishism, all men feel some male–male desire.

In a very different register the French feminist theoretician Luce Irigaray also argues for the dominance of male–male desire. It is difficult to know how culturally specific Irigaray is being – particularly as she starts from Claude Lévi-Strauss's universalist argument about the exchange of women and the origin of society, which he put forward in *The Elementary Structures of Kinship* (1949) – but the very tendency of her argument towards the universal suggests the extent of the naturalisation of the importance of male–male desire in post-Second World War Western thought. Following Lévi-Strauss, Irigaray begins by asserting that 'the society we know, our own culture, is based upon the exchange of women'.[1] She goes on to explain that:

> The use of and traffic in women subtend and uphold the reign of masculine hom(m)o-sexuality, even while they maintain that hom(m)o-sexuality in speculations, mirror games, identifications, and more or less rivalrous appropriations, which defer its real practice. Reigning everywhere, although prohibited in practice, hom(m)o-sexuality is played out through the bodies of women, matter, or sign, and heterosexuality has been up to now just an alibi for the smooth workings of man's relations with himself, of relations among men.[2]

The latter part of this description provides a theoretical counterpoint for the cultural-historical argument I have been developing, that women's bodies have been constructed by men as phallic substitutes. Elsewhere, again following Lévi-Strauss's argument about the exchange of women, Irigaray makes the point that 'the exchanges upon which patriarchal societies are based take place exclusively among men'.[3] It follows that 'all economic organization is homosexual'.[4] Here it seems that Irigaray is making a general argument about patriarchal economies. However, her theoretical point can be reworked once again as a historical description of the post-1850s Western capitalist economy which is overdetermined by the male experience of cultural fetishism.

Irigaray argues that male homosexual relations 'challenge the nature, status, and "exogamic" necessity of the product of exchange'.[5] She goes on to suggest that 'once the penis itself becomes merely a means to pleasure, pleasure among men, *the phallus loses its power*'.[6] This suggests that men experience the penis as the material equivalent of the symbolic phallus. In this argument the proscription of homosexuality serves to preserve phallic power. This theorisation fails to explain why men should desire other men rather than women. In contrast, the cultural-fetishism argument is premised on the idea that men actually experience themselves as *lacking* the phallus. Men's desire for other men needs to be understood as the fetishistic consequence of the fear invoked by men's experience of this lack.

One recognition of the social privileging of male homosexuality in modern society can be found in Dean McCannell's *Empty Meeting Grounds*:

> The normalization of the ideology of homosexual superiority; the prestige accorded to its adherents; the denigration of heterosexual pleasure, a denigration engaged in by homosexuals and heterosexuals alike; the highly stereotypical way in which the fear of homosexuality manifests itself and is represented; the *de facto* establishment of the single-parent family as the social norm; the aggressive experimentation with medical technologies that detach reproduction from parenting; the promotion of arbitrary beauty standards as the only basis for heterosexual attraction; all these attitudes and actions are well developed among modernized peoples for whom capitalism is established as the only economic mode.[7]

McCannell's claim is that the ideology of male homosexuality operates to help keep down population size, thus preserving per-capita wealth, and to reinforce homosocial forms of organisation which are central to the practice of capitalism, such as the gang, the corporation, and the state, which are central to the practice of capitalism by deligitimising the family and heterosexual relations generally. Whilst I do not agree with McCannell's causal argument, it is worth noting his recognition that late, or corporate, capitalism – he uses both terms – is dominated by an ideology which valorises male–male desire.

The latter part of the nineteenth century saw the development by men of two ideals of manhood. Both express, in different ways, the male desire for the phallus. They came into existence at the same time as the formation of the category of the homosexual and became integrated into it. During this same period, as Bram Dijkstra points out, the male bourgeoisie were beginning to express a tremendous fear of women. This is not surprising, given their fetishisation by men: as we have seen, fetishism combines both pathological desire and pathological fear. Dijkstra has usefully distinguished the two male ideals as the 'blond god' and the 'ephebe'. He describes how the blond god was thought of as the perfect adult male. He grows out of the other ideal of manhood, the adolescent ephebe. Dijkstra writes of the 'grown male, the "blond god", his lingering freshness [as the ephebe] enhanced by muscular development and physical strength'.[8] This is the active ideal of the male, the strong and powerful man who has the phallus and, metonymically, can represent the phallus. Dijkstra describes how 'a very large groups of poets and artists throughout Western culture', including Oscar Wilde, had

> a dream of the Nietzschean superman forging ahead ever more securely toward a new state of being in which the mind of man might transcend its physical prison. These men saw the ideal they were searching for in the supremely powerful musculature of the triumphantly predatory male god of imperialist achievement, the miracle man who could at any time prove his mastery in the struggle for existence.[9]

This is the fantastic representation of phallic power. It is with this image that men, experiencing their phallic lack, identify narcissistically.

For obvious reasons it is this image of the male ideal which has been closely associated with totalitarian, including fascist and Nazi, political practices. These populist and demagogic politics inscribed very clear roles for both men and women in the family and the state, giving men the phallic, patriarchal power and making the leader, as nearly as possible, equal in power to the state itself. As a consequence he was experienced by the members of the state as approaching in power the originating, primal Father. At the same time, these political ideologies have heavily proscribed homosexuality. Whilst Nazi propaganda celebrated the strong Aryan body and encouraged Platonic camaraderie among men, the party was sending homosexuals to the concentration camps.

The other ideal of manhood, the ephebe, was the adolescent boy who epitomised the characteristics that men felt women should have but which, it was considered, they all too often fell short of. As Dijkstra describes it:

> in a world in which arousal spelled doom to the male in search of the ideal, in which the adult woman and even her pubescent daughter all too often had abandoned her responsibility to be a Madonna, a state of restful detumescence – of peace, the absence of temptation, of removal from carnal involvement – seemed available only when the artist sought the outlines of the ideal in those real forms which unavoidably, it would seem, still retained the shapes of innocence which had been abandoned by woman, by the temptress Eve. ... Thus, it seemed legitimate to seek in the male child those shapes of the ideal which in the feminine body became so rapidly contaminated by base desires.[10]

In this way the adolescent boy took on 'feminine' associations. In order to fully appreciate the implications of this we need to remember that, by this time, the pubescent girl had become much sought after by bourgeois men. There is here a convergence. Where pubescent girls were given a phallic overtone and were feared as well as desired, it was thought that men could celebrate the adolescent boy, without desire, for the feminine virtues attributed to him. This ambiguous male figure rapidly became eroticised. Writing about painting, Dijkstra has commented that 'it was soon clear that even in this realm passion could rear its ugly head'.[11] Among many examples he cites is a painting entitled *The Wet Cupid* by the celebrated French artist Bouguereau, exhibited at the salon in 1891. As Dijkstra describes it: 'No more sexually enticing adolescent could have been offered by the master, but unlike Oscar Wilde who was jailed after being prosecuted for pederasty, Bouguereau was given official accolades and honors.'[12] One difference was that, where Bouguereau's painting remained safely in the realm of fantasy, Wilde acted the fantasy out.

As early as 1780, men who desired other men were thought to be effeminate. In Britain during this period such men were designated as Mollies, Madge-culls and Mariannes.[13] This idea of effeminacy became an important component in the developing myth of the

homosexual. Indeed, the discursive connection was so strong that
the three major English campaigners for the acceptance of homosexuality around the turn of the twentieth century, J. A. Symonds,
Havelock Ellis, and Edward Carpenter, all 'insisted that "effeminacy", the usual caricature for male homosexuality, was not necessarily linked with homosexuality'.[14] During the late nineteenth
century a confusion developed between the notion of effeminacy
and the new ideal of the feminine male as encapsulated in the
ephebe. The ephebe began to be thought of not only as manifesting
these feminine qualities in his behaviour but as exhibiting them in
his looks:

> [Around 1900 a] new admiration developed for the special
> [physical] beauty of the male. Man, it was now argued, with
> numerous quotations from Plato, had all the 'soft', physical
> attractions of woman, plus the male's exclusive capacity for
> intellectual transcendence. The ephebe, the sensitive male
> adolescent, not woman, was the true ideal of aesthetic beauty.
> Indeed, the young, fully grown male, the 'blond god', his
> lingering freshness enhanced by muscular development and
> physical strength, seemed to many artists and intellectuals
> fleeing woman the personification of the magnificent,
> aggressively evolving mind of man.[15]

The difference between a man possessing feminine qualities and an
effeminate man was one of essence versus masquerade. To have
feminine qualities entailed an ability to express them from the
inherent constitution of the adolescent male. On the other hand,
effeminacy was the effect of a man behaving in a way that it was
believed women behaved.

From the point of view of the fetishistic male desire for the
phallus, the ephebe and the blond god occupy distinct positions. As
we have seen, the image of the ephebe derives from the male appropriation of what were considered to be feminine qualities. Reinfor-
cing this was the placing of these qualities in the adolescent boy.
Unlike the all-powerful adult blond god, the adolescent boy was
thought of as lacking in power, physically weak, and therefore passive. In short, he was positioned as a woman. From a heterosexual
perspective this made him potentially and dangerously desirable.
As a consequence, in the discourse of homosexuality the ephebe
came to characterise the object of homosexual desire. The adult
male desire for the ephebe was transformed into one of the perverse
characteristics of the homosexual. The establishment of this desire

was to play an important role in Oscar Wilde's prosecution, which, as we shall see, can be viewed as crucial in helping to define the characteristics of the homosexual. The fetishistic desire for the ephebe, like that for the female body, is a sexual desire focused on appropriation and consumption. However, unlike women, who had to phallicised, the ephebe was already male, and therefore could be more easily thought of as a phallic fetish. He could be possessed/consumed to provide the possessor with the phallus.

On the other hand, the blond god provides a site for narcissistic phallic identification. He exemplifies the phallus. Historically, this was expressed in his spiritual striving. Dijkstra sums up the late-nineteenth-century attitude towards the ideal man by referring to 'his goal of evolutionary transcendence and muscular male mastery'.[16] He discusses Joseph Le Conte, an American follower of Charles Darwin among others, who argued in *Evolution: Its Nature, Its Evidences, and Its Relation to Religious Thought* (1888-91) that 'there can be no doubt that we are on the eve of a great revolution'. Dijkstra explains: 'This revolution was to take the form of man's transcendence into a new realm of material being, in which he would move from an "outer lower life" to an "inner higher life", not shedding the "necessary work-clothes" of materiality, but letting the "life-force" inherent in all material things and representative of God in nature distil itself, as it were, into an embodied spirit.'[17] During the twentieth century this image of a spiritual phallic being, whose body expressed its mental transcendence, gradually gave way to an increasing emphasis on the body itself as a spectacular expression of the phallus. In Chapter 6 we shall see that this new emphasis became particularly apparent from the late 1960s, with the increasingly general spectacularisation of the male body. As the discourse of male homosexuality began to be constituted, so the two images rapidly took on the aspects of the active and the passive homosexual.

One site where there has been an attempt to unite the blond god and the ephebe is in the American superhero. If Superman falls into the category of the blond god then his everyday-life alter ego, Clark Kent, is a version of the ephebe. Likewise, where Batman plays out the role of the blond god, Robin, for all his pretensions, is an ephebe. With both these sets of characters, the structure of desire one would expect is played out from a male viewpoint. Lois Lane desires Superman but wants to have Clark Kent for a friend, and the question of a homosexual desire between Batman and

Robin is constantly raised but impossible to resolve.

In my first chapter I discussed the British Criminal Law Amendment Act of 1885, an Act arising out of the moral panic over the prostitution – and apparent white slavery – of young girls. The Act raised the age of consent. One of the points I made about this was that it reflected an increasing preoccupation among men with pubescent girls – the time in their lives when females most nearly approached a male shape. In addition to raising the age of consent the act also contained what has become known as the 'Labouchère amendment'. It was this amendment which outlawed unspecified relations between men and, in doing so, contributed significantly to the modern construction of the category of the homosexual. The amendment provided that:

> Any male person who, in public or in private, commits, or is a party to the commission of, or procures or attempts to procure the commission by any male person of any act of gross indecency with another male person, shall be guilty of a mis-demeanour, and being convicted thereof shall be liable at the discretion of the court to be imprisoned for any term not exceeding two years, with or without hard labour.[18]

The key phrase here is 'any act of gross indecency', a phrase which formalised a shift from a concern with the physical act of buggery to a wider, and much less defined, group of activities. As Ed Cohen has put it, the amendment provided 'the first legal classification of sexual relations between men not predicated on earlier ecclesiastical and moral injunctions against specific sexual acts'.[19] What this shift signals is that the discourse of homosexuality embraces not only – and not even necessarily – a focus on specific sexual acts but, also, a range of images and behaviours. Cohen has remarked: 'To some interpreters, this section has seemed so entirely inconsistent with the act's primary concern for controlling cross-sex practices that it appears to have been included by its author, Henry Labouchère, in order to discredit the act as a whole'.[20] However, Jeffrey Weeks has argued that the regulating of male same-sex and cross-sex practices in the same act was a consequence of the fact that 'the social purity campaigners of the 1880s saw both prostitution and male homo-sexuality as products of undifferentiated male lust'.[21] In Chapter 1, I also argued that this new concern with male lust was an effect of the deployment of cultural-fetishistic supplementation of male desire. That both Labouchère's amendment (Section 11, as it is also widely known in Britain) and the age-of-consent legislation appeared in the same Act also demonstrates the different effects of the spread of cultural fetishism; both concerns of the Act express different facets of the new phallic orientation of male desire. In fact, reflecting the problematic nature of the idealisation of the adolescent boy as the ephebe, the problem of adult men's desire for adolescent boys seems to have been one of Labouchère's concerns when he framed his amendment. Weeks notes:

> Childhood sexuality became an important political issue. The 1885 Act had succeeded in raising the age of consent for girls to sixteen, and Labouchère at least claimed that his most . famous Amendment was directed at preventing the corruption of youth. The theme of corruption of youth is constant, and the public-school controversy kept it on the boil. Working-class boys were involved in all the major scandals.[22]

I have already indicated that integral to the discursive construction of the homosexual was his desire for adolescent boys.

The nineteenth-century notion of the undifferentiated nature of male lust missed the historical point that the extension of male sexual desire from women's bodies to men's bodies was a new development. As Cohen indicates, previous British laws regulating male desire had had a quite different purpose and had been concerned neither with non-sexual aspects of male demeanour and interaction nor with specifically male-male sexual relations. Certainly this does not prove that 'homosexuality' did not exist earlier but, at the least, it suggests that there was little public concern with those men who formed same-sex liaisons. For religious reasons it had been specific sexual acts involving the penis which were singled out for proscription. Weeks has described how, in British law before 1885, 'the only legislation which directly affected homosexual acts was that referring to sodomy or buggery'.[23] This legislation referred to all forms of buggery, whether with other men, women, or animals. Not singling out male–male buggery as a particular problem suggests that there was little concern with male–male sexual desire as such. Furthermore, what the law proscribed was a specific sexual activity, and this was not thought to be the practice of a particular kind of person. As Foucault so succinctly puts it in his account of the transformation in the construction of sexuality which took place in the second half of the nineteenth century: 'The sodomite had been a temporary aberration; the homosexual was now a species.'[24] One signifier of this reconstruction was the rhetorical shift which takes

place in Labouchère's amendment. It is no longer the physical act of
buggery which is concentrated on; rather, it is activities which relate to
some general moral criterion which can define 'gross indecency'.
Furthermore, unlike the earlier legislation which outlawed all buggery, Labouchère's amendment concentrates specifically on male–
male relations. It is, for example, not interested in male–female
buggery.

These two changes mark an important discursive shift which
forms part of the construction of the category of the homosexual,
but which also signals (as part of this new construction) a new preoccupation with a particular orientation of male sexual desire. For
the first time there is a concern about male desire for other men.
This shift occurred throughout Europe. Weeks describes how there
was 'a sharpening definition of and hostility towards homosexuality in the late nineteenth century, not only in Britain but in other
European countries, especially Germany'.[25] A dual process was in
train. One aspect was the discursive construction of the male homosexual as a person with a specific range of characteristics, focused
ultimately on a particular act which was constructed as a sexual act
and which was the end result of male sexual desire for other men.
The other was the proscription of this act and the classification of
the homosexual species as deviant.

Weeks argues that there is a connection between the proscription of homosexuality and the nineteenth-century establishment of
the bourgeois nuclear family as the normative family form: 'What
is apparent is that, as social roles became more clearly defined, and
as sexuality was more closely harnessed ideologically to the reproduction of the population, so the social condemnation of male
homosexuality increased.'[26] Here, the proscription of male homosexuality is accounted for as a consequence of its perceived threat to
the family. The belief in such a threat would only be reasonable if
male sexual desire for other men was thought to be, in the end,
greater than male desire for women.

Examining the growth in usage of the term 'homosexual',
Cohen notes that it was 'coined in 1869 by the Austro-Hungarian
translator and *littérateur* Karl Maria Kertbeny and popularised in
the writing of the German sexologists'. He goes on to explain that it

> made its first widespread British appearance in Charles
> Chaddock's 1892 translation of Krafft-Ebing's seminal
> *Psychopathia Sexualis*. Here, as the descriptive assessment of
> a 'contrary' or 'inverted' 'sexual nature', 'Homosexual' came

to signify a pathological deviation from monogamous, pro-creative sexual intercourse within marriage, which Krafft-Ebing unhesitatingly called 'the sexual instinct'.[27]

The description of male same-sex sexual desire as inversion marks it as the opposite of the 'natural' sexual instinct. As Cohen explains: 'That this new characterisation of sexual relations between men not only (negatively) confirmed the dominance of the "instinctual" sexual norm but also, to some extent, produced it can be seen in the concurrent emergence of the word "heterosexual"'.[28] 'Heterosexual', it seems, also made its first English appearance in the translation of *Psychopathia sexualis*, where it was used to describe the desired outcome of the therapeutic treatment given to males whose pathology included 'the impulse to masturbation' and 'homo-sexual feelings and impulses'.[29] Here we see that male sexual desire for women is first given a name as the description of the 'natural' state of affairs which should be produced in men with a tendency to inversion. The nomination of male desire for women is a consequence of – and determined by – the discursive construction of the homosexual. If, with Foucault, we can talk about the emergence of the species of the homosexual, then we can also talk about the emergence of the species of the heterosexual. In both cases the terms were first used to describe the project of male desire; they were only subsequently applied to women. More generally, if male heterosexual desire was defined in opposition to its proscribed opposite, it was also the case that the image and behaviour which are the practice of the discourse of male heterosexuality are themselves constituted in opposition to their proscribed opposites. From this point of view the species of the heterosexual also comes into existence in the second half of the nineteenth century, and we can see how, once again, male–female desire in its form as heterosexual desire is constituted as secondary to male–male desire.

Through the latter part of the nineteenth century and into the twentieth century, the construction of male sexual desire for women underwent a change in which, for the first time, despite the claim that it was natural, it became a nominated category of sexual behaviour defined reciprocally by its 'opposite', male same-sex desire. It is important to note here that women's desire does not enter this scheme. It was male desire which was thought to be active and determining – as it was in Freud's work. 'Heterosexual' was a term originally used to describe male desire for women, not, as it has become, a general term which describes other-sex relations and which, on this definition, now has an applicability to both women and men. In this system for categorising desire, which is dominated by a concern, born of the spread of cultural fetishism, with male desire, the discourse of female homosexuality – lesbianism – is an absent rather than an excluded term. This can be understood partly in relation to cultural fetishism. The construction of the species of the homosexual and the heterosexual around male sexual desire reflected an interest in identifying and privileging 'normal' male sexual behaviour against the male's implicit fear that men might actually find other men preferable as sexual choices. Male sexual desire was characterised by an idea that it was active and genitally focused. As epitomised in Freud's work, women's sexual desire was supposed to be passive, or non-existent. Moreover, alternative expressions of libidinal desire were not considered.

It is easy to demonstrate the novelty of the term 'homosexual' as the description of a particular species:

> An eminent doctor, Sir George Savage, described in the *Journal of Mental Science* (October 1884) the homosexual case histories of a young man and woman and wondered if 'this perversion is as rare as it appears', while Havelock Ellis was to claim that he was the first to record any homosexual cases unconnected with prisons or asylums.[30]

In these medical accounts, which are contemporaneous with the Labouchère amendment's use of the term 'acts of gross indecency', there is made plain the problem of identifying a member of a category the discursive construction of which is still taking place. In this circumstance the problem of self-identification would have been just as great as that of 'expert' – or, for that matter, 'lay' – identification.

The construction of the category of homosexuality closely linked it, historically, to masturbation. Weeks has traced the connection in England between male same-sex attraction and masturbation back to the late eighteenth century. However, with the later nineteenth-century spread of the homosexual category, it took on a new meaning. Weeks describes how 'the most horrific disease that masturbation opened up for the nineteenth-century pessimist was homosexuality', and he goes on: 'Both in the United States and Britain there was a frequent linking of masturbation, 'the secret sin', with homosexuality.'[31] We have already seen that in the second half of the nineteenth century male desire was associated with an increase in prostitution and with a perceived need to raise the age of consent. The inclusion of masturbation suggests an understanding of male desire as being excessive, and the connection with homosexuality suggests, further, an idea that this 'excessiveness' is associated with a desire for other men. Masturbation was thought to be enfeebling. Krafft-Ebing described how 'with tainted individuals the ... latent perverse sexuality is developed under the influence of neurasthenia induced by masturbation, abstinence and otherwise'.[32] Marriage provided a healthy solution for the problems of active male desire, but that desire seemed to overflow this limiting, heterosexual environment. These problems all privilege the male and, by implication, his erection as the source of sexual desire. Desire is not thought to be produced by, for instance, a specific woman or a specific man, but, rather, is something the male innately has and which is exemplified by the erect penis.

The importance of the erect penis lies in the cultural experience of the penis as the (always inadequate) material form of the phallus. If men feel that they lack the phallus, then one expression of this lack of power will be through a sexual fear that their penises, when erect, are not big enough. Big enough for *what* is – inevitably, given that this is a cultural pathology – unclear. The concern with penis size has become an important element in male sexual mythology. The fascination with size is played out in many ways. There is, for example, Jeff Stryker, who, in the late 1980s and early 1990s, became the most celebrated star of gay male porn videos because of the size of his erection. A cast has even been made of it and used to make two types of Stryker dildo.[33] Asked if gay men are too obsessed with size, Stryker replies: 'They are until they have to deal with it, then it is a different story. But I would say men and women are equally ... um, interested.'[34] Here we have an illustration of how the concern with size spreads across gay men as well as heterosexual men, and then to women. Stryker himself is described as 'tanned, heavily pumped'.[35] He falls into the category of the blond god; his penis size literalises the phallic image presented by his body, and his body image reinforces the phallic power associated with his penis.

One of the uses to which men have begun to put cosmetic surgery in the early 1990s is to increase their penis size. At present this is mostly limited to increasing the penis's thickness. The feeling of phallic lack which drives men's concern with their penis size is well summed up in this quotation from a thirty-six-year-old who had cosmetic surgery on his penis:

All my life I've been thinking that I'd like to be a bit bigger. I don't really have a small one but it was never the size I wanted. It was always a little dent in my self-esteem. I go to the gym a lot, and in the showers it's nice to have something that is a good size. I always want to look better than everyone else.[36]

Here, also, we have an example of how the preoccupation with penis size (even when flaccid) is, ultimately, directed at other men. Whilst it is often suggested, particularly since women's sexual satisfaction has become an important item on the cultural agenda, that men's concern with penis size is connected with a desire to satisfy women, in this quotation we can appreciate that size is also – and perhaps primarily – related to men's interaction with other men. In other words, size is an expression of phallic power, and, to repeat, men's experience of their lack of phallic power is expressed in their concern over the physical size of their erections.

The construction of the species of the heterosexual man was founded on a negative: he was a man who (naturally) desired women but who definitely did not desire men. The category of the homosexual and the proscription of homosexuality – the practice and experience of the category – were necessary to preserve male–female desire as the dominant cultural form of male sexual desire. In the binary construction of heterosexual and homosexual, the homosexual was given the structural characteristics of 'woman'. The allying of the homosexual with the female took place at the same time that the female body was becoming fetishised. The distinction between the active male and the passive female, which was central to this fetishistic order, was also mapped on to the heterosexual–homosexual division. Heterosexual men are active; homosexual men are passive. In this stereotyped binary distinction all homosexuals are thought to be effeminate. Heterosexual men are able to have feminine qualities, but homosexual men are effeminate. There is, here, no place for an active, dominant homosexual. This role, of the homosexual who actively desires and who, in this sense, fits the role of the heterosexual male, is the term most concealed in this binary structure. John Marshall writes:

This distinction [between active and passive homosexuals] had actually been challenged [as early as] Havelock Ellis, but the image was to have a long career and a deep impact upon many homosexual men. Moreover the strict adoption of an active role in sodomy allowed many men to engage in homosexual behaviour without coming to regard themselves as 'really' homosexual.[37]

The lack of clear social boundaries between the active homosexual and the heterosexual becomes problematic only when the category of the active homosexual is expressed. Paralleling this is the socially accepted position which denies that the blond god could desire the male body. He embodies the phallus, so he will have no fetishistic desire for other men. In gay porn, though, as the example of Jeff Stryker shows, the blond god is both desired and desiring. However, in non-transgressive circumstances, whilst he himself might not desire, he is narcissistically desired and, as a spectacle, he takes on the passivity of an object of desire which gives his image an erotic charge.

Heterosexual men are strong, taking an active role in the material production of society; homosexual men are weak and found not, of course, in the female domain of the home, but in the materially non-productive area of the arts. In this world in which women's bodies are fetishised and structural power operates on a continuum ranging from the invisible, unmarked, heterosexual (white) male to the visible, marked woman, the effeminate homosexual is presumed to display his difference through his manner and his clothes. He is a man whose manner is that of a woman. As I have already remarked, the trial of Oscar Wilde, the writer and aesthete, in 1895 was fundamental to the formation of the homosexual image. I have already implied that, from the dominant cultural perspective, the same set of binary distinctions were constructed within the category of the homosexual as between the categories of homosexual and heterosexual. There were considered to be two varieties of homosexuals who played out either the 'male' role as in active heterosexual desire (and who were, therefore, the penetrators) or the 'female' role, and who were perceived as effeminate (and who were, therefore, the penetrated). At the same time, from the point of view of the dominant culture, all homosexuals were effeminate, and were, ideally, visible and identifiable as homosexuals.

In Chapter 3 we saw that one aspect of the history of the eroticisation of the female body was bound up in the reconstruction of the *flâneur*. However, there is another, and parallel, history of the advent of the visible, effeminate male as the homosexual. This history is founded on the reconstruction of the dandy. Where the *flâneur* was the man set apart gazing upon the world, but became, ultimately, all (heterosexual) men gazing upon women, the category of the dandy began its career describing the man who displayed himself to be gazed upon.

Baudelaire is frequently credited with being the first theoriser of the *flâneur*. What he also did was to appropriate the dandy, and to give him an aesthetic function. Having done this, Baudelaire took some of the qualities which he associated with the dandy and gave them to the *flâneur*. In *Le Peintre de la vie moderne* (The Painter of Modern Life), Baudelaire provides a portrait of the modern artist as both *flâneur* and dandy. He discusses 'G.', Constantin Guys, whom Ellen Moers describes as 'the brilliant draughtsman and illustrator … for many years known personally to Baudelaire but at the time almost unknown to the general public'.[38] Moers outlines how Baudelaire reconstituted Guys's passion for anonymity as an element in his theorisation of the dandy:

> G.'s mania for anonymity is, for Baudelaire, the dandy's imperious aloofness. To the insensitive and the uninitiated, the form of G.'s life may appear to be absolute idleness. As the apparently idle man, however, G. again approaches dandyism: he is the stroller and onlooker, the dandy as *observateur passionné* and *parfait flâneur*.[39]

Baudelaire's essay was published in 1863. As yet dandyism – and the effeminacy associated with it – were not yet connected with homosexuality, a category which was, in any case, still being constituted. Baudelaire was able to combine dandyism and the behaviour of the *flâneur* because he thought of the dandy as being epitomised by a particular way of experiencing the world:

> Through his refusal to sketch for money G. escapes the stigma of *specialist*, which for Baudelaire is comprised in the word *artist*. Rather let us call him a *man of the world*, 'c'est-à-dire homme du monde entier, homme qui comprend le monde et les raisons mystérieuses et légitimes de tous ses usages'. Better still, let us call him a *dandy*, for – and here Baudelaire brings a new dimension to that already weighted term – 'car le mot *dandy* implique une quintessence de caractère et une intelligence subtile de tout le mécanisme moral de ce monde'.[40]

Baudelaire sets aside the outward trappings of dandyism and makes use of the way of being in the world which he believes to characterise the dandy. He thinks of the dandy as one who sets himself apart from the world to gain a better understanding of it. This critical capacity is founded on an acceptance and an appreciation of the new,

modern world of the unknown urban crowd, and the necessary corollary, the concentration on and interpretation of signs. It is this
reconstruction of the dandy as commentator which Baudelaire
yoked together with the idea of the gaze taken from the *flâneur*.
Nevertheless, Baudelaire does not consider Guys to have the entire
sensibility of the dandy. He adds that, 'with another part of his
nature however, the dandy aspires to insensitivity, and it is in this
that Monsieur G., dominated as he is by an insatiable passion – for
seeing and feeling – parts company decisively with dandyism'.[41]

What Baudelaire's discussion of dandyism is most noteworthy
for is its departure from the dominant tradition of thinking of dandyism descriptively, instead attributing to the dandy a sensibility.
Elsewhere in *The Painter of Modern Life* Baudelaire discusses the
dandy as one of the subjects which Guys sketched. Here the dandy
is described as having a 'burning need to create for [himself] a personal originality, bounded only by the limits of the proprieties. It is
a kind of cult of the self which can nevertheless survive the pursuit
of a happiness to be found in someone else – a woman for example;
which can even survive all that goes by in the name of illusions.'[42]
Baudelaire does not give this aspect of personal creation to Guys,
only the dandy's deep understanding of the world which enables
him to recreate himself as a spectacle. In his description of G. as the
man of the crowd, a theoretical revision of the *flâneur*, Baudelaire
subordinated the aesthetic function he attributed to the dandy to
the practice of the *flâneur*. This may be one reason why, as in
Benjamin's work, the dandy has been conspicuously absent as a
term to help theorise the modern urban experience whilst the
*flâneur* has become such an important idea.

The idea of the man of the world as a removed, critical commentator was subsequently to be reworked in the homosexual
aesthetic of camp. Central to this development was, again, the trial
of Oscar Wilde. Here, there was a confluence of the ideas of the
dandy, effeminacy, sensibility, and the aesthete with the production of
the species of the homosexual. Jonathan Dollimore has provided a
useful discussion of camp:

> The definition of camp is as elusive as the sensibility itself,
> one reason being simply that there are different kinds of
> camp. I am concerned here with that mode of camp which
> undermines the categories which exclude it, and does so
> through parody and mimicry. But not from the outside: this
> kind of camp undermines the depth model of identity from

inside, being a kind of parody and mimicry which hollows out from within, making depth recede into its surfaces.[43]

Using the techniques of parody and mimicry and, as Dollimore adds a little later, pastiche and exaggeration, camp (in the sense that concerns Dollimore) provides a commentary on dominant, heterosexual culture from a position that is simultaneously one of exclusion, being located in the proscribed category of homosexuality, and one of inclusion, given that the construction of today's – post-1850s – culture is in part dependent on the formation of the heterosexual through the definition of his homosexual opposite.

Baudelaire's discussion of the dandy came at a time when that category was in flux, at least partly due to its embourgeoisement at the hands of such as Baudelaire himself. He saw the dandy as a disappearing species: 'But alas, the rising tide of democracy, which invades and levels everything, is daily overwhelming these last representatives of human pride and pouring floods of oblivion upon the footprints of these stupendous warriors.'[44] It would seem that the dandy as a self-created spectacle was disappearing under the pressure of democratic, normative mediocrity, whilst leaving behind his sensibility to be taken up and reworked by the artist-as-*flâneur*. In order to transform the dandy and the *flâneur* into a unified, ideal modern artist Baudelaire downplayed the 'passive' element of display in the dandy, that is his costume, in order to privilege his critical purchase on the world. Moers notes: 'The perfect dandy, Baudelaire wrote in the 'sixties, valued costume merely as a symbol of spiritual aristocracy. "Aussi, à ses yeux ... la perfection de la toilette consiste-t-elle dans la simplicité absolue, qui est, en effet, la meilleure manière de se distinguer."'[45] Here, the dandy's clothes are not a display in their own right but a signifier of his inner qualities. In this way Baudelaire does away with what had been, perhaps, the most important aspect of the original dandy and which, ultimately, was the source of continuity between the dandy and the sub-species of the effeminate homosexual. What Baudelaire wished to get rid of was the increasingly uncomfortable fact that the dandy had been an object of display, somebody who was gazed upon – but not, as we shall see, with an eroticised gaze.

The term 'dandy' is British, and Moers argues that 'dandyism as a social, even political phenomenon, with repercussions in the world of ideas, was the invention of the Regency, when aristocracy and monarchy were more widely despised (hence more nastily exclusive) than ever before or since in English history'.[46] The Regency lasted from 1800 until 1820, when the Prince of Wales was crowned George IV. Moers argues that 'dandyism was a product of the revolutionary upheavals of the late eighteenth century. When such solid values as wealth and birth are upset, ephemera such as style and pose are called upon to justify the stratification of society.'[47] However, the dandy is better understood as the product of the last gasp of an older aristocratic system which paired display and power. Before the advent of the state and disciplinary power – one foundation of which was the visibility of those disciplined – power was associated with being visible rather than invisible. Foucault puts it like this: 'Traditionally, power was what was seen, what was shown and what was manifested and, paradoxically, found the principle of its own force in the movement by which it deployed that force.'[48] In that world display was an integral part of asserting power.

The fashionable London aristocracy of the period described themselves as 'the exclusives'. In 1830 the name became the title for a novel outlining their world. Moers comments:

> It is the nature of High Society to exclude undesirables. What marks Regency society as unique is the determined way it went about exclusion, the innumerable hedges against intruders, the explicit, almost codified rules for membership, and the elaborate sub-rules for the behaviour of members.[49]

What Moers is describing is a pale and paranoid version of the aristocratic society of the *ancien régime*, known to its members as *le monde*. Unlike *le monde*, which ended with the French Revolution, the exclusives were living in a state increasingly dominated and ordered by the bourgeoisie. Hence their sense of threat and their self-description as exclusives rather than as the world. It makes sense that the fashionable language of these people should have been sprinkled with French words and phrases. This, then, was the world of the dandy, the most famous of whom was George Bryan Brummell, nicknamed Beau.

Brummell was born in 1778. His father, not an aristocrat, was for many years secretary to the prime minister Lord North. Brummell's way into high society was smoothed by the sponsorship of the Prince of Wales. After Eton and Oxford, Brummell joined the Tenth Hussars. Upon resigning from the regiment in 1798 he took a house in London and began to establish himself as a member of high society, joining clubs and going to the great social gatherings. Brummell lived off his inheritance; but the cost of his lifestyle was greater than he could afford and, in 1816, he left England to escape his debtors. For the next fifteen years he lived in Calais, where he was visited by members of the exclusives on their continental journeys. In 1830 Brummell was appointed the English consul for Caen. After he lost this position in 1832 he went into a long decline. 'At sixty-one, an imbecile, disgusting old man, forgotten and unwanted by everyone but the Sisters of Charity, Brummell was carried off to a sanatorium on the outskirts of Caen.'[50] He died there on 30 March 1840.

In his heyday in England Brummell was renowned for his dress and his repartee. As Moers describes him: 'The dandy has no occupation, and no obvious source of support. Money does not strike him as a subject worthy of his attention.'[51] In this way the dandy asserted the aristocratic contempt for the bourgeois capitalist dominated by salary, savings, investment and a firm Protestant hand on expenditure. The dandy was a man who remade himself as a site of display:

> The dandy's achievement is simply to be himself. In his terms, however, this phrase does not mean to relax, to sprawl, or (in an expression quintessentially anti-dandy) to unbutton; it means to tighten, to control, to attain perfection in all accessories of life, to resist whatever may be suitable for the vulgar but is improper for the dandy. To the dandy the self is not an animal, but a gentleman.[52]

In short, the dandy was the naturalisation of the gentleman, cast as an object of display with no other life than his public life as the arbiter of taste. One of the characteristics of the dandy was an indifference to the sexual charms of women or, for that matter, men. Brummell's first biographer, Captain Jesse, wrote that he 'had too much self-love ever to be really in love'.[53] Thomas Carlyle, in *Sartor Resartus*, described the dandy as 'a Clothes-wearing Man, a Man whose trade, office, and existence consists in the wearing of Clothes'.[54]

From the 1830s onwards the circle of the exclusives, and therefore the milieu which gave meaning to the dandy, began to decline. Brummell's most famous successor, the Count D'Orsay, straddled the fundamental transition in the meaning of the dandy which culminated in Oscar Wilde's trial. D'Orsay was born in Paris in 1801. After Napoleon's escape from Elba, his parents moved with him to London. His life spanned Paris during the period of the rise of the *flâneur* and London during the period of the decline of the dandy:

> Trained to dandyism in the reign of George IV, but flourish-
> ing under William IV and Victoria, he was the essential link
> between two eras. Born into an Anglo-French borderland of
> émigrés and tourists, reigning in post-Regency England,
> dying in France under the hesitant patronage of his friend
> Napoleon III, he carried dandyism forth and back across the
> Channel.[55]

D'Orsay provides the connection between the earlier dandy as the
site of aristocratic display and the later dandy who was thought of
as a part of the *fin-de-siècle* movement of aesthetes and decadents.
As Moers puts it: 'Pride of the aristocracy but also friend of virtually every distinguished literary man in his period, he fathered the
literary tradition of dandyism.'[56] D'Orsay came under the financial
protection of Lord and Lady Blessington, with whom he lived until
Lord Blessington died. His association with writers marks the beginning of the reconstruction of the role of the dandy. Discussing this
new positioning, Rita Felski argues that, 'like woman and like the
work of art, the dandy can be perceived in aestheticist doctrine as
quite useless: exalting appearance over essence, decoration over
function, he voices a protest against prevailing bourgeois values
that associate masculinity with rationality, industry, utility, and
thrift.'[57] Felski's example of the dandy being transformed into a
work of art is Dorian Gray's connection with his painted image in
Oscar Wilde's story *The Picture of Dorian Gray*. Her description
shows well how the new discursive formation of the dandy emphasised his image as a masquerade, a shift from the earlier emphasis
on his spectacular self-creation *per se*. The new understanding of
the dandy implicates it in a moral critique which, ironically,
includes a moralising of the masquerade of effeminacy.

In his will Lord Blessington appointed D'Orsay his executor
and major heir on condition that he married one of Blessington's
daughters from his previous marriage. D'Orsay's sexual arrange-
ments with both Lord and Lady Blessington were the subject of
much unsubstantiated gossip. The point is that, unlike Brummell,
D'Orsay was thought of as a sexual being. Moers notes: 'Women
generally did not take to D'Orsay. They were disturbed by the sexual
ambivalence not only of his relationship with Lady Blessington but
also of his butterfly variety of dandyism.'[58] She goes on: 'Like Lady
Holland, many found his costume "effeminate"'; and, making what

was going to become the crucial but complex distinction between effeminacy and the feminine in men: 'Camilla Toulmin, a silly English miss of a novelist ... found D'Orsay "mannish rather than manly, and yet with a touch of effeminacy quite different from that woman-like tenderness which adds to the excellence of a man".'[59] Not only sexual, then, D'Orsay was also thought of as effeminate rather than as exhibiting feminine qualities. Simultaneously, we are told, 'men were powerfully drawn to D'Orsay (Byron called him a *cupidon déchaîné*) or occasionally repelled (Cobden called him a "fleshy, animal-looking creature")'. Moers sums up the male experience of D'Orsay: 'Enchanted or offended, however, they all found his dandyism a daring blend of the masculine and feminine graces.'[60] This seems to conflate the important distinction between the exhibition of feminine qualities and effeminacy. Brummell had not been thought of as effeminate[61] – the association of dandyism with effeminacy began with D'Orsay. D'Orsay was effeminate; he also produced both strong attraction and repulsion in men. It would seem that the fetishising experience of phallic lack was producing in these *littérateurs* a complex desire for this man whose presentation of self was now being eroticised as effeminate.

The high point of D'Orsay's career as a dandy was during the 1830s. He died in 1852, having been appointed Director of Fine Arts in the Second Empire under Napoleon III. Where Brummell was the dandy as an asexual display of power, D'Orsay's dandyism was surrounded by male, rather than female, desire. At the same time his display was read as effeminate. D'Orsay was being structured into an economy of male desire which excludes women and out of which was coming the species of the homosexual. However, these discursive shifts did not finally come together for another forty years; until they were formalised in Oscar Wilde's trial. At this time it was still the case that 'D'Orsay's superficial or essential effeminacy bothered the Victorians less than his parasitical way of life'.[62]

The *flâneur* and the dandy both had aristocratic origins. They were also both male roles. In the case of the dandy, the context out of which Beau Brummell came was an aristocratic world in which men and women equated male display with power in the fashionable, public world of 'society'. A woman could not be a dandy because her display was always experienced by the observer in relation to men: through it, for example, she expressed her husband's social position, or the fact that she was looking for a husband. In this sense an aristocratic woman's display was of limited power 'in its own right' and could never express general power in the society, only her power as a fashion arbiter for women. The Brummellian dandy existed as a display for men, an object of impossible emulation materialising the social gentleman. Baudelaire's subsumption of the dandy into the *flâneur* reflects the ending of the possibility of the Brummellian dandy. Baudelaire wanted to keep what he considered to be the sensibility of the dandy whilst eradicating what had been the defining quality of the Brummellian dandy, his display.

In Chapter 3, where I discussed the *flâneur*, I argued that, by the middle of the century, the male gaze was becoming eroticised, and women were becoming fetishised spectacles. The aristocratic social world of the exclusives was being bypassed by the new bourgeois establishment, and display was being relegated to women: 'Everyday male dress in the 'sixties was probably the ugliest ever worn: black settled over the Victorians like a pall, cloth wrinkled into deep, greasy folds, and huge straggling beards turned men at the height of their powers into solemn patriarchs.'[63] Jennifer Craik confirms this transformation, explaining that the concentration on the suit as the major item of respectable male dress 'was accompanied by denunciations of clothes and adornment which threatened "traditional masculinity or masculine values" and sustained "ridicule of occasion-specific styles such as the frock coat"'.[64] Referring to J. Finkelstein's book, *The Fashioned Self* (1991), Craik sums up the shift: 'By the late nineteenth century, there was a relentless trend towards plain dress characterised by the uniform choice of colour, style and fabric.'[65] D'Orsay's display was experienced as having a dubious sexual quality to it. The eroticising male gaze was that of the fetishist seeking the phallus. Men could no longer display themselves for if they did they might find each other desirable spectacles. This was the context in which, in Britain, Labouchère got passed into law in 1885 his amendment proscribing acts of gross indecency between men.

Oscar Wilde came down from Oxford in 1878. He was 'resolved to make himself famous'.[66] He moved to London and reconstructed himself as the Professor of Aesthetics. This entailed a transformation in his appearance:

> When an undergraduate at Oxford, Wilde had dressed in the prevailing style: tiny bowler hats with curled brims tipped squarely over the eyes in the Swell manner, bright tweeds and loud checks patterned uniformly over coat, trousers and waistcoat all cut along heavy lines. Now he styled himself

Professor of Aesthetics and adopted a costume for the part –
the knee breeches, drooping lily, flowing green tie, velvet coat
and wide, turned-down collar which first made him famous.[67]

Moers explains that this new style was not intended to impress the
aristocracy. Unlike Brummell, Wilde was not, in the first place,
seeking an entry into high society; what he was looking for was
much more bourgeois – literary fame and fortune. Wilde thought
of himself as a commodity, transformed himself into a spectacle,
and sold it: 'If Frank Harris [author of *Bernard Shaw*] is for once to
be believed, Wilde was always ready to discuss his scramble for
fame. He would compare himself to the best-selling Pears soap and
enumerate the qualities on which self-advertisement rested.'[68]
Wilde's display was fundamentally different in intent and context
from that of Brummell.

Where Baudelaire had dispossessed the dandy of his costume,
Wilde appropriated it. Like Baudelaire, Wilde recognised the new
importance of appearance and this became central to his definition
of aesthetics: 'What Wilde the aesthete admired in high society was
the artificiality, the decorous surface, the mannered ritual. "The
canons of good society", he wrote, "are ... the same as the canons of
art. Form is absolutely essential to it."'[69] However, the aristocratic
preoccupation with appearance was quite different from the new
bourgeois preoccupation with spectacle, founded on male fetishistic
desire and expressed through spectacularising surveillance.

On 28 February 1895, Oscar Wilde went to his club, the
Albemarle, and was given an envelope which contained the Marquis
of Queensberry's calling card. On the back of the card was written:
'For Oscar Wilde Posing as a Somdomite [sic].' What is extraordinary is that this statement does not describe Wilde as a sodomite but, rather, describes his pose – his costume and his manner,
his masquerade we might say – as being that of a man who engages
in buggery. In this statement we have evidence of the discursive
shift that was constructing a particular, self-conscious manner as
being effeminate and was associating this manner with male display
and also with male same-sex sexual activity. Whilst this may be
clear in hindsight, Wilde did not have that advantage. He became
angry and filed charges under the 1843 Criminal Libel Act. The case
came to court. By the time Wilde's barrister Sir Edward Clarke rose
to withdraw the prosecution against Queensberry during the opening speech for the defence, Wilde had already been publicly tried in
the newspapers. On 5 April Wilde was arrested and charged, under

Section 11 of the Criminal Law Amendment Act, with acts of gross indecency. As Cohen puts it, as a result of the case against Queensberry that Wilde had brought, 'in the three days prior to his arrest Wilde's person had been publicly redefined so that both in the court and in the press he came to exemplify the "kind" of man who had a "tendency" toward the commission of "certain" (sexual) acts with other men'.[70]

By the time Wilde was found guilty his costume and manner were firmly associated in the public mind with men likely to indulge in same-sex sexual activity. They began to give a form to the new species of the homosexual. Cohen argues that the 'supplementing of "aesthetic" effeminacy with connotations of male sexual desire for other men is ... one of the consequences of the newspaper representations of the Wilde trials'.[71] This assertion makes both too much and too little of the case. The cultural context for the combining of effeminacy and male same-sex sexual desire was already present, as it was for the proscription of male display. What the trials did was to provide a situation in which all these connections could be made explicit and become the public knowledge of the homosexual. From this time on, in Britain at least, male display in costume or manner was associated with effeminacy and with same-sex sexual activity. In addition to his relationship with the Marquis of Queensberry's son, Lord Alfred Douglas, Wilde was supposed to have had sexual relations with a number of young working-class men. The portrayal of Wilde as the active partner in sexual activity meant that, in this key instance, effeminacy was connected with the active homosexual. The male display, in general, had – like the female – been transformed into a sexualised spectacle of male desire. Wilde, though, was not constructed as desirable but as an effeminate man who desired other, younger men. That his own desirability was never raised as an issue enabled the general problem of excessive and undifferentiated male desire – that is, the supplementary desire of cultural fetishism – to remain suppressed whilst the rules for the patrolling of that sexual desire were established.

## NOTES

1   L. Irigaray, 'Women on the Market', in *This Sex Which is Not One* (Ithaca, Cornell University Press, 1985), p. 170.

2   *Ibid.*, p. 172.

3   Irigaray, 'Commodities among Themselves', in *This Sex which is Not One*, p. 192.

4   *Ibid.*, p. 193.

5   *Ibid.*, p. 193.

6   *Ibid.*, p. 193.

7   D. McCannell, *Empty Meeting Grounds: The Tourist Papers* (London, Routledge, 1992), p. 59.

8   B. Dijkstra, *Idols of Perversity: Fantasies of the Feminine in Fin-de-siècle Culture* (New York, Oxford University Press, 1986), p. 200.

9   *Ibid.*, pp. 200–1.

10   *Ibid.*, pp. 198–9.

11   *Ibid.*, p. 200.

12   *Ibid.*, p. 200.

13   J. Weeks, *Coming Out: Homosexual Politics from the Nineteenth Century to the Present* (London, Quartet Books, 1977), p. 37.

14   *Ibid.*, p. 49.

15   Dijkstra, *Idols of Perversity*, pp. 199-200.

16   *Ibid.*, p 216.

17   *Ibid.*, pp. 216–17.

18   Quoted here from Weeks, *Coming Out*, p. 14.

19   E. Cohen, *Talk on the Wilde Side: Towards a Genealogy of the Discourse on Male Homosexuality* (New York, Routledge, 1993), pp. 91–2.

20   *Ibid.*, p. 92.

21   J. Weeks, 'Discourse, Desire and Sexual Deviance: Some Problems in a History of Homosexuality', in Ken Plummer (ed.), *The Making of the Modern Homosexual* (London, Hutchinson, 1981), p. 87.

22   Weeks, *Coming Out*, p. 20.

23   *Ibid.*, p. 11.

24   M. Foucault, *The History of Sexuality*, trans. R. Hurley, vol. 1 (New York, Pantheon, 1978), p. 43.

25   Weeks, *Coming Out*, p. 15.

26   *Ibid.*, p. 6.

27   Cohen, *Talk on the Wilde Side*, p. 9.

28   *Ibid.*, p. 9.

29   Quoted from *ibid.*, pp. 9–10.

30   Weeks, 'Discourse, Desire and Sexual Deviance', p. 83.

31   Weeks, *Coming Out*, p. 25.

32   Quoted in Weeks, *Coming Out*, p. 26.

33   J. McClellan, 'Mister Big', in *The Face*, no. 57 (June 1993), p. 84.

34   *Ibid.*, p. 85.

35   *Ibid.*, p. 82.

36   C. Bowen-Jones, 'Men, Sex and Surgery', in *Cosmopolitan*, September 1992, p. 132.

37   J. Marshall, 'Pansies, Perverts and Macho Men', in K. Plummer (ed.), *The Making of the Modern Homosexual* (London, Hutchinson, 1981) p. 147.

38   E. Moers, *The Dandy: Brummell to Beerbohm* (London, Secker and Warburg, 1960), p. 277.

39   *Ibid.*, p. 279.

40   *Ibid.*, p. 279.

41   C. Baudelaire, *The Painter of Modern Life and Other Essays*, ed. and trans. J. Mayne (New York, Garland, 1978), p. 9.

42   *Ibid.*, pp. 27–8.

43   J. Dollimore, *Sexual Dissidence: Augustine to Wilde, Freud to Foucault* (Oxford, Clarendon Press, 1991), p. 310.

44   Baudelaire, *The Painter of Modern Life*, p. 29.

45   Moers, *The Dandy*, p. 272.

46   *Ibid.*, p. 12.

47   *Ibid.*, p. 12.

48   M. Foucault, *Discipline and Punish: The Birth of the Prison*, trans. A. Sheridan (New York, Vintage, 1979), p. 187.

49   Moers, *The Dandy*, p. 41.

50   *Ibid.*, pp. 30–1. All the material in this brief sketch of Brummell's life comes from Moers, *The Dandy*, pp. 24-31.

51   *Ibid.*, p. 18.

52   *Ibid.*, p. 18.

53   Quoted in *ibid.*, p. 37.

54   Quoted in *ibid.*, p. 31.

55   *Ibid.*, p. 147.

56   *Ibid.*, p. 147.

57   R. Felski, 'The Counterdiscourse of the Feminine in Three Texts by Wilde, Huysmans, and Sacher-Masoch', *PMLA*, 106:5 (1991), p. 1096.

58   Moers, *The Dandy*, p. 161.

59   *Ibid.*, p. 161.

60   *Ibid.*, p. 161.

61   *Ibid.*, p. 36.

62   *Ibid.*, p. 161.

63   *Ibid.*, p. 226.

64  J. Craik, *The Face of Fashion: Cultural Studies in Fashion* (London, Routledge, 1994), p. 186. Craik is quoting from J. Paoletti, 'Ridicule and Role Models as Factors in American Men's Fashion Change 1880–1910', *Costume*, 29 (1985), 121–34.

65  *Ibid.*, p. 186.

66  Moers, *The Dandy*, p. 295.

67  *Ibid.*, p. 295.

68  *Ibid.*, pp. 298–9.

69  *Ibid.*, p. 300.

70  Cohen, *Talk on the Wilde Side*, p. 174.

71  *Ibid.*, p. 136.

# 5

# The phallicised female body and its consumption

As I have explained, the female body comes to be positioned as the key phallic fetish. This fetishistic phallicisation of the female body has a dual effect on men's relations with women. The fetishistic context makes women both more sexually desired – their bodies appearing to acquire a heightened desirableness – and more feared – whilst simultaneously their bodies become the site of a fetishistic terror which complements, but is quite different in origin from, the fear of castration provoked by the recognition of women's 'lack' of a penis. The cultural overdetermination of cultural fetishism means that women may be constructed in two ideal–typical ways by men. First, and dominant, is the spectacle of the 'passive', phallicised woman, the woman who appears compliantly to express, for men, the spectacle of the phallicised body. Second, there is the spectacle of the 'active', phallic woman who, from a male perspective, re-works the phallic power attributed to her into a spectacle which men experience as threatening to their own, already lacking, feeling of phallic power.

There are two aspects to the reformation of the experience of consumption in the latter part of the nineteenth century. One is a consequence of the increasing production of commodities and the ideological shift which accompanied the transition to a consumption-oriented capitalism. The other can be described psychoanalytically as the desire to appropriate, possess, and internalise which is provoked by the feeling of, ultimately, phallic lack. In the twentieth-century experience of consumption these aspects are conflated. To take the shift in the ideology of capitalism first: where previously the term 'consumption' had been thought of as a using-up of something, from the middle of the eighteenth century onwards it began to be used in texts on political economy to describe the acquisition of material goods.[1] The earlier meaning of consumption remained through the nineteenth century and was implicit in its long-standing use as a name for tuberculosis. Susan Sontag has noted that the *Oxford English Dictionary* 'records "consumption" as a synonym for pulmonary tuberculosis as early as 1398'.[2] In the nineteenth century, although many men including Keats died of it (as did Kafka in 1924), tuberculosis came to be thought of as an illness of women. Its effect was to create the spectacle of an increasingly emaciated (female) body. In the mythology, 'the dying tubercular is pictured as made more beautiful and more soulful'.[3]

Expressing the new concerns of spectacularising surveillance, tuberculosis became a spectacle and was voyeuristically consumed, appropriated, by the male attendants on the woman. In tuberculosis we have a cultural genealogy for anorexia nervosa. As in anorexia the emaciated tubercular body is described as wasted; it is consumed, used up, by the illness. Signalling its connection with spectacle, Kim Chernin describes anorexia nervosa as having 'a distinctly exhibitionistic quality'.[4] By the middle of the twentieth century hysterical illnesses – which, as we saw in Chapter 3, were historically associated with the establishment of spectacle – had become rare. Anorexia nervosa – and, I would add, bulimia – is the last, and most culturally profound, of the spectacular forms of hysteria. It literally embodies a fundamental cultural contradiction. On the one hand the spectacle of the anorexic body epitomises the male fetishistic fantasy of the phallicised (pubescent) female body. On the other hand the same body spectacularises the woman's resistive refusal of the new imperative to consume. Bram Dijkstra makes apparent some of the distinctions between the old and new meanings of consumption, and their complex relations to tuberculosis:

> Many middle-class women, impressed with the lesson that they were of value only as consumer goods, came to see it as their primary purpose in life to enhance their own status in marriage by surrounding themselves with other expensive consumer goods.... Thus, woman, having been consumed in the marriage market, then having become consumptive as a wife through lack of respect, exercise and freedom, took her revenge by becoming a voracious consumer.[5]

Structurally, anorexia might be described similarly, except that it has historically affected younger, in fact pubescent, women – daughters rather than wives.

Anorexia suggests the extent to which the different meanings of consumption are played out around the body, particularly the female body. Mark Seltzer notes that 'one of the most evident paradoxes of the insistently paradoxical notion of a culture of consumption is the manner in which a style of life characterised by its excessiveness or gratuitousness – by its exceeding of, or disavowal of, physical and natural and bodily needs – is yet understood on the model of the natural body and its needs'.[6] When the body consumes food, it uses the food up and transforms the residue into waste product. The model for consumption remains eating; the model for the desire to consume is hunger. As we shall see, eating is also the dominant cultural metaphor for the appropriation, assimilation, internalisation, and consumption of the phallic fetish.

In cultural fetishism, consumption operates as the active metaphor to describe the way the male's phallic 'lack' is resolved. Unlike individual fetishism, in which the male imposes a fetish on to what he perceives as the woman's lack, in cultural fetishism the male feels that he himself is lacking. In order to acquire what he lacks he must assimilate the fetish supplement which he constructs. On the model of the functioning of the body, assimilation takes place through drinking and eating, which, of course, are also thought of in terms of consumption. In the desiring structure of cultural fetishism, then, such consumption acquires a renewed libidinal charge. I say renewed because Freud pointed out that, in the oral stage of childhood psychosexual development, food intake carried a libidinal charge. This was finally repressed, like other bodily pleasures, in latency. The film of *Tom Jones* (1963), reworking what is a recurrent metaphor in Henry fielding's novel (1749), is well known for making obvious use of eating as a metaphor for sexual intercourse. And this was at the time when Britain's consumer culture was taking off, leading into the celebration of consumption in the late 1960s which often goes by the shorthand of 'Swinging London'.

In the late eighteenth and through the nineteenth century, in bourgeois everyday life, women were expected to eat little. In her book *Women in American Society*, published in 1873, Abba Goold Woolson wrote: 'The familiar heroines of our books, particularly if described by masculine pens, are petite and fragile, with lily fingers and taper waists; and they are supposed to subsist on air and moonlight, and never to commit the unpardonable sin of eating in the presence of man.'[7] *Female Fetishism*'s authors, Lorraine Gamman and Merja Makinen, argue that many, if not all, cultures make a connection between a desire for food and sexual desire. Quoting a variety of examples, they suggest that: 'What is especially interesting, in such cross-cultural data, is the way that sex and food are gendered. Food is seen as the women's realm and sex as the men's.'[8] They discuss how in Western consumer culture the "displacement" of the direct pleasures of eating on to the pleasure of economic consumption creates conflicting messages about female identity'.[9] This displacement happens in the context of a new eroticisation of consumption which focuses on the female mouth, often emphasised by bright-red lipstick, something now so naturalised in advertising that there is no reason to give specific examples.[10] The question of why men find the female mouth so desirable is often accounted for on ethnological and psychological grounds, it being claimed that full lips, apparently engorged with blood, signal that a woman is sexually turned on. The reverse does not seem to apply. Here I want to argue for a more localised, cultural explanation.

Because a central aspect of cultural fetishism is the appropriation and (metaphorical) consumption of the phallic fetish, the mouth has become the most libidinally energised site. The projection of this energy focus on to the fetishised female body constructs the female mouth – rather than, as in individual fetishism, the vagina - as the key site of men's desire and fear. In short, men desire to consume (the phallic fetish) and are frightened of being consumed (as the phallic fetish). This desire and fear is repressed and acted out around a fascination with the female mouth - that is, the mouth of the phallic fetish herself. Combined further with the connection between eating and commodity consumption in a culture that valorises commodity consumption, the female mouth has become a complex source, for both men and women, of contradictory desires and fears. The fetishistic eroticisation of the female mouth has led to its conflation with the vagina, conflating also the desire for food and sexual desire. One of the most obvious examples of this can be found in René Magritte's 1945 surrealist painting The Rape, in which a face doubles as the female body. The eyes are the breasts and the mouth is the vagina. Set in the context of cultural fetishism, with its male preoccupations of appropriation, assimilation, internalisation, and consumption, the shift from the vagina to the vaginal mouth combines with the association of hunger with sexual desire. This theme has come into its own in the consumption culture of the post-Second World War period.

The male fantasy of the vaginal mouth emphasises the lips and represses the teeth. This mouth is thought to desire, and offer itself to, the penis. At the hard-core pornographic limit of male sexual fantasy we find the film *Deep Throat,* released in 1972. It formed part of the move of hard-core pornography into the mainstream. As Linda Williams writes: 'For the first time cinematic works containing hard-core action were reviewed by the entertainment media and viewed by a wide spectrum of the population, including, most significantly, women'.[11] By the time *Deep Throat* had lost its censorship battle in March 1973, it had already been seen by over a quarter of a million people in New York alone.[12] In *Deep Throat* the lead character is supposed, by a freak of nature, to have her clitoris positioned at the back of her throat. This image literally embodies the transference of male sexual desire from the vagina to the mouth. It provides the film with its excuse for a series of episodes of fellatio. Williams notes how, beginning with the tremendous popularity of *Deep Throat,* fellatio took on a new importance in hard-core pornography. She writes: 'Fellatio – culminating in a money shot in which ejaculation occurs on the woman's face and mouth – becomes, in the wake of *Deep Throat*'s enormous popularity, the privileged figure for the expression of climax and satisfaction (reaching, in fact, a kind of apotheosis in *Behind the Green Door,* made later that same year)'.[13] In this preoccupation the mouth has taken on the sexual role of the vagina.[14] For the reasons I have been outlining, it would not be at all surprising if fellatio now had a new importance as an everyday sexual practice in the population at large.

With the eroticisation of the female mouth, the male fear of the active, aggressive vagina – the *vagina dentata* – now also occurs, and is culturally though not individually privileged, in relation to the mouth. The idea of the *vagina dentata* is, again, located in the association between eating and sexual intercourse. Peter Mason has discussed the idea of the *vagina dentata* as one common to many societies:

> As Lévi-Strauss has remarked, the terms 'eat' and 'copulate' are identical in a very large number of languages. This already indicates a linking of the sexual and alimentary codes, and enables us to pass from the orifices of the digestive system (mouth, anus) to those of the genital system (vagina and penis). This homology between the two domains is sustained by the widespread mythical theme of the *vagina dentata,* the toothed vagina.[15]

Setting aside this universalistic claim, in a capitalism which fetishises the female body and which also privileges consumption the *vagina dentata* takes on new meanings. At its most general it expresses a male castration fantasy. In a Freudian society this male fear is positioned within the organisation of the Oedipus complex. In our patriarchal order the mother is the only woman whom the boy accepts as being able to exercise power. She is also the object of Oedipal desire. The effect of this combination of power and desirability is to produce the vagina as a place of castrating threat as well as pleasurable satisfaction – something reinforced by the castration complex, the belief that the mother has herself been castrated, perhaps in the very incestuous act that the son desires. The idea of the *vagina dentata* is, in the first place then, a product of a male fear.

Where, in the myth of the *vagina dentata*, the quality of the mouth, its teeth, is transferred to the vagina, in the eroticisation of the mouth the vagina's sexual quality is transferred. The fear of the mouth, which of course implies the desire for fellatio, has a rational legitimation. The mouth has teeth. The male fear is that the passive and submissive female mouth will become active and consuming. The mouth *dentata* has become the signifier of the phallic woman, the virago, as opposed to the phallicised woman whom men want to assimilate, consume. In *Idols of Perversity* Dijkstra presents us with an early example of the phallic woman drawn from the time when the conflation of vagina and mouth was taking place. He describes how, in the latter part of the nineteenth century, 'the Medusa, with her bouffant of snakes, paralyzing eyes, and bestial proclivities, was the very personification of all that was evil in the gynander'.[16] The term 'gynander' was introduced by Joséphin Péladan in the late nineteenth century to describe the woman men most feared, 'the predatory woman, the autoerotic or lesbian woman who consorted with males in a futile attempt to absorb or syphon off their masculine energies in order to "become masculinized", but who otherwise chose to conjoin herself only with other women in an orgy of degenerative, self-extinguishing regression into the absolute of femininity, a journey back into the primordial earth'[17] – the phallic woman, in fact. In Dijkstra's book there is a picture of a lithograph entitled *Istar* by Fernand Khnopff, made in 1888 and inspired by Péladan's outline of the gynander. As Dijkstra explains: 'He showed a bestial Venus, arrogantly self-possessed even while chained in punishment to the walls of subterranean lust, while the polyplike tentacles of a giant Medusa head, screaming in frustration, covered the feminine loins whose barren symbol, whose aggressive "vagina dentata", the Medusa's head was widely thought to be, with its masculine, phallic, yet hypnotically ingestive powers'.[18] That the Medusa's head was a widely used image for the *vagina dentata* must have meant that the mouth already carried a sexual charge. In the Khnopff lithograph the connection is made explicit, with the Medusa's snake hair substituting for Istar's pubic hair whilst the Medusa's head is strangely positioned somewhat down Istar's right leg. It has an open mouth with bared teeth. From a woman's point of view, therefore, the connotations of the mouth *dentata* can be positive – power, freedom, independence, and such like.

The conflation of the mouth and the vagina is pervasive. In one example, Andrew Wernick has discussed how cars came to be given fronts which could be read as a human face: 'Figuration in so blatant a form, however, declined after the Ford Edsel – a car whose spectacular marketing failure (in 1958) was perhaps best explained by customer comments that its grille looked like a vagina (replete, we may add, with teeth)'.[19] Here we find both the easy association of face and female genitals, focusing on the mouth/vagina conflation, and the male fear of the vagina/mouth *dentata*. The vaginal mouth *dentata* has become a common fear. One example can be found in *Eve of Destruction* (1990), where Eve's gynoid double bites off a man's penis. In John Irving's novel *The World According to Garp* (1978) the wife accidentally bites off her lover's penis when her husband accidentally rams the car they are in from behind. In fact this is a literary version of a common urban myth involving a car, fellatio, and the accidental biting-off of the penis. The fetishistic fear which underlies this rational fear is of women's consumption of the phallus, giving them the power men desire.

From a perusal of post-Renaissance European paintings of the female nude such as those of Rubens, and, in fact, very early photographic evidence, we find that in the seventeenth, eighteenth, and early nineteenth centuries the dominant bourgeois male image of the preferred female body was that of a woman in her late twenties with an amount of fat on her which would enable her today to be described as voluptuous. Naomi Wolf has summed up this history, explaining that 'various distributions of sexual fat were emphasised – big ripe bellies from the fifteenth to seventeenth centuries, plump faces and shoulders in the early nineteenth century ... generous dimpled buttocks and thighs until the twentieth century'.[20] In the latter half of the nineteenth century the preferred female body underwent a radical shift. It became slimmer, whilst large breasts and buttocks became problematic. This change could have been the effect of women's own wish to alter their body image as they entered the public domain. If a 'full' body could be read in terms of the wholesome motherly figure of the domestic domain, the slimmer body minus these 'female' characteristics would appear more 'masculine', and would have a better cultural fit in the male public domain, as women began to enter the professions and take their place in the middle-class workforce. This is an important argument, but it only tells a part of the story. First of all, women's entry into the middle-class workforce did not take place in any significant numbers until after the Second World War, whereas the change in body form began to take place in the latter part of the nineteenth century. Second, as we have already seen in Chapter 3, women did appear, literally, in the public domain, on the streets as shoppers, from the middle of that century. As we have also seen, whilst this new presence gave women a freedom of movement that they had not previously enjoyed, it came at a price, and that was the increasingly spectacularising surveillance of these women's bodies by men. In other words, these women became objects of desire in a new desiring structure – that of the phallic economy of cultural fetishism. It may be the case that many women found the new clothing fashions and the new body image more appropriate to their new public situation; it remains, however, that these changes took place amid a new spectacularisation of the female body which was libidinally driven – its eroticisation or, as we found Wilson describing it, the 'over-sexualisation' of women.

The spectacularising surveillance of women's bodies led to a reconstruction of the preferred image towards a more phallicised look. As we saw in Chapter 1, one important way in which this took place was through a privileging of the body image of the pubescent girl. As a consequence, the image of the desirable female body has got younger as well as slimmer. Whilst this look is, culturally speaking, the male's preferred look, this does not mean that it cannot be used by women in their own interests - or indeed, more obviously, criticised, ignored, or even deliberately denied. All these are possible; and in day-to-day life, contradictory combinations of cultural pressures and these critical and appropriating positions are a part of women's experience.

One exemplification of the late-nineteenth-century shift in the

dominant male fantasy image of the female body, and a reinforcement of it as the preferred body, was the so-called 'Gibson girl'.
Charles Dana Gibson, twenty at the time, began to draw his ideal
woman for the American magazine *Life* in 1887. So popular was
Gibson's image of the youthful wasp-waited, full-bosomed girl that
in 1903 he 'signed a $100,000 contract with *Collier's* (1886-1957) to
render a series of double-page "cartoons" over four years' time,
yielding even further exposure for his historic creation'.[21] Many of
Gibson's portrayals of his girls had them as seaside girls, on the
beach.[22] As the popular expression of male fantasy, the Gibson girl
was followed in 1933 by George Petty's 'Petty girl', to be found in
the first and subsequent issues of *Esquire,* appearing on a foldout
page from early 1941 until her unexplained demise in December
1941.[23] Unlike the comparatively demure Gibson girl, the Petty girl
was often naked or nearly so. She was youthful, long-legged, flat-
stomached, and small-buttocked, with full but not overlarge breasts.
Her body's connotations of adolescence belied the age implied by
her breasts and face, and her disproportionately long legs gave her
an elongated, phallic look.

The late-nineteenth-century shift was not absolute. Roberta
Pollock Seid writes that, although there was a vogue for slenderness
in the United States in the latter half of the nineteenth century, 'by
the close of the century, in the Edwardian period, the fashionable
ideal was Junoesque: an amply bosomed, tall, statuesque figure'.[24]
Then: 'Rather suddenly, in 1908, the voluptuous hourglass figure
fell out of favor. It was replaced by a body type closer to the one we
admire today: slender, long-limbed, and relatively straight. We don't
often see such radical shifts in popular taste.'[25] Seid explains that
the shift in taste was precipitated by the new fashion look of Paul
Poiret, a Paris designer: 'In 1908 he introduced his sleek, "natural"
look, soon called neo-Empire, and by 1910 it had become the fashionable silhouette.'[26] Here it is important to distinguish between
short-term fashion changes and long-term social shifts in the idea
of the desirable body. Seid's surprise at the radical change in up-
market popular taste precipitated by Poiret's designs becomes
understandable if we consider that through the last half of the
nineteenth century bourgeois women were already beginning to
internalise the male preoccupation with the pubescent female body
– and here we should recall the Gibson girl as a pointer. Poiret
developed a look which coincided with this interest.

One of the most important aspects of Poiret's look, unlike that

of the Gibson girl, was that it de-emphasised breasts. Seid quotes
Madame Poiret remembering her husband announcing: 'From now
on, the breasts will no longer be worn.'[27] Through the twentieth
century, as the desirable and desired female body has become more
and more phallic, so the most problematic region of the female
anatomy has been the breasts. As the girl develops through puberty
it is the breasts which provide the most visible sign of her maturity
as a woman. From the fetishistic male point of view of the woman as
spectacle, breasts have an ambiguous quality. They define the body
as that of a woman – and this before any oral associations of the
breast with nurture. But breasts also detract from the phallic quality of
the female body. Large breasts, then, reassure the man that the
'male', phallicised body before him is, in fact, female. In short we
can say that, as a consequence of cultural fetishism, men want
women both to have breasts and to have no breasts. The situation is
compounded by the fact that the effect of reducing body size to fit
the fantasy phallic image tends also to reduce breast size. We can
find one reason for the current prevalence of breast enlargement
surgery in this contradictory male desire for a phallic body with
clearly defined breasts.

After the First World War, the fashion introduced by Poiret
took a further step towards an erotic androgyny, evolving 'into the
boyish look of the flapper': 'Skirts shortened to calf length, waists
loosened and lowered to the hip, breasts were to be flat and were
often bound to make them seem small, and women discarded one of
the most cherished marks of their sex – their long hair'. Seid
explains: 'For the first, but not the last time, fashion suppressed the
female shape, exalting instead boyish or prepubescent forms'.[28] At
the same time, the acceptance of the generalised eroticisation and
spectacularisation of the female body can also be found in the post-
First World War spread of beauty contests in the United States.
Using bathing suits, which resonate with the myth of the seaside
girl, the first Miss America contest was held in 1921.[29] If the striptease was the non-respectable development of the *tableau vivant* in
respect of the fetishised female body, the beauty contest represented the respectable, morally acceptable, side.

In the United States, following the introduction of assembly-
line production, the 1920s and 1930s were the first period when a
major cultural emphasis was placed on consumption. The second
period occurred in the 1950s. After the Second World War, there
was a further expansion of the ethos to the American working class,

to Europe, and to the other Western countries. At this same time we find that 'rather suddenly after World War II, interest in weight loss crescendoed, penetrating more deeply into the culture and into the daily lives of ordinary Americans'.[30] This correlates with a renewed emphasis on women as consumers, spurred by advertising's use of the idea of women's bodies as lacking, and the use of 'attractive' women's bodies as adjuncts in advertising campaigns aimed at men. In these different ways women's place in the phallic economy of consuming desire was reinforced.

During the 1950s there was a twofold development in the phallicisation of the female body. First there was a renewed cultural emphasis which increased the body's phallicisation. One small example of the gradual diminution in the acceptable size of the female body can be found in the changes in dress sizes. Seid describes how, in the late 1940s, advertisements in women's magazines 'had usually been for 10s to 18s, with occasional 8s. By the mid-50s, they were 8s with occasional 6s, and they went up to 14, sometimes 16, but rarely to 18 or 20'.[31] She comments that the effect of this shift was that women had to slim down.

Second, from being a clothing fashion trend the phallicising drive was internalised to the body itself. This is most evident in the increased social acceptance of slimming. In other words, the actual shape of the body changed. Equally importantly, and complementarily, the emphasis on the phallicised female body spread from the bourgeoisie to the working class, pervading the whole of society. As with the apparent suddenness of the bourgeois shift in body preference related to Poiret's new fashion style, this shift in the 1950s also only *appeared* to be sudden. It was one culmination of a long-term transition and came about in the context of the post-war spread of the new consumption-driven culture.

During the post-Second World War period the category of the teenager also spread from its origins in middle-class youth of the 1920s United States to become a general Western category. Many accounts have been written of the relation between the deployment of the new category of the teenager and the spread of consumerism. Describing youth as 'a cultural expression of social relationships and a product of a specific set of historical conditions', Paula Fass writes that in the 1920s 'youth appeared suddenly on the social scene'.[32] Fass shows the development of a new set of concerns and values among white middle-class American young people during this period. As she argues: 'Many of these values grew from the leisure which the young enjoyed in abundance, and many were directed toward the approved consumption of leisure time – sports, dates, sociability, and congeniality'.[33] These leisure activities were increasingly centred around material consumption. One marker for the spread of the category of the teenager was the development of the 'youth problem' film in the mid-1950s. The key films here were *The Wild One* (1954), *Rebel Without a Cause* (1955), and *Blackboard Jungle* (1955). Elsewhere I have summed up the relation between the categories of adolescent and teenager:

> As a part of the development of a consumption-oriented social order emanating from America in the early part of this century and spreading to other developed countries in this period following the Second World War, the period of adolescence was invested with a new set of ideological determinations – such as hedonism and leisure – which formed the thematic basis of the new consumerism.[34]

Here I want to emphasise the association of commodity consumption with the sexualised teenager of both sexes. We should recall again Nabokov's *Lolita,* and Lolita's transformation into a teenage consumer in the 1962 film.

In the early 1960s in England the most famous model was Jean Shrimpton. Her nickname was 'the Shrimp', which was a shortened version of her name but also an echo of her thinness. Shrimpton, who appeared on the cover of *Vogue* in 1963, was credited with popularising the mini-skirt. However, the acceptance and celebration of her body size marked another shift towards the dominance of the image of the pubescent girl. Jean Shrimpton was followed by Twiggy, whom Seid describes as 'an emaciated seventeen-year-old girl'.[35] In 1967 Twiggy was five feet seven and a half inches tall and weighed ninety-one pounds.[36]

By the 1980s the phallicised female body was being transformed by aerobics and weight training into what became known as the hard body, an even further literalisation of the phallic fetish:

> At heart, the muscled look was androgynous. Traditionally, fashion has accentuated the differences between the sexes ... In the seventies unisex styles and thin bodies had begun to erode sexual differentiation in dress and, to a lesser extent, in bodies themselves. Everyone was to look like a just-budding adolescent. The look of the eighties was more androgynous

still. Women were not just dressing like men; they actually
were trying to develop the musculature of men, and the
physical strength it brought.[37]

It is deceptive to describe what was taking place as a move to
androgyny. There was no movement to a mean between the sexes.
Rather, women came to look more and more like adolescent boys.

In the early 1990s this image was encapsulated in the 'waif
look' pioneered by Kate Moss and, subsequently, Emma Barlow.
Kate Moss was discovered by the English magazine *The Face* when
she was 16 and appeared twice on its cover in 1990. In an article
entitled 'London Girls' in the June 1992 edition of *The Face*, the
new waif look was contrasted with the look of supermodels such as
Claudia Schiffer, Christy Turlington, and Linda Evangelista. The
article claims two things: that the 'innocent' and 'soft' waif look will
supersede the look of the supermodels, and that the new waif
models are really just ordinary girls. For example, Kate Moss is
described as 'the faintly gangly, freckled kid from Croyden with the
"moonchild" face'.[38] By this means the look of the thin, almost
breastless, pubescent adolescent – all the five 'waif' models discussed in the article were under 20 – is naturalised as being how
every young girl looks. The fetishistic power of this apparently
helpless, juvenile spectacle – and its nineteenth-century heritage –
is made clear in a reading by Stacey D'Erasmo in the New York
*Village Voice*:

> In fact, the imagery in which Moss and her imitators are
> embedded is much older than the '60s. These are very deca-
> dent images, images of virgins who could at any minute turn
> into succubi, like the pre-Raphaelite non-heroines of Francis
> Ford Coppola's *Dracula*, and not unlike their ravenous, man-
> stabbing elder sisters in *Basic Instinct*. Be careful not to get
> one as a roommate'.[39]

In fact, in the film *Single White Female* (1992) this is exactly what
happens. Here the seeming passivity of the look is counterbalanced
by claims that it has male-threatening vampiric connotations.

The increasingly slim body form, and in particular the looks
popularised over the last thirty years by the likes of Jean Shrimpton
and Kate Moss, have been credited with exacerbating the problem
of anorexia nervosa among young women. Towards the end of the
nineteenth century this illness began to be distinguished from the
other 'protean symptoms' of hysteria. At least two of Breuer's and

Freud's patients, Anna O. and Emmy von N., had symptoms of anorexia among their other problems, and Breuer describes a twelve-year-old boy who developed a condition in which he 'refused food and vomited when it was pressed on him'.[40] Anorexia nervosa combined the spectacularisation of the body, its context of a developing social preoccupation with the phallicised female body-look, and the day-to-day problems experienced by the bourgeois adolescent girl trying to negotiate familial, social, and personal demands. Amongst other things, the illness plays on the substitution of the desire for food in place of the desire for love. The metaphor which connects the two is, once again, consumption and its complex meanings.

Simultaneously with the advent of anorexia nervosa, the other forms of hysteria which proliferated in the second half of the nineteenth century seemed to begin to disappear. Rather than actually disappearing, however, hysteria became a social commonplace, a part of everyday life. It was internalised. No longer played out on the body, hysteria came to be acted out in the repetitions of childhood trauma which are of such importance to psychoanalysts and other therapists. In therapeutic terms this shift takes place between Charcot and Freud. Where Charcot's patients staged their hysteria on their bodies in the frenzy of the visible, Freud's patients, who were, in the main, bourgeois women, tended, as time went on, to act out their hysterical symptoms. It is as if the very expression of the problems which generated the hysterical symptoms was internalised and became a part of the lived experience of everyday life. The period of 'imperfect' body control occurred at the time of the 'over-sexualisation' of women's bodies when they were becoming the focus of spectacularising surveillance. At this time, it would seem, women's experience of alienation from their bodies – the cultural process, discussed in Chapter 3, which Freud describes as latency – was being reinforced as a consequence of the new fetishisation of those bodies. The reassertion of bodily discipline shifted the symptoms from 'bodily' display to 'mental' acting out – with the important exception of anorexia.

Anorexia nervosa was described almost simultaneously by the English physician Sir William Gull, who was doctor to Queen Victoria, and the French neurologist Charles Lasègue. In an address to the British Medical Association in 1868, during a discussion of the diagnosis of abdominal problems, Gull referred to a kind of indigestion in young women which he called hysteric apepsia. His point was that hysteric apepsia needed to be distinguished from indigestion brought on by intestinal disease. In April 1873 Lasègue published a description of what he called *l'anorexie hystérique* in the *Archives Générales de Médecine*, and it was published in English in the *Medical Times and Gazette* in September 1873. The following month, Gull read a paper to the Clinical Society in London entitled 'Anorexia Hysterica'. It was published a short time later under the title 'Anorexia Nervosa (Apepsia Hysterica, Anorexia Hysterica)'. In this paper Gull acknowledged Lasègue's work and focused on anorexia as a mental problem. He rejected Lasègue's use of the term 'hysteria' on the grounds that males as well as females were affected by the illness.[41]

Where Gull concentrated on the aetiology of the illness in individuals, Joan Jacobs Brumberg points out that Lasègue emphasised the importance of the family context:

> It was Lasègue, not William Gull, who provided the first real glimpse of the pressurized family environment in anorexia nervosa. Unlike Gull, who hoped to isolate a new disease, Lasègue was part of an influential group in early French psychiatry – the *médicins-aliénistes* – who were interested in delineating each of the symptomatic groups under the broad rubric of hysteria'.[42]

The recognition of anorexia nervosa, then, occurred in the context of attempts to distinguish forms of hysteria. Gull's removal of the term hysteria from the name for the illness disguised the fact that it was, and is, in the main, adolescent girls who develop the problem. The removal also tends to detract from the recognition that, in anorexia as in other hysterias, the body displays the individual's experience of a social conflict.

It is not surprising, given the understanding of anorexia nervosa as a spectacular illness, that Gull himself illustrated the three case histories which he provided in his paper with before-and-after head-and-shoulder photographs of the girls concerned. In 1895 Doctor Lockhardt Stephens published in the *Lancet* a photograph of a sixteen-year-old girl who had died from anorexia nervosa whilst under his care seven years earlier. In the picture the girl is arranged naked except for a sheet covering her genitals. Brumberg describes the picture as 'devoid of eroticism', whilst recognising the pleasure that Victorians – she does not gender them – gained from photographs of the nude, 'particularly soft, opalescent, womanly flesh and the budding bodies of young women on the brink of their sexual potential'.[43] Such an assertion begs the question of why Stephens took the trouble to arrange the body and take the photograph – particularly when we learn that William Playfair, the professor of obstetric medicine discussed in Chapter 3, was also 'the collector of [an] album of anorexic photographs'.[44] The predatory fascination with the female body expressed in these photographs becomes clearer when we remember that it was during this same period that that most notorious of nineteenth-century London murderers, Jack the Ripper, killed five, if not more, prostitutes, 'removing vagina and womb with all the professional skill of … a medical man'.[45]

Female madness and ecstasy were equated by men as both being one step away from death. In Germany, Albert von Keller 'visited the morgue to paint the bodies and facial expressions of dead women so that he might more successfully depict the extreme religious joy of the nuns he liked to portray at the very moment of their ecstatic self-sacrificial demise'.[46] Dijkstra also describes how 'Hans Rosenhagen, in a monograph on Keller published in 1912, reported that the artist had determined, as a result of his field research, that at least "in the case of girls and women who had died a natural death", if one "studied their faces intensively one could see them take on an expression of pain made so noble and almost so sympathetic by their suffering that it allowed an otherworldly happiness to shine through which could often only be compared to the miraculous expression of a woman who is in love to the point of ecstasy"'.[47] Here, Edmund Burke's association of the sublime with bodily pain, put forward in *A Philosophical Enquiry into the Origin of Our Ideas of the Sublime and the Beautiful*, published in 1757, has become gendered and, showing also a Sadeian heritage, has been connected with ecstasy. As the mention of Sade indicates, what is being repressed is an association of women's death with female orgasm. Where death, as we saw in Chapter 2, is a characteristic of the fetish, orgasm suggests the sexual being of women. Presented as a spectacle, it seeks to legitimise the eroticising gaze of the male viewer.

Dijkstra has documented the late-nineteenth-century vogue for pictures of mad women and dead women. The context for the photographs and paintings of dead women lies in the connection made in Chapter 2 between the fetish, death, and photography. At the Salpêtrière, 'Charcot saw [the] patients as a huge neurological laboratory of material for his experiments, his famous clinical lectures, and his subsequent publications'.[48] The Salpêtrière photographs of the manifestations of hysteria are a scientific inflection of the genre of the mad woman, which included a multitude of paintings of Shakespeare's Ophelia. Dijkstra shows how female madness was thought of as the extreme self-sacrifice of love; as in Ophelia's typifying case, it paved the way for death, the final and ultimate self-sacrifice. He describes Ophelia as 'the later nineteenth century's all-time favorite example of the love-crazed self-sacrificial woman who most perfectly demonstrated her devotion to her man by descending into madness, who surrounded herself with flowers to show her equivalence to them, and who in the end committed herself to a watery grave, thereby fulfilling the nineteenth-century male's fondest fantasies of feminine dependency'.[49] Dijkstra argues that, by the turn of the century, a literary pretext was no longer necessary. As evidence he provides a painting from 1899 by Pierre-Georges Jeanniot called *The Madwoman*. This painting, 'quite straightforwardly the portrayal of a deranged woman', has, in Dijkstra's words, an 'emotional impact [which] is made ambiguous by the morbidity and exploitative prurience of its focus'.[50] It is here that we have the more precise connection with Charcot's photographic laboratory, and with Gull's and Stephens's photographs of anorexics.

Stephens's photograph, like Keller's paintings, is part of a genre of representations of dead young women which develops from around 1850. The paintings have titles such as those of Joseph Noel Paton's *The Dead Lady* (c. 1850) and Paul-Albert Besnard's *The Dead Woman* (1880s).[51] Dijkstra notes that Sarah Bernhardt '[carted] about with her on her *tournées* what she described as her own coffin, and by letting it be known that she was not averse to sleeping in this rather narrow cot [emphasised] the (to her admirers evidently delicious) fact of her own mortality'.[52] He adds that photographs of Bernhardt lying in her coffin 'did the rounds of afficionados and appropriately thrilled men everywhere'.[53] Dijkstra recognises in Besnard's paintings that 'his fascination with dead and dying women was mingled with a morbid eroticism'.[54] Bernhardt's photographs circulated in the 1870s, shortly before Stephens took his photograph. As the female body became fetishised, so the spectacle of the dead woman became a libidinally powerful site of the male gaze.

Sander Gilman argues that 'one of the favorite images of late nineteenth-century medical art is the unequal couple transmogri-

fied into the image of the aged pathologist contemplating the exqui-
site body of the dead prostitute before he opens it'.[55] In this image
we find summed up many of the concerns involved in the
spectacularisation of the female body. There is the gendering of
sight, and its relation to power and to class. Bourgeois males gaze on
the (dead) bodies of working(-class) women. As viewers of these
pictures we too are invited to gaze with the pathologists. The beauty
of the female corpse encourages the desire of the gaze. That the
woman was a prostitute both enhances the sexual overtones and
seeks to excuse the gaze on her semi-naked body. That she was a
prostitute also reminds us of the association of women with commodities. Finally we can ask what it is that the pathologist in the
picture is looking for in the body. Elisabeth Bronfen suggests that:
'Woman serves allegorically as the site of a truth which is beyond
man's reach. What he can't know, namely woman's lack (be it in
respect to death or sexuality), translates into a lack in his knowledge'.[56] In the modern period the most significant Otherness that
women had for men – and what they desired to appropriate – was
women's ability to reproduce. But, perhaps also, the male pathologist is, like the spectator at the striptease which was shortly to
come into being, looking for what a woman does not have, a penis,
and what she is not but is being fetishised as, the phallus.

In 1924 Kafka published a story called 'A Hunger Artist'. Seid
notes that it is based on a short tradition of spectacular male starvation: 'From the 1880s until World War I, "hunger artists" captivated
American and European audiences'.[57] She traces this tradition to
Henry Tanner, who in 1880 'began a much-publicized forty-two
day fast in New York City under the supervision of "regular physi-
cians"',[58] and suggests that Tanner and his followers were testing
how long it was possible to go without food. With hunger artists,
starvation was being commodified as a spectacle and as an endur-
ance test. However, there is more we can say about these male
hunger artists. First, they were men, whereas, historically, it has
been women who have accounted for the vast majority of cases of
anorexia nervosa. The fascination with the hunger artist's performance may be understood as a recognition of the way it provided an
idiosyncratic commentary on consumption. A female hunger artist
would not have been acceptable. Men could be hunger artists
because they stood outside the fetishistic order which their desire
organised. They could, therefore, provide a commentary on it.
Women, however, fetishised and commodified, were always already

implicated within it. Where the hunger artist provided a commentary from without, the anorexic inscribed her personal experience of the fetishisation and commodification of women's bodies on her own body. During the time that anorexia was being discovered as a female illness, male hunger artists were performing for paying audiences.

Kafka tells the story of a man who is placed in a cage and fasts for forty days. He does this regularly and crowds pay to watch him. Forty days is the maximum his manager will allow – after this time, the crowd begins to lose interest. The hunger artist's denial of his personal consumption, visible in his body, was something people paid to watch. This spectacle was, in the first place, a commodity. This is a quite different motivation from that of the female anorexic. In Kafka's story the hunger artist starves himself to death. He says that he has to fast because he cannot find any food he likes: 'If I had found it, believe me, I should have made no fuss and stuffed myself like you or anyone else.' In this comment Kafka gives his hunger artist an anorexic's rationalisation. The fetishisation of the female body leads, finally, to a male fascination with women's death, and, as we shall see, sometimes to her literal consumption. By contrast, in Kafka's story the crowd loses interest in the male hunger artist approaching death because he is not an object of desire. Their interest in him, as in hunger artists generally, has more to do with his self-control, manifested in his voluntary denial of the consumption of food at a time when commodity consumption was beginning to be encouraged through a new emphasis on hedonism. Unlike the late-nineteenth-century anorexic, no male doctor would take a photograph of his tastefully displayed body.

Beside the male hunger artists, in the later years of the nineteenth century there were a number of cases of 'fasting girls', as they were known in Britain and the United States. These girls had much in common with those cases which were given the new classification of anorexia nervosa, but they also tended to include some older religious or mystical concerns. Often the length of their fast was attributed to divine intervention. These girls attracted many visitors, who often donated money,[59] but their key difference from the hunger artists is that they did not perform for money before an audience - they did not commodify the spectacle of their starvation. Instead they were thought of as a problem and, increasingly, as suffering from an illness.

In the midst of the general emphasis on consumption it has

become more and more difficult to distinguish 'normal' dieting for weight loss from a pathological dieting which can be identified with anorexia nervosa. A part of the problem here lies in the way that what is considered to be a 'normal' female weight has altered steadily downwards through the twentieth century. In 1922 Florence Courtney, an American beauty writer, recommended that a five-feet seven-inch woman should weigh 148 pounds.[60] In 1983 a local pageant committee for the Miss California contest was urging the winner, who had put on some weight, to reduce down to 115 pounds. She was also five feet seven.[61]

Although anorexia nervosa was described and distinguished from other forms of hysteria in the 1860s and 1870s, it did not become a relatively common illness until after the 1950s. It is extremely difficult to put a figure on the percentage of women suffering from anorexia nervosa for a number of reasons. First, diagnostic awareness differs historically and geographically. Second, as a hysterical illness, its symptoms are likely to vary. Third, as a hysterical illness – as a social illness – there is an important sense in which its symptoms *are* the illness; the body spectacularly produces the illness. Fourth, anorexia nervosa has to be situated within the spectrum of demands which the present order makes on its female members in terms of an emphasis on thinness and a concern with diet. It is clear, though, that the incidence of the illness is increasing. In one study in Switzerland the incidence for females between the ages of 12 and 25 increased from 3.98 per 100,000 in 1956-58 to 16.76 per 100,000 in 1973-75. In another study it was calculated that one in every 250 girls enrolled in a London private school would suffer anorexia nervosa.[62] In Munroe County, New York, a study of psychiatric case registers between 1960-69 and 1970-76 showed almost a doubling of diagnosed cases.[63] As the male body is becoming spectacularisingly surveilled, so young men too are beginning to suffer from anorexia in increasing numbers.

In the nineteenth century the middle-class family meal became the most heavily ritualised and disciplined of all interpersonal interactions of family members. It brought the members of the family together in a regular secular ritual which established the familial rule of the father's law. Kafka, author of 'The Hunger Artist', also wrote a *Letter to His Father*:

> For me as a child everything you shouted at me was positively
> a heavenly commandment, I never forgot it, it remained for

> me the most important means of forming a judgement of the
> world.... Since as a child I was together with you chiefly at
> meals, your teaching was to a large extent teaching about
> proper behaviour at table ...[64]

It became common to limit food consumption to three meals a day and to discipline not only the familial interaction but the food intake also. In *Health Fragments, or Steps Towards True Life*, published in New York in 1875, George Everett and Susan Everett wrote: 'Eat only at regular hours, and never then unless you are hungry, nor oftener than three times a day'.[65] Brumberg points out that, in the middle-class household, it was easy to conflate love and food. This is especially so when children were, and are, forced to eat things 'for their own good' or when food, or rather its withdrawal, was, and is, a frequent form of punishment, as in 'You must go to bed without any supper'. One common strategy aimed at getting a child to eat more is to suggest to them that they think of the less fortunate, the starving, who would be grateful for the food. Here, love and food are combined with guilt and implicated in excessive consumption. The child is expected to eat regardless of whether or not their hunger is satisfied. To not want to eat is understood as a failure of the desire to consume. The starving are usually situated somewhere like Africa, in a country peripheralised in relation to the economic core of Europe and the United States, the 'West'. Famine and starvation are conceptualised as occurring on the frontier of capitalism, an event which can be ended by the acceptance of 'modernising' capitalism which will bring abundance. In this way the stories of starvation in the 'peripheral' countries operate in the 'core' as homilies about consumption, and about capitalism and its associated practices – such as democracy – which, it is claimed, make possible the abundance on which consumption is premised.

One fascination with emaciation is with the ability of the 'mind' to control the appetitive desire of the 'body'. Susan Bordo has extended this argument, writing that anorexia 'could ... be seen as an extreme development of the capacity for self-denial and repression of desire (the work ethic in absolute "control")'.[66] It is also apparent that there is a certain general fascination with emaciation in a well-fed society, a fascination which is still present in the reception of images of famine victims. The title of Katherine Gilday's film about anorexia nervosa, *The Famine Within* (1990), makes the connection clear. The male erotics of the thin or emaciated female body articulates with the dichotomous relation of control of appetite and the celebration of consumption. We are, then, brought back to the spectacle of Stephens's carefully arranged photograph and Playfair's photograph album. During the later years of the nineteenth century the effects of female starvation began to articulate with a masculine erotic pleasure which became increasingly normalised in the middle years of the twentieth century.

Appetite and sexual desire, and their connections with consumption, are, then, central to a discussion of the historicity – and cultural specificity – of anorexia nervosa. In Margaret Atwood's novel *The Edible Woman* (1969), the connections between anorexia, male sexual desire, and appetite are quite explicit. Towards the end of the novel, Marian McAlpin has been becoming increasingly anorexic as her marriage to her fiancé Peter gets closer. Finally she bakes him a cake in the shape of a woman and offers it to him: '"You've been trying to destroy me, haven't you," she said. "You've been trying to assimilate me. But I've made you a substitute, something you'll like much better. This is what you wanted all along, isn't it?"'[67] Marian's comment is an accurate description of the form that male sexual desire takes in cultural fetishism. She recognises that Peter's desire to possess her body sexually is also a desire to consume her. It is this, and the power relation which underpins it, which provoked Marian's anorexia. Peter's other passion is photography.

The equivalence that developed between eating and sexual intercourse as actions which violate the 'objectness' of the body is well illustrated in a statement by Evan Jacob, the father of the Welsh fasting girl Sarah Jacob, who died of starvation in 1869. Replying to advice to force-feed his daughter, Jacob asked: 'How can you London doctors make my child eat, without making a hole in her?'[68] The anorexic does not intend to die; death is a by-product of the expression of desire manifested in the spectacular wasting of the body. The individual anorexic works with a very personal agenda of conflicts but she does so in terms of a pre-established set of cultural concerns. Hunger asserts both the physicality of the body and its objectness. Where sexual desire was constituted in modernity as pervasively psychosocial, and male, anorexia demonstrates that hunger, reconstructed as appetite, is the province of the female.

Conversely, anorexia can be understood as a pathological appropriation of this disciplinary order. The pubescent girl starves herself and does not enter the post-Oedipal, adult world of women's bodies as spectacular objects. Paradoxically, though, her very act of starvation recognises her place in this order because her body becomes the site of spectacular display. Alternatively or simultaneously, she may have internalised the male desire for the phallicised pubescent female body. In *The Obsession: Reflections on the Tyranny of Slenderness*, Kim Chernin describes her own anorexic experience:

> I reverted to a fantasy about my body's transformation from this state of imperfection to a consummate loveliness, the flesh trimmed away, stomach flat, thighs like those of the adolescent runner on the back slopes of the fire trail, a boy of fifteen or sixteen, running along there one evening in a pair of red trunks, stripped to the waist, gleaming with sweat and suntan oil, his muscles stretching and relaxing, as if he'd been sent out there to model for me a vision of everything I was not and could not be.[69]

Once more we have the image of the male adolescent as an object of beauty, this time as having the body that this anorexic woman desires.

The male consumption of the female body which takes place through spectacularising surveillance is sometimes literalised in cannibalistic consumption. In Western culture the consumption of the female body by men – whether through surveillance or eating – is, of course, overdetermined as an effect of the cultural-fetishistic desire to acquire the phallus. In this world dominated by consumption, the desire of appetite and sexual desire meet in cannibalism. Freud describes how a child goes through two pre-genital phases of psychosexual development, the oral and the anal-sadistic, during the time before latency. He writes: 'The first of these is the oral or, as it might be called, cannibalistic pregenital sexual organization. Here sexual activity has not yet been separated from the ingestion of food'.[70] The child wants to eat whatever it desires. Freud is here emphasising the bodily, sensual pleasure of eating. It is this pleasure that modernity denied in the process which Freud identifies as culminating in latency. Bodily pleasure was reduced to genital, sexual pleasure. Freud argues that in the oral stage hunger and sexual desire are conflated. Cultural fetishism provides a context in which this repressed experience returns in a newly energised way. In this context, from the late nineteenth century on, the theme of cannibalism has taken on a new cultural salience. Freud's use of it as a metaphor in his discussion of the oral stage can be understood as a late-nineteenth- and twentieth-century male sexual fantasy of adult life.

Consider again Freud's myth of the origin of society: 'One day the brothers who had been driven out [by the primal father] came together, killed and devoured their father and so made an end to the patriarchal horde'.[71] When I discussed this story in the Introduction I concentrated, as most people do, on the killing of the Father. Here, I want to focus on his cannibalistic consumption. In Freud's story the sons are, literally, internalising the phallic power of the Father. Freud writes: 'The violent primal father had doubtless been the feared and envied model of each one of the company of brothers: and in the act of devouring him they accomplished their identification with him, and each one of them acquired a portion of his strength'.[72] In the Introduction, I discussed this societal origin myth as a way of thinking about the experience of the modern state, and I proposed the male experience of the patriarchal and phallic modern state as the cause of the development of cultural fetishism. Now we can see that, in addition, Freud's myth literalises the consumption of the phallus as a male cannibal meal. Read in the context of Freud's story, today's myth of cannibalism is, ultimately, a male fantasy of men acquiring power by consuming the phallus. In the spectacularised cultural order, the fetishised female body substitutes for the impossible dream of consuming the primal phallus.

The case which perhaps most clearly sets out what is at issue in present-day cannibalism occurred in 1981. A Japanese student, Issei Sagaua, completing his doctorate in Paris, became friendly with a young Dutch woman. The Japanese man wanted a more sexual relationship. The woman did not. One night he invited the Dutch girl round for a meal. When she arrived he taped her reading some poetry. Whilst she was reading he shot her. He then had sexual intercourse with her body. Later he dismembered it, taking a number of Polaroid photographs – yes, photography again – as he did so, and retained some edible parts. Eating some of these, he placed the rest in the fridge and disposed of the remainder of the body. Over the next few weeks he cooked various meals with the parts he had reserved. When he was caught he is quoted as saying, 'I have always dreamed of being able to eat a pretty young girl'.[73] Baudrillard has taken an interest in this case. He remarks that 'the silence of metaphor accompanies the cruel act, thus the Japanese cannibal passed directly from the metaphor of love to the devouring of that marvellous young Dutch girl'.[74] In television interviews Sagaua has been more explicit, saying that his sexual desire for the woman amounted to desiring to eat her. The first thing to notice about this case is that it is the male who eats and the woman who is eaten. In Western culture it is only the male lover who means to flatter when he says, in adoring tones, 'You look so good I could eat you'.[75] In the Sagaua case we can see the conflation of eating and sexual satisfaction. As Jonathan Friedman puts it: 'His consumption of her body was also the consummation of his love'.[76]

The French decided that Sagaua was insane and deported him to Japan. In Japan, after spending some time in an asylum, it was decided he was sane and he was freed. Sagaua now lives off writing books and giving interviews for which he charges. He has become a celebrity, something which illustrates the general fascination with what he did. The inability to decide whether he was sane or insane suggests the cultural complexity of his act. His murder and cannibalism are indeed shocking – but do they not act out something men structured into cultural fetishism find understandable? Finally, it must be remembered that Sagaua is Japanese and the woman was Dutch. Inflecting this fetishist's behaviour is a postcolonial revenge. Sagaua says that he only wants to eat white women. They are, of course, the most desirable – delicious? – for him.

The structure of cultural fetishism constructs men as the eaters and women's bodies – or, indeed, other men's bodies – as the eaten phallic fetishes. From the perspective of a different argument, Joy McEntee writes that recent 'feminist analysis has revealed the material dependence of public masculine power on the consumption and abjection of women in private'.[77] From this point of view it is not surprising that so many male serial killers, who seem to act out many of Western culture's fantasies, eat parts of their female victims. Over the last twenty years or so cannibalism has become a more common, though still relatively rare, practice in films. Most obvious in horror films but gradually spreading to mainstream films, it reached mainstream acceptance with *Alive!* (1992), the dramatised story of an actual event in 1972 when the members of a Uruguayan rugby team, having survived a plane crash in the Andes, had to eat the bodies of their team-mates whilst they waited to be rescued. Cannibalism is a central theme in films as varied as *Cannibal Apocalypse* (early 1980s), *Eating Raoul* (1982), *Cannibal Women of the Avocado Jungle of Death* (1988), *Lucky Stiff* (1988), *Parents* (1989), *Eat the Rich* (1987), and *The Cook, The Thief, His Wife and Her Lover* (1989). In *Alive!*, where men eat men, the fantasy expression of consuming male–male desire is masked by the assertion of factual truth. Even though the plot revolves around the rescue of the survivors, the film reaches a climax when the first piece of flesh is taken from one of the frozen bodies and eaten. Many cannibal films, especially those including female cannibals, are comedies, the horror of the cannibalism being undercut by the comedy. *Cannibal Women of the Avocado Jungle of Death* has *Playboy* pin-up Shannon Tweed as a star and combines the spectacle of desirable female bodies with the satirical irony that these bodies belong to a tribe of radical feminist cannibals who eat men.

*The Cook, The Thief, His Wife and Her Lover* has a transgressive, revengeful climax in which Georgina, the abused wife, forces her gangster husband to eat the body of her lover, whom he has had killed. After he has taken a bite, Georgina shoots him. In her discussion of this film McEntee concentrates on Georgina's destruction of Spica's masculine privilege.[78] However, I would suggest another reading. Spica treats Georgina like a spectacular, eroticised commodity, but he is not that sexually interested in her himself. Instead, he concentrates his energy on the abuse and subjection of his male subordinates – as well as Georgina. This constant abuse suggests his insecurity with his own power. At the same time, his homosocial preoccupations may be read as a repression of a fetishistic homosexual desire, a desire, in this case, born of a need to reassure himself of his complete authority. Spica's authoritarian order can be read as an analogy of the homosocial world of the social contract, and the public domain of the modern state. What Spica cannot express is exactly his fetishistic need to consume his subordinates in order to give himself the patriarchal power of the Father he is so fearful he lacks. When Georgina forces him to eat her lover the circuit of Spica's sexual/abusive desire is closed. His death at Georgina's hands may be read by men as far more than simply her revenge. It is an expression of the male fear of the phallic woman and of the possible consequences of female empowerment.

In *Parents* a ten-year-old boy discovers his parents' secret – they eat people. One of the recurring images in the film is the son's discovery of his parents making love whilst simultaneously eating (human) meat in what is clearly itself an erotic act. In this film it turns out that cannibalism is handed down through the male line. The husband seduced his wife into becoming a cannibal. This narrative operates within the structure of consuming cultural-fetishistic desire, which, as we have seen, is male-driven but which women are also interpellated into as consumers. From the point of view of individual development, the film follows a Freudian course constructing cannibalism as the repressed aspect of sexual desire – an aspect of the oral stage which is past and its memories repressed during latency. (This is something which could be said about the Sagaua case also.) The film's narrative is focused on the adolescent son and his horror at his discovery. In this film's patriarchal ordering of cannibalism one of the victims is the son's female psychiatrist from school, who, concerned about the son's behaviour, has come to the house and discovered the family's secret. Michael, the son, is forced by his parents to eat her, implying that, through this ingestion of the phallic fetish, he will grow up and take on adult male responsibilities. Interestingly, after appeals from his mother, Breuer's anorexic twelve-year-old boy told how: 'While on his way home from school he had gone into a urinal, and a man had held out his penis to him and asked him to take it in his mouth. He had run away in terror, and nothing else had happened to him'.[79] The boy's symptoms appeared from this time. Of course, it is possible that this event actually happened, but the story reads very much as a metaphor for accepting male adulthood through the ingestion of the penis/phallus. Even if the story is true the hysterical reaction has this as a cultural component. The boy's symptoms disappeared as soon as he had told the story. In *Parents* Michael rebels and stabs his father with a knife. When his mother comes to Michael's aid his father kills her and, subsequently, Michael kills his father, in the process setting fire to the house. Michael's virtuous rejection of his parents is also, ironically, a rejection of his own manhood as well as a destruction of the nuclear family. When he is sent to be looked after by his kindly grandparents until he is an adult, they feed him a sandwich of human meat. Michael, it seems, cannot escape.

In some of these cannibal films, such as *Parents* and the cannibal comedy *Lucky Stiff*, there are cannibal families in which cannibalism is inherited; whether culturally or biologically is unclear. In this way the cannibal narrative is made safe: cannibal tendencies are something that other people (ultimately men) have, rather than something which permeates our culture. In *Lucky Stiff* sexual desire and cannibalism are combined when the attractive daughter of the very patriarchal cannibal family goes off to search for a man, suitable for Christmas dinner, to seduce. The family is incestuous by generations, so it will be her brother/lover who will kill and dress the chosen man. The film focuses on the daughter, constructing her as active and phallic, and producing both desire and fear in the male audience. It is driven by the male fear of the sexually active woman who will not only seduce him – that is what he would like – but, as a virago, will, in this case literally, consume him. This is set within a larger structure which establishes cannibalism as, ultimately, men's concern: it is the father who rules the family (in a phallic challenge to the state he allows one of his sons to kill the local sheriff for further provisions) and the eldest son who prepares the victims.

One schlock-horror film in which the horror is provoked by the male concerns of fetishistic male desire, making use of both the cannibalism theme and the vaginal-mouth theme, is *Bloodsucking Freaks* (1982). This film has become a cult classic. As McEntee remarks in her brief discussion of it: 'Cannibalistic revenge as a woman's art is confined to arthouse films and Z-grade porno flicks, like *Bloodsucking Freaks*'.[80] (Female eating of men seems to be still too powerful a transgression for mainstream horror films.) The film's narrative concerns Sadu, the gay Master of the Theater of the Macabre, who runs an off-off-Broadway theatre specialising in the sadistic torture of naked women. He also has a very lucrative international white-slavery business. In the cellars under the theatre he keeps a group of naked women in a cell, where they have become animalised by their experience. Sadu wants his theatrical work to be recognised as art, and to this end kidnaps a well-known ballerina and an eminent theatre critic. However, the narrative takes second place to the set-piece scenes intended to provoke horror and, sometimes, male desire. Sadu and his offsider eat the women they kill and make the kidnapped theatre critic eat them also. At one point a corrupt doctor is repaid for his services by being allowed to do anything he likes to a woman. He extracts her teeth before forcing her to suck him off. Afterwards, in a vampiric echo, he drinks her brains through a straw in her skull. The caged women have also become cannibals and, when Sadu wants to get rid of the doctor, he is given to them. At the end of the film the corrupt policeman investigating Sadu is eaten by the caged women, who, now released, go on to eat Sadu and his offsider. In the final shot one of the women has a penis – we presume it is Sadu's – in a hot-dog bun and is about to consume it; the vaginal mouth forced on the tortured woman by the patriarchal doctor is now transformed as the freed women assert their new power, in a transgressive echo of the original cannibalistic meal suggested by Freud, by eating the penis of the patriarch, the Master, who dominated them.

The cultural genealogy of films whose central theme is cannibalism lies in the vampire fantasies of the second half of the nineteenth century. Starting with Polidori's story *The Vampyre* (1818), the vampire theme rapidly became a commonplace of horror, climaxing in Bram Stoker's *Dracula*, published in 1897. Dijkstra connects the spread of the vampire myth with the claimed life-enhancing properties of blood during this period. In addition to tuberculosis, anaemia 'plagued and weakened so many middle-class women, and … was deemed a principal source of the weakness of effeminate males'.[81] Dijkstra goes on:

> What better way to strengthen one's blood, it was reasoned, than to drink the blood of others – not that of humans, to be sure, but the blood of strong animals like oxen. This blood should be as fresh as possible. In consequence, slaughter-houses everywhere began to attract 'blood drinkers', anemics who came to ingest their daily cup of ox blood.[82]

These drinkers would have been, in the main, female. However, with the exception of Sheridan Le Fanu's eponymous vampire in 'Carmilla', a short story first published in 1879, the vast majority of these creatures were male, though Stoker's Dracula, signalling an excessive, phallic desire, had a small harem of three female vampires whom he had inducted. The point is that the effect of the structuring system is such that, where the female vampire presents the threat of the active, sexually aggressive woman, the male vampire provides a male transgressive fantasy of the consumption, if not of the female body then at least of her blood – with the further *frisson* of the transgression of Christian ritual.

The vampire myth may have had some historical connection with a cure for female anaemia, but it also presented a partially repressed expression of the new male desire to consume women. Projected on to women, the female vampiric act was clearly sexualised. For example, in a 1922 popular guide, *Married Life and Happiness*, William Robinson, M.D., chief of the Department of Genito-Urinary Disorders and Dermatology at the Bronx Hospital, wrote: 'Just as the vampire sucks the blood of its victims in their sleep while they are alive, so does the woman vampire suck the life and exhaust the vitality of her male partner – or victim'.[83] Here we have an equivalence drawn between the vampire's mouth and the woman's vagina, an equivalence which expresses the gradual eroticisation of the mouth and its conflation with the vagina which has already been described.

Whilst the main character is usually male in vampire stories, his victims – true to heterosexual desire – are without fail female. Dijkstra notes that in the late nineteenth century men's fear of the sexually active woman had found its image in the female vampire: 'By 1900 the vampire had come to represent woman as the personification of everything negative that linked sex, ownership and money'.[84] The post-First World War phallicised female form of the easy-going pleasure-seeking flapper – a version of the 'passive' female spectacle that men desired – formed a seamless pair with the earlier image of the vamp – a version of the 'active' female spectacle that men both desired and feared:

> The serpentine slimness that at the turn of the century had been associated with the femme fatale – the dangerous but exciting vamp with an insatiable appetite for money, power, and sex, the exotic outlaw who enticed men to their ruin – had suddenly become mainstream and fashionable. The young flappers tried to cultivate this flavor of the exotic and mysterious sexuality portrayed so well on the silent screen by Theda Bara, Pola Negri, and later by Greta Garbo. The term *sex appeal* entered the vernacular, and sex appeal, not modesty, demureness, or regal elegance became the goal for many women in both fashion and behavior.[85]

Where Dijkstra identifies the female vampire as being associated with sex and money, Seid here provides a similar description of the vamp. Dijkstra adds ownership: the point is really the symbolic power which accrues to the spectacle of commodity ownership. Seid adds power, which overlaps with this spectacle but, in Seid's context, also includes the more general sense of a power that is active, acting on the world – phallic power. Aptly, Seid describes these women using a term applicable to both vampirism and cannibalism, writing that they have an 'insatiable appetite'. They are consumers. For men, on the one hand, the vamp epitomised the combination of desire and fear which is found in the active phallic fetish. On the other hand, the category of the vamp provided women with a context for a new public assertiveness and independence – drinking, smoking, travel, and so forth – which were a part of the everyday-life gains fought for by first-wave feminism and summed up in the descriptive term New Woman.

In this chapter we have discussed the eroticisation of the female mouth, the phallicisation of the female body, and both in the context of consumption. With the spread of consumption capitalism the meaning of consumption has been transformed. It no longer means to waste or use up, but rather to acquire or accumulate. This meaning fits well with the organisation of cultural-fetishistic desire, in which the desire is to possess and assimilate the fetish. The articulation together of cultural-fetishistic desire and consumption capitalism has produced a dominant cultural structure in the West which is played out in everyday life through men's consumption of women's bodies by sight or by cannibalism and through women's consumption of commodities by sight or purchase.

## NOTES

1   On the shifts in meaning surrounding the term, see the entry 'Consumer' in R. Williams's *Keywords* (London, Fontana, 1976).

2   S. Sontag, *Illness as Metaphor* (New York, Vintage Books, 1979), p. 9.

3   *Ibid.*, p. 16.

4   K. Chernin, *Womansize: The Tyranny of Slenderness* (London, Women's Press, 1983), p. 46.

5   B. Dijkstra, *Idols of Perversity: Fantasies of Feminine Evil in Fin-de-siècle Culture* (New York, Oxford University Press, 1986), p. 355.

6   M. Seltzer, *Bodies and Machines* (New York, Routledge, 1992), p. 153.

7   A. Goold Woolson, *Women in American Society* (Boston, 1873), p. 136. Here quoted from Dijkstra, *Idols of Perversity*, p. 29.

8   L. Gamman and M. Makinen, *Female Fetishism: A New Look* (London, Lawrence and Wishart, 1994), p. 146.

9   *Ibid.*, p. 153.

10   J. Craik, in *The Face of Fashion: Cultural Studies in Fashion* (London, Routledge, 1994), explains that in the 1930s, spreading outwards from their use by film stars, 'cosmetics became an accepted part of women's "beauty" routines as a technique of self-presentation and prestigious imitation' (p. 160). She goes on to discuss Revlon's 1952 'Fire-and-Ice promotion', which offered women 'a range of lipsticks and nail polishes in "passionate' reds" ( p. 161).

11   L. Williams, *Hard Core: Power, Pleasure, and the "Frenzy of the Visible"*, (Berkeley, University of California Press, 1989), p. 99.

12   *Ibid.*, p. 100.

13   *Ibid.*, p. 111.

14   There is another point to make about *Deep Throat*. To quote Williams in *Hard Core* again: 'In just about every sense, *Deep Throat* can be said – for all its talk about the clitoris – visually to fetishise the penis' (p. 112).

15   P. Mason, *Deconstructing America: Representations of the Other* (London, Routledge, 1990), p. 139.

16  Dijkstra, *Idols of Perversity*, p. 309.

17  *Ibid.*, pp. 273–4.

18  *Ibid.*, p. 310.

19  A. Wernick, *Promotional Culture: Advertising, Ideology and Symbolic Expression* (London, Sage, 1991), p. 74.

20  N. Wolf, *The Beauty Myth* (New York, W. Morrow, 1991), quoted in Gamman and Makinen, *Female Fetishism*, p. 156.

21  M. Gabor, *The Pin-up: A Modest History* (New York, Universe Books, 1972), p. 47.

22  Illustrations in *ibid.*, p. 46.

23  *Ibid.*, pp. 76–7.

24  R. P. Seid, *Never Too Thin: Why Women are at War with their Bodies* (New York, Prentice Hall, 1989), p. 71.

25  *Ibid.*, p. 81.

26  *Ibid.*, p. 81.

27  *Ibid.*, p. 81.

28  *Ibid.*, pp. 90–91.

29  *Ibid.*, p. 93.

30  *Ibid.*, p. 103.

31  *Ibid.*, p. 110.

32  P. Fass, *The Damned and the Beautiful: American Youth in the 1920s* (New York, Oxford University Press, 1977), p. 6.

33  *Ibid.*, p. 221.

34  J. Stratton, *The Young Ones: Working Class Culture, Consumption and the Category of Youth* (Perth, Black Swan Press, 1992), p. 189.

35  Seid, *Never Too Thin*, p. 137.

36  *Ibid.*, p. 148.

37  *Ibid.*, p. 250.

38  L. Baker, 'London Girls', in *The Face*, no. 45 (June 1992) p. 41.

39  S. D'Erasmo, 'Poison Flower Child', *Village Voice*, June 15, 1993.

40  J. Breuer and S. Freud, *Studies on Hysteria (1893-1895)*, in *The Standard Edition of the Complete Works of Sigmund Freud*, translated under the general editorship of James Strachey in collaboration with Anna Freud (London, Hogarth Press/Institute of Psycho-Analysis), vol. 2 (1958), p. 212.

41  All this information is drawn from J. J. Brumberg, *Fasting Girls: The History of Anorexia Nervosa* (New York, New American Library, 1989), chs 4 and 5.

42  *Ibid.*, p. 127.

43 *Ibid.*, p. 162.

44 *Ibid.*, p. 150.

45 S. Heath, *The Sexual Fix* (London, Macmillan, 1982), p. 25.

46 Dijkstra, *Idols of Perversity*, p. 54.

47 *Ibid.*, p. 54.

48 I. Veith, *Hysteria: The History of a Disease* (Chicago, University of Chicago Press, 1965), p. 230.

49 Dijkstra, *Idols of Perversity*, p. 42.

50 *Ibid.*, pp. 48, 49.

51 *Ibid.*, pp. 50–63.

52 *Ibid.*, p. 45.

53 *Ibid.*, p. 45.

54 *Ibid.*, p. 54.

55 S. Gilman, *Sexuality: An Illustrated History: representing the sexual in medicine and culture from the Middle Ages to the age of AIDS* (New York, Wiley, 1989), p. 249.

56 E. Bronfen, *Over Her Dead Body: Death, Femininity and the Aesthetic* (New York, Routledge, 1992), p. 264.

57 Seid, *Never Too Thin*, p. 77.

58 *Ibid.*, p. 77.

59 Brumberg devotes a chapter to 'Fasting Girls' (*Fasting girls*, ch. 3).

60 Seid, *Never Too Thin*, p. 97.

61 *Ibid.*, p. 262.

62 These figures are quoted in W. Stewart Agras, *Eating Disorders: Management of Obesity, Bulimia, and Anorexia Nervosa* (New York, Pergamon, 1987), p. 4.

63 P. Garfinkel and D. Garner, *Anorexia Nervosa: A Multidimensional Approach* (New York, Brunner/Mazel, 1982), p. 101.

64 Quoted in P. Stallybrass and A. White, *The Politics and Poetics of Transgression* (London, Methuen, 1986), p. 165.

65 Quoted in Brumberg, *Fasting Girls*, p. 319, n. 18.

66 S. Bordo, 'Reading the Slender Body', in M. Jacobus *et al.* (eds), *Body/Politics: Women and the Discourse of Science* (New York, Routledge, 1990), p. 99.

67 M. Atwood, *The Edible Woman* (Toronto, Seal, [1969] 1978), p. 271.

68 Quoted in Brumberg, *Fasting girls*, p. 68.

69 K. Chernin, *The Obsession: Reflections on the Tyranny of Slenderness* (1981), quoted here from N. Caskey, 'Interpreting Anorexia Nervosa', in S. R. Suleiman (ed.), *The Female Body in Western Culture: Contemporary Perspectives* (Cambridge, Mass., Harvard

University Press, 1986), p. 178.

70  S. Freud, *Three Essays on the Theory of Sexuality*, in *The Standard Edition*, vol. 7 (1953), p. 198.

71  S. Freud, *Totem and Taboo*, in *The Standard Edition*, vol. 13 (1955), p. 141.

72  *Ibid.*, p. 142.

73  This outline is taken from J. Friedman, 'Consuming Desires: Strategies of Selfhood and Appropriation', in *Cultural Anthropology*, 6:2 (1991), pp. 154–63. The quotation from I. Sagaua (the Japanese man) is from the *Paris-Match* of 27 May 1983.

74  Quoted in M. Bane, *Baudrillard: Critical and Fatal Theory* (London, Routledge, 1991), p. 61. The quotation is from Baudrillard's *Cool Memories* (Eng. trans. 1990).

75  Reminiscent of Marian's ploy in *The Edible Woman*, there are now novelty cake shops which make cakes in the shape of women's torsos. In Sidney Mintz's study of the place of sugar in modern history, *Sweetness and Power* (New York, Penguin, 1986), there is an undated photograph with an inscription which reads: 'Etienne Tholoniat, a great French sugar baker, puts the finishing touches on a life-size chocolate nude with spun-sugar hair. She is lying on a bed of six hundred sugar roses.'

76  Friedman, 'Consuming Desires', p. 154.

77  J. McEntee, 'Ladies, Bring a Poisoned Plate: Cinematic Representations of the Vengeful Woman', in *Media Information Australia*, no. 72 (May, 1994), p. 42.

78  *Ibid.*, pp. 42-5.

79  Breuer and Freud, *Studies on Hysteria*, in *The Standard Edition*, vol. 2, p. 212.

80  McEntee, 'Ladies, Bring a Poisoned Plate', p. 47.

81  Dijkstra, *Idols of Perversity*, p. 337.

82  *Ibid.*, p. 337.

83  Quoted in *ibid.*, p. 334.

84  *Ibid.*, p. 351.

85  Seid, *Never Too Thin*, p. 92.

6

# The spectacularisation
# of the male body

In Chapter 4 we saw how the discursive construction of the male homosexual was, in part, dependent on the new circuit of male desire which was formed as an aspect of the spread of cultural fetishism. The desire to acquire the phallus led to a cultural situation in which the supplementary desire for women's bodies which constructed them as fetishised, spectacular phallic substitutes was one instance of a generalised fetishistic desire which was ultimately ordered by a homosocial male desire in which other men were either narcissistically identified with as being/possessing the phallus, or else could be consumed to provide the phallus. However, for reasons I discussed in that chapter, male–male desire was proscribed and the female body was fetishised as the most important phallic substitute. In the desiring structure I have been describing, women's bodies were made visible, constructed as a spectacle, whilst men became the invisible source of the fetishising gaze. At the same time that their bodies were spectacularised women were also becoming constructed as consumers, firstly as their attempt to complement their phallic 'lack', an experience which was imposed on them by men, and, secondly and complementarily with this overdetermining structure, narcissistically. In this fetishising and consuming system men's bodies were made to be invisible. Any display of the male body might entice a homoerotic desire from a male population in the thrall of cultural fetishism. The spectacular display of the male body was limited and ghettoised in homosexual pornography.

In the mid-to-late-1960s two events took place, the complex connections between which form a context for this chapter. One was the liberalisation of attitudes towards male homosexuality. In

Britain, the Sexual Offences Act of 1967 decriminalised male homosexual activities in private for adults over the age of twenty-one.[1] Across Europe and in the United States similar reforms were taking place. The New York Gay Liberation Front was founded in 1969 and, confirming the new visibility of male homosexuals, the first Gay Pride march took place in New York in 1970. The London Gay Liberation Front was founded in 1970, and from this period there was a constant campaign for homosexuals to 'come out of the closet'. The change in terminology from 'homosexual' to 'gay' marks this shift. Weeks writes that the latter word 'had been used by homosexuals in the United States at least since the 1950s, but in Britain, though it was known, it tended to have an upper-class connotation'.[2] Through the 1970s 'gay', a word chosen by homosexuals themselves, increasingly became the generally acceptable term.

The second event was the spreading acceptance of male consumerism. Robert Bocock suggests that gay men 'have been defined as pleasure-seeking consumers, hedonists, *par excellence*'[3] in recent Western culture. He argues that it was the acceptance of male homosexuality in the late 1960s and 1970s which provided a context in which gay men could pioneer the acceptability of male consumerism:

> There developed … more clothing stores for men; men in general were a growing market for clothing, and gay men often set up, or worked in, such shops. Newspapers, magazines and books related to gay issues developed; discos for gay men were started. Even particular holiday resorts developed for gays in Europe, north Africa, Asia and the United States, for instance.[4]

For the first time, men in general were being targeted as consumers in the expanding consumption order of capitalism. This development drove the spectacularisation of the male body, and gays were in the forefront.

There is a prehistory to the general acceptance of men's consumption in Britain, and this is to be found in the male participants in youth cultures. Working-class teddy boys and lower-middle-class mods both revelled in the new availability of quality, tailor-made clothes that made them look stylish and sharp.[5] To quote the title of George Melley's early discussion of British pop culture and youth culture, it was a 'revolt into style'.[6] Indeed, by the late 1960s the male fashion styles of the mods were being appropriated and reworked for mainstream acceptability. By the time of punk in the late 1970s male clothing fashions had become so generally accepted that punks could only make their spectacular, oppositional statement by establishing an anti-style with ripped clothes, safety pins, and non-clothes such as plastic binliners.[7] It is because of the changed context of consumption in which punk was staged that it can be described as the last of the traditional post-Second World War British youth cultures. After it, youth cultures in Britain have become segmented style groupings within a wider spectrum of consumption-oriented youth styles.

The spectacularisation of the female body and of the male body had different sources. Where the female body was spectacularised as the effect of cultural fetishism, the male body was placed on display for men as a consequence of the expansionary attempt to create a new male consumer market. This produced a relation of visibility in which, for the first time, men gazed on male bodies. Unlike women, however, men were culturally constructed as having an active sexual desire. Where the cultural order asserted that women could gaze without sexual desire on other female bodies – only identifying with them narcissistically – men's active, and indeed fetishising, sexual desire created the possibility that men might be stimulated into desiring other men. At this point we need to extend our discussion of the gaze in order to theorise the conditions under which men gaze on the male body. In Chapter 3 I briefly outlined Laura Mulvey's psychoanalytic argument about the gaze of the film viewer: 'The determining male gaze projects its phantasy on to the female figure which is styled accordingly'.[8] The male fantasy that Mulvey refers to here is a product of the male experience of the castration complex. She argues that 'woman as representation signifies castration, inducing voyeuristic or fetishistic mechanisms to circumvent her threat'.[9] My point was that, reworking Mulvey's generalising psychoanalytic account as a culturally specific, historical account, we can take her work as a description of how the fetishising male gaze operates across all visual media to eroticise the female body, reforming it into a libidinally charged spectacle.

In an article entitled 'Masculinity as Spectacle' Steve Neale has taken up Mulvey's argument, examining how the male gaze looks at other men.[10] Neale begins by extending a point of Mulvey's, that the male viewer identifies with the main male protagonist: 'Narcissism and narcissistic identification both involve phantasies of power, omnipotence, mastery and control'.[11] He notes: 'It is easy enough to find examples of films in which these phantasies are heavily prevalent, in which the male hero is powerful and omnipotent to an extraordinary degree.'[12] Neale's examples include Clint Eastwood's spaghetti westerns and the *Mad Max* films. To these we can add the male 'body' films of the 1980s which I will discuss later in this chapter, including those of Arnold Schwarzenegger and Sylvester Stallone and the martial-arts films of the same period starring the likes of David Carradine (for part of his long career), Chuck Norris, and Jean-Claude Van Damme. This discussion of identification should not stop at narcissism, however. The reason why male narcissism involves those fantasies Neale lists is because the man with whom the male viewer is narcissistically identifying exhibits, either in his body or in his actions, phallic power. The description of the narcissistic fantasy is, in fact, of the power of the phallus which men lack. The narcissistic identification with a hero as played by Clint Eastwood or Sylvester Stallone is a strategy of fantastic identification with the power of the phallus. What we have here, then, is another version of the 'blond god' myth discussed in Chapter 4.

Further on in his article Neale quotes from D. N. Rodowick's discussion of Mulvey's argument: 'Mulvey discusses the male star as an object of the look but denies him the function of an erotic object.'[13] Taking up this idea, and by way of a discussion of Paul Willemen's article 'Anthony Mann: Looking at the Male',[14] Neale argues that the male viewer's pleasures from watching the hero 'are founded upon a repressed homosexual voyeurism'.[15] In Neale's words, Willemen argues that 'the repression of any explicit avowal of eroticism in the act of looking at the male seems structurally linked to a narrative content marked by sado-masochistic phantasies and scenes'.[16] Commenting on Willemen's position, Neale writes: 'The (unstated) thesis behind these comments seems to be that in a heterosexual and patriarchal society, the male body cannot be marked explicitly as the erotic object of another male look: that look must be motivated in some other way, its erotic component repressed.'[17] Thus, for example, the sadism and mutilation which often occur in Mann's films – and in many other films such as Clint Eastwood's spaghetti westerns and, I would add, many of the films of Stallone, Norris, and the other male 'body' stars – provide a way of repressing homoerotic desire and of disqualifying the male body from being an object of erotic contemplation.

It is important to note in Neale's argument how the narcissism discussion spills over into the discussion of repressed sexual desire. The reason we can give for the connection between these two aspects is that both are motivated by the same fetishistic desire, to internalise, consume, possess the phallus. Since, as we have seen, this is one of the fundamental elements in the modern construction of homosexuality, it is not surprising that Neale should subsequently make the connection with homosexuality:

> I would certainly concur with Mulvey's basic premise that the spectatorial look in mainstream cinema is implicitly male: it is one of the fundamental reasons why the erotic elements involved in the relations between the spectator and the male image have constantly to be repressed and disavowed. Were this not the case, mainstream cinema would have openly to come to terms with the male homosexuality it so assiduously seeks either to denigrate or deny.[18]

As I explained in Chapter 4, in post-1850s everyday life the problem of the male gaze on other men was dealt with by making male fashion colourless and by prosecuting those who desired (or seemed to desire) other men. In addition, social and legal pressures were placed on those – identified as homosexuals – whose dress had the potential for marking their bodies as the site for a homoerotic gaze. Oscar Wilde's trials not only constructed an image of the homosexual; they also asserted that that visible image should be hidden, made invisible. Homosexuals were caught in a double bind where, expected to be effeminate, they were expected to exhibit themselves like women, while at the same time such exhibition was considered to be transgressive and its proscription was heavily policed. Only women were allowed to present themselves to the male spectacularising gaze. In these ways, at the same time that women's bodies were becoming spectacularised, so men's bodies were being hidden from sight and men who desired other men's bodies were prosecuted for acts of gross indecency. From the mid-1960s onwards this fetishistic structure of visibility and invisibility became increasingly problematical.

Around the middle of the nineteenth century, the experience of the dandy underwent a change. He became eroticised, his visual spectacle was marked as effeminate, and, with Oscar Wilde's trial, this persona became identified as that of the homosexual. Rosalind Williams argues that the dandy represented the last gasp of male elitist consumption. Writing about Huysmans's novel *A rebours*

(1884), in which the hero, des Esseintes, was based on the dandy and fanatical collector Robert de Montesquiou, she suggests:

> Its immense popularity, or notoriety, indicates that it struck a responsive emotional chord in many readers of the time. *A rebours* is a work of fiction which even more than the biography of an actual dandy illuminates the pleasures and perils of elitist consumption; it portrays a lonely and agonized attempt to salvage the elitist ideal in an age of mass consumption.[19]

Elite consumption had been a male preserve at a time when power related to visibility.

Following a suggestion of Rachel Bowlby's in *Just Looking*, Rita Felski makes the point that 'the aesthete and the dandy [share] with women an identity as consumer'.[20] Since the aesthete and the dandy were being constituted as homosexual we can add that the proscription of the homosexual was, simultaneously, a proscription of the male as consumer. Felski makes the further point that 'it becomes imperative for the [aesthete/dandy] to signal the superior taste and the qualitative difference of his own aesthetic response'[21] from that of women. In Oscar Wilde's description of his possessions in *De profundis*, possessions to be sold as a consequence of his forced bankruptcy, we have a good example of this combination of the aesthetic with consumption:

> all my charming things were to be sold: my Burne-Jones drawings: my Whistler drawings: my Monticelli, my Simeon Solomons: my china: my library with its collection of presentation volumes from almost every poet of my time, from Hugo to Whitman, from Swinburne to Mallarmé, from Morris to Verlaine: with its beautifully bound editions of my father's and mother's works, its wonderful array of college and school prizes: its *éditions de luxe*, and the like … [22]

This catalogue of precious consumables through which Wilde constructed his life as a visible work of art has, itself, a fetishistic quality. Each item adds to the image being constructed to produce a total image which is necessarily more impressive than the person who is putting the image together. In other words, Wilde is constructing himself as a spectacle. Here, the difference between the aesthete/dandy as consumer and women as consumers is that, where the latter operate in the realm of fashion, the former constructs himself as a work of art (paralleling the masquerade of the effeminate homosexual) through his aesthetic sensibility.

*De profundis* is cast in the form of a letter from Wilde to his friend, and the cause of his downfall, Bosie – Sir Alfred Douglas. In his description of their relationship Wilde spends much time providing an account of the money he spent on Douglas's pleasures – from expensive meals, and trips abroad, to paying for his gambling excesses. Douglas, cast in the role of the ephebe by Wilde, is the young man who, no matter how much he consumes, will always fall short of fulfilling his phallic desire; he will never transform himself into a 'blond god'. Wilde describes the extreme hatred Douglas had for his father, something not surprising on this reading. As unthinking consumer, Douglas has a lot in common with Nabokov's characterisation of Lolita, and both have consumer goods lavished on them by older men trying to buy their love. Both narratives are, in different ways, about transgressive desire and its relation to consumption. Both can be read as moral tales about the impossibility of buying the phallus for either of the parties in both of the relationships.

Andrew Wernick argues that the targeting of men as consumers took place on two fronts. First, there was the breakdown of the traditional gender division of labour which placed women in the home as the consumers and men in the workplace as producers. As more women were drawn into the workplace since the 1960s, so, 'even if slow to adapt, male partners have gradually been forced to take greater responsibility for domestic chores so that few of either sex are now unfamiliar with the joys of supermarkets and shopping malls'.[23] To this change in family life Wernick adds 'the growth in the number of students, the rise in the age at first marriage, the increase in divorce rates, and the open emergence of gay households'.[24] However, these changes do not expand by very much consumption itself. This can be achieved either by increasing the amount that is consumed of what is on offer or by increasing the variety of products on offer whilst at worst holding present consumption levels of each commodity steady and thereby increasing overall consumption. Given the limitations on disposable income, even with the increased availability of credit, the expansion of commodity consumption by targeting men was an ideal solution. As Wernick puts it: 'Beyond the general extension to men of consumer status, there has been an extension in the range of commodities aimed especially at them.'[25] In the period up to and including the 1950s, the list of consumer goods aimed at men was quite short, comprising little more than cars, alcohol, and tools:

The list, today, is much longer. Men confront an ever increasing array of leisure goods (including erotica); their clothing has been fully incorporated into the world of fashion; and mounting efforts have been made to sell them all manner of personal-care products and accessories, from jewellery and athletic trainers, to bath-oil, deodorants, and hair-dye.[26]

What has happened in this expansion of consumer targeting at men is that the male body – like the female body before it – is now being overtly constructed as a site of lack. It is being described in advertising as an incomplete or inadequate body which can be improved by buying these new male-oriented consumer goods.

It has become a Freudian platitude to say that men experience fast cars or machine tools as phallic, but it is important to examine why men might feel a need for such phallic accessories. Simply, it is a further effect of cultural fetishism. The car, or other commodity, is fetishised and consumed as a fantastic attempt to acquire the phallus which the man feels he lacks. In the history of the integration of women into consumption, the fetishisation of women's bodies was followed by the commercial attempt to supplement their feeling of lack with more specific claims about inadequacy which could be solved by the purchase of particular commodities. The male fetishistic preoccupation with women's bodies, which transformed them into a spectacle, thus spilled over into a commercial use of women's bodies which combined male desire with the female sense of lack and with narcissism. Starting from the female body, consumer goods aimed at women, and the associated advertising, have expanded to commodities not connected with the body – from items in the domestic domain such as fridges or kitchen aids, to, more recently, holiday travel and, indeed, cars. In this historical development the 'lack' was first associated with the female body (as a spectacle) and subsequently generalised.

For men, advertising kept away from the male body as much as possible. As in everyday life, it remained hidden, invisible. The male consumer goods most accepted by the male population, and most advertised, were those which were not to do with body image as such – such as cars and tools – or which, like cigarettes and alcohol, were not to do with the visual display of the body, but had more to do with self-image. Commodities which were not to do with the body were mostly advertised using women's bodies as a way of making the commodity more desirable to men. The exploitation of men's fear of their phallic lack was disguised by an apparently straightforward transference of male heterosexual desire from the desirable woman's body to the commodity. The recognition that the spectacularisation of women's bodies was a consequence of their fetishistic phallicisation enables us to appreciate how the 'heterosexual' desire for women's bodies could reinforce the desire for a car or a tool as a phallic substitute. The use of the female body to sell commodities to men distracted the male audience from the male body and worked as a displacement for the repressed male body which could not be shown. With the extension of male consumption to the male body this situation could no longer be preserved, especially as, it must have seemed to the advertisers, if lack could be used to sell to women it could also be used to sell to men.

The spectacularisation of men's bodies in the context of the expansion of male consumption has been difficult because it involves the recognition of men's repressed fear of their 'lack'. In other words, we have two structures here which overlap. First, there is advertising's use of the construction of lack to sell products to fill that lack. As we have already seen, one of the most important changes in the development of modern advertising was the shift from providing information to the attempt to persuade people that a previously unknown, or unthought-about, commodity is, in fact, necessary to them. Second, there is the male experience of phallic lack. The former to some extent develops out of the latter. However, the utilisation of phallic lack in advertising to men, which is part and parcel of the spectacularisation of the male body, involves great fear as well as desire. It is often disguised by the narrative claim that, by using a particular commodity, men will become more attractive to women. This heterosexual emphasis draws attention away from the reason why men would previously not have been attractive to women – that is, within this neurotic male narrative, because of their phallic lack. In day-to-day life this fear of male inadequacy often manifests as a fear of effeminacy, with its negative connotations of the 'weak' male and of homosexuality. Discussing the spread of consumer goods for the male body in the late 1960s, Wolfgang Haug has noted the general concern with overcoming men's fears of seeming to be effeminate if they use such products. He argues that (in the early 1970s):

> In the overall market for male cosmetics, it is still mainly shaving and hair lotions that do the biggest business. A common factor is that their advertising, especially of hair

preparations, is associated with a pseudo-medical rationalization which helps to overcome the masculine inhibitions and
fears of appearing effeminate.[27]

Haug notes how, in 1967, in the cosmetics industry 'the amount
spent on advertising men's perfumes was seven times that on
ladies'[28] and adds, quoting a report, that 'many men shied away
from using cosmetics for "fear of being considered homosexual, or
effeminate"'.[29] This was the acknowledged context when, also in
1967, the first photograph of a male nude was used in advertising
products to men:

> Since the beginning of May 1967, Sélimaille ('Ceinture
> noire') has advertised in France using nude photos of Frank
> Protopapa, who was famous world-wide as the first publicly
> displayed male nude.... Protopapa's nude photos were shot at
> close-up and printed sharply: what his nudity revealed most,
> however, was capital's efforts at profit-making in a particular
> competitive situation. Now, for once, male nudity had turned
> up and had gained entry – if only as a back view at first – into
> the editorial section of magazines, into the theatre and films.[30]

Where late-nineteenth-century male clothing fashion hid the male
body from the problematic, fetishising gaze of other men, the late
1960s began to display that body to other men, rather than to
women. Haug quotes from a 1967 issue of *Der Spiegel*: 'half-naked
men entice us to buy Ronson cigarette lighters and Prestige
perfumes. In France a full-nude has already appeared – albeit rather
out of focus and necessarily at a distance – advertising Pierre
Cardin's perfume for men.'[31]

As the male body began to be displayed as desirable to other
men – with all the homoerotic complexities I have been outlining –
so it also began to be displayed to women. It is important to note
here that the male body was first displayed for other men and then
displayed for women. It is often suggested that the display of the
male body for women was one minor effect of the feminist movement of the late 1960s and 1970s. To some extent this is correct, but
the environment in which this could take place was already developing with the use of desirable male bodies to advertise commodities to men. Whilst it is certainly the case that magazines such as
*Playgirl* and *Viva* modelled the general idea for their images of
male bodies on the female bodies in the likes of *Playboy*, *Penthouse*, and *Mayfair*, the context for this development was the use

by advertising of male bodies which, because of their desirability, carried a complex (homo)erotic charge. In April 1972, the New York edition of *Cosmopolitan* 'featured a centrefold illustration of the actor Burt Reynolds, completely nude though not frontally exposed, and its London counterpart *Cosmopolitan* simultaneously featured Paul de Feu [Germaine Greer's ex-husband] in a similar state.'[32] In Australia, *Cleo* began as a magazine for the new liberated woman in 1972. Its first editorial explained whom it was aimed at:

> We decided that you're an intelligent woman who's inter-
> ested in everything that's going on, the type of person who
> wants a great deal more out of life. Like us, certain aspects of
> Women's Lib appeal to you but you're not aggressive about it.
> And again like us, you're all for men – as long as they know
> their place![33]

*Cleo* also included a nude male centre-spread. The first was of the Australian actor Jack Thompson. *Playgirl* and *Viva*, both more centrally concerned with providing photographs of the naked male body, began in 1973.

Male strippers for women were popularised through the success of Chippendales, a Hollywood nightclub opened in 1979 which featured 'a cast of male exotic dancers and a women-only policy at the door'.[34] Interestingly, in their description of the act Jane and Michael Stern write that, 'like the singing group the Village People, Chippendales' men come on stage dressed as archetypal studs: a construction worker, a cowboy, a cop, a lifeguard, a chauffeur'.[35] In both cases what is put into visibility is the male body as a spectacle. Both the Village People and Chippendales use stereotypical male images which draw on the blond-god myth of phallic power. The Village People were a 1970s American gay disco group, whose major international hits came in 1978 ('Y.M.C.A.'), and 1979 ('In the Navy' and 'Go West'). Their use of such imagery highlights the homosexual ambiguity around such images. Homosexual effemi-nacy mimics a version of what is culturally considered to be female behaviour. Effeminacy demonstrates itself as inauthentic – as camp – and this was how the Village People used the blond-god/stud images they appropriated. Appealing, in the first place, to the men who were a part of the gay disco scene, much of the humour in their performances was lost on audience members who took their spec-tacular style at face value. The connection with male body display for women is that, because of its passivity as a spectacle, these men, who put on the phallic image of the blond god as stud, and in doing so make themselves desirable to the consuming gaze of women, also take on connotations of homosexuality. Since Chippendales, groups of male exotic dancers and male strippers became much more common in the 1980s, reflecting the increased acceptability of the female gaze on the male body. In all cases, though, it is the well-built, blond-god phallic body which is displayed as the object of women's desire.

Once the male body began to appear in advertisements associated with lack, or, more correctly – like women's bodies – as signifiers of the ideal to which male readers could aspire if they bought the product being advertised, then male desire became a problem. Wernick has discussed the changing cultural situation of the male body by comparing a 1959 advertisement with an advertisement for Braggi aftershave which appeared in *Penthouse* in September 1975. In the Braggi advertisement a slim, self-confident, and naked man is shaving with his back to us. We can see his face in the mirror above the wash basin as he watches himself using the razor. Seated next to him is a woman, also poised and self-confident, who is wearing a sophisticated kimono-style bath-robe. She is staring at us as we gaze on the picture. Wernick argues that what is most striking about this advertisement is that, like analogous advertisements for women's cosmetics, it is structured narcissistically. Not asking why it is that the female narcissistic look is not homoerotic, Wernick argues that: 'the ad's treatment of narcissism is especially norm-breaking':

> The homoerotic desire which is always implicit in taking one-self as a sexual object, and which conventional masculinity is largely constituted as a reaction against … , is here fully exposed. And not only (though they are doubtless one of the target markets) in a way designed to appeal to gays. For as our eye strays to inspect the man's body, it is constantly inter-rupted by the eyes of the woman who is herself always looking on. Those eyes both judge and condone. But they provide, both for him and for us, a crucial heterosexual cover.[36]

In providing a heterosexual cover they help repress the phallic yearning which structures the address of the advertisement for a male reader, whether 'homosexual' or 'heterosexual'. It is also important to note here that Wernick reads the advertisement as appealing to both gays and heterosexuals.

By assuming the inevitability of homoerotic desire as a consequence of viewing oneself (other men) as a sexual object, Wernick
bypasses the problem of why a man viewing himself in the mirror,
or looking at the advertisement, *should* see himself as a sexual
object. The answer lies in the economy of desire of cultural fetishism. Wernick explains that the insert picture in the advertisement
of a bottle of Braggi held in a man's hand 'is the aroused penis of the
masturbating male'.[37] In Chapter 4, I noted that, in the post-1850s
reconstruction of male desire, masturbation was associated with
prostitution and homosexuality as a signifier of excessive male
desire. The bottle in the man's hand may connote an erect penis but
this disguises its further connotation as the phallic addition the man
needs to possess the phallus. In the advertisement the man's penis is
itself hidden from view. Instead we see his own lean and muscled
physique, emphasised by his taut buttocks. For the male reader, the
man's body is the signifier of the phallus. We can now understand
how male fetishistic desire structures the male reading of the advertisement. The male reader desires the man's body because, as a
spectacle, it performs as a metonym of the phallus the reader lacks.
Ideally, the bottle of Braggi will serve as a substitute. The woman,
then, is not only a cover for the homoerotic gaze but, at a deeper
level, may be read as the prize which legitimises the man as having/
being the phallus. As a final point, as an object of male desire herself,
the woman also functions in the advertisement as a phallic fetish.

The attempt to market successfully a male style and fashion
magazine has been going on since the early 1970s. However, it
seemed that the narcissistic discussion of men's new consumerist
concerns required the reassuring cover of pictures of naked women
to provide a legitimising justification, and reassurance of the
heterosexual nature of male desire. Such a description fits *Playboy*
perfectly. It was started by Hugh Hefner in November 1953. As
Adrian McGregor tells it, Hefner 'made two inspired decisions':

> One was on the magazine's title, which clicked with a genera-
> tion of American males looking for advice about male fashion,
> drinks, cars, hi-fi's – in short, about lifestyle. In place of moral
> barriers and social taboos, Hefner offered his versions of taste
> and sophistication – Chivas Regal, a smoking jacket and cool
> jazz.[38]

The second inspired decision was to buy the famous nude photograph of Marilyn Monroe, originally taken for a calendar company,

and to make her 'Sweetheart of the Month'. In the era of mass consumption, men could read articles and advertisements aimed at male consumerism whilst reassuring themselves of their heterosexual desire by gazing at female nudes. Of course *Playboy* also fitted into that modern tradition of magazines whose reason for existence is the portrayal of naked female bodies and which I discussed in Chapter 3.

The first successful youth consumer – as opposed to music – magazine was the British production *The Face*, which focused on youth cultural consumerism. It began in May 1980; and out of it, in 1986, came the first successful general-interest youth fashion magazine for (heterosexual) men, *Arena*. Nevertheless, even *Arena*, Jonathan Rutherford suggests, punning on its name, is 'a gladiatorial stadium where two contending meanings of male heterosexuality battle it out'.[39] He argues that there is a split between 'pictures of young male models … portrayed in passive, "feminised" poses, exposed to the camera' and the text, which contains articles that 'confirm a traditional male view of the world': 'The mirror is thrown away for the old objective authority, the interviews with wealthy fashion moguls, articles on money and sex.'[40] Rutherford wants to find in the fashion pictures an intimation of a new, sensitive man. In fact, what we have is another reworking of the modern active/passive, gazer/gazed-upon, male/female split: the male, both feminised and spectacularised – that is, doubly and reassuringly, passive – is counterbalanced by the active, macho text. There is a reworking of the blond-god and ephebe myths here. The images make use of the ephebe because he lacks the phallic power. The ephebe is the better myth for selling personal commodities to men because he can be shown to be more attractive, more phallic, by the addition of the personal commodity. (More attractive, more phallic, to whom? To women, the advertisement claims; but in being portrayed as the ephebe he stimulates homoerotic desire in the male reader.) As advertising took up the ephebe he lost his enticing sexual innocence and, instead, became a man who desires, and is desired by, women. The text of *Arena*, on the other hand, positions the reader as the bearer of phallic power and invokes the blond-god myth. Those who incarnate the blond-god myth do not need to be sexually attractive – and certainly do not need to increase their sexual attraction – because they can get what, and whom, they want as an expression of phallic power.

I have argued that the discourse of homosexuality is closely bound up first with the proscription, and subsequently with the spread, of the visible male body as spectacle. Whilst *Playboy* provides one history because of its emphasis on male consumerism, to find the precursors for the style of *Arena*, and the other men's fashion magazines such as *Gentleman's Quarterly* (now *GQ*), the revamped *Esquire, Loaded, Hommes, Vogue International Mode, Attitude*, or the Australian *Studio for Men*, we should look not to the women's magazines such as *Cosmopolitan* and *Cleo*, but to the gay magazines of the late 1960s and early 1970s. Of Britain, Weeks writes:

> Many of the youths who worked or shopped in the trendy boutiques of Carnaby Street or the Kings Road, Chelsea, might be seen, in the height of fashion, at the new gay bars in the evenings. The magazines that began to appear at the very end of the 1960s, such as *Timm, Spartacus* and *Jeremy*, reflected this new affluence and a muted openness, though there were subtle differences in emphasis.[41]

Weeks describes *Jeremy* as 'trendier and glossier' than *Spartacus*. He goes on: 'The boys in the photographs were younger, and there was more of an emphasis on high fashion. Articles wove a web of excitement around new clothes, travel, and sexual success.'[42] Apart from its sexual orientation, this sounds remarkably like Rutherford's description of *Arena*. Historically, we find in these magazines a reformation of the concerns of the Wildean aesthete in the construction of a new fashion-driven canon of taste. Returning to Bocock's point, we should note the extent to which gay male consumption pioneered the acceptance of male consumerism.

Typically it is the ephebe who is used to sell personal consumer products to men. First, this is because the age of the ephebe is closer to that of the youth male market but, second, it is because, as a site of identification, the ephebe is less threatening than the blond-god male. Third, what is being sold is visual appearance: style, not self-image. As we have seen in the discussion of Neale's article, the narcissistic identification with the blond-god hero in films is driven by the pleasure of experiencing the power a man lacks in his daily life. This can be generalised. The blond-god male is the man men want to be, and because his body is so perfect – so much the phallus – he needs nothing more. When he is used in advertisements he is usually partly or completely naked. His most enduring image comes from *The Terminator* (1984) where, at the beginning of the film, Arnold Schwarzenegger, playing the eponymous cyborg terminator, having just travelled back in time, strides naked towards a trio of heavily dressed punks to demand their clothes – not, of course, because he is ashamed of his naked body, but because he needs to blend in with the ordinary, human population. The blond-god adult male is the ideal to which men are supposed to aspire but, precisely because he has/is the phallus, he is also the patriarchal threat. From an advertising point of view, for the selling of personal consumer goods, the ephebe is a much better bet. Men find him unthreatening because, to the extent of his 'feminine' quality, he too lacks the phallus. He needs clothes, after-shave, skin-care products, and so forth to help him on the way to becoming (as powerful as) the blond god.

In Britain the best-known advertisements of the 1980s featuring a man were those made using Nick Kamen for Levi jeans. Kamen, a male model, has the slim figure coupled with perceptible muscle definition that characterise the sexualised ephebe image. This coupling combines the myths of the blond god and the ephebe; the phallic power of the blond god is made safe – that is, non-threatening – for men by its packaging in the adolescent, 'feminine' body of the ephebe. In one advertisement, set in a 1950s laundrette, Kamen stripped down to his boxer underpants, taking off his Levi 501s, and put his clothes in the washing machine. These advertisements were extremely successful. In them, Frank Mort argues: 'male sexuality is conjured up *through the commodity*, whether jeans, hair-gel, aftershave or whatever':

> Though Kamen stripped to his boxer shorts and white socks and 'bath' [another advertisement] began with a naked torso, it was the display of the body *through the product* that was sexy… . And so the sexual meanings in play are less to do with macho images of strength and virility (though these are certainly present) than with the fetishised and narcissistic display – a visual erotica.[43]

When Mort describes the Kamen advertisements in terms of a 'fetishised and narcissistic display' he is highlighting the homo-erotic desire which, in this case, is a consequence of identification not with the 'lacking' ephebe's body but with that body supplemented by the commodity it is selling. It is the commodity which gives the sexualised ephebe a supplemental phallic quality, his 'look' as a male adult which provokes an additional (fetishistic and narcissistic in Mort's terms) sexual desire, and it is this experience of the commodity which sells to men.

In the United States the male model equivalent to Nick Kamen is Marky Mark. Marky Mark started out as a white pre-teen pop rap idol, and turned down an offer to join the teen pop group New Kids on the Block. In the early 1990s he signed a deal with Calvin Klein for $100,000 to do commercials and photographs to advertise their products[44] – as, in fact, did the waif model Kate Moss. These advertisements have him either nude or semi-nude; one very well-known one has both him and Kate Moss together nude. In an article in *The Face* entitled 'Man Child', Mark is described as 'the body beautiful of pop, 5 feet 8 inches and nearly 13 stone of pectorals and abdominal muscle, a boy with a man's body, the Madonna of rap'.[45] Elsewhere in the article he is a 'man-child pin-up'. The article also points out that Marky Mark's image is a favourite with the gay community but has Mark himself insisting that he is not gay: 'Yo, if you're gay you're in the house, just don't do that shit around me! Don't try to fuck me!' At the same time, Mark's insistent heterosexual orientation is overlaid by a preoccupation with his penis. His eponymously titled book is 'dedicated to my dick'.[46] Mark comes over, like Kamen, as the renovated ephebe. No longer innocent, he has a vaulting heterosexual desire which simultaneously asserts his own heterosexuality and enables the male spectator to deflect his homoerotic desire into a displaced heterosexual desire.

As the male body began to be spectacularised the blond god provided the alternative image. In Chapter 4 I have already made the connection between the political invocation of the blond-god myth and the totalitarian state. Richard Dyer's book *Only Entertainment* has a photograph of Schwarzenegger in nothing but his posing briefs, standing in imitation of a classical Greek statue known as the Poseidon of Artemision, muscles pumped, left arm raised at a 75° angle, head looking along it, and with his right arm up and ready to punch. At his feet sit three clothed black men. The photograph connects the late-nineteenth-century blond-god ideal with the racist Nazi, Aryan myth of the superman whilst now emphasising the phallus as embodied in the spectacular, body-built, male body. In this fantasy the blond god can, literally, embody the phallic state. This spectacle is something for men to desire to identify with, not to consume.

The blond god is a more threatening spectacle to gaze on than the ephebe because of its incarnation of phallic power. Dyer argues that 'muscularity is a key term in appraising men's bodies'. He suggests that this 'comes from men themselves': for men, 'muscularity is the *sign* of power – natural, achieved, phallic'.[47] He outlines Margaret Walters' argument in her book *The Nude Male* (1978), to the effect that the hardness of the muscled male body is phallic 'not in the direct sense of being like an erect penis but rather in being symbolic of all that the phallus represents of abstract paternal power'.[48] Writing in 1982, and not engaging with the new film spectacles of Stallone and Schwarzenegger, Dyer suggests that 'the penis isn't a patch on the phallus':

> The penis can never live up to the mystique implied by the phallus. Hence the excessive, even hysterical quality of so much male imagery. The clenched fists, the bulging muscles, the hardened jaws, the proliferation of phallic symbols – they are all straining after what can hardly ever be achieved, the embodiment of the phallic physique.[49]

His example is Humphrey Bogart. It was Clive James, the television critic, who once made the phallic association with Schwarzenegger's body by describing his muscles as looking like 'condoms stuffed with walnuts'.

It has been unusual to find the blond-god male body used in advertising. When this body is used, it is rarely to sell personal consumer products to men. Rather, it usually sells something generally reassuring which falls into the male-dominated public domain – such things as insurance. Wernick has discussed two 1950s advertisements, for Union Carbide and Morgan Guaranty Trust, which both use the image of a giant male hand. He characterises this hand as 'the hand of God'.[50] At this time, before the male body was spectacularised, the hand of the blond-god male was about all that could reasonably be shown. By the late 1980s, equivalent advertisements were using pictures of the whole male body – usually naked. In these advertisements, God is revealed in his patriarchal and phallic splendour. In one Australian advertisement from this period for MLC, an insurance company, a very body-built and symmetrically proportioned man held a very young baby; both were naked. Here the baby's weakness and need for protection was counterpointed by the blond god's phallic and also patriarchal power in a very obvious way. The man, whose omnipotence is expressed in his size and his naked muscularity, is portrayed as providing comfort, care, and sanctuary; he keeps the world well-ordered.

As I have already explained, blond gods do not need consumer goods to supplement their phallic lack because they are not lacking. This myth is used to emphasise the strength and power of the commodity being advertised. Thus, truck advertisements or those selling clothes as work-wear sometimes use the myth in a watered-down version. In the same way it is invoked to show the traditional attributes of 'masculine' men – such as drinking beer. The most celebrated use of the blond-god myth in an advertisement – and its celebration may well have to do with the invocation of the myth in its full, albeit clothed, form – is that of the Marlboro Man. An American advertisement, it has become recognisable over much of the world. Selling Marlboro cigarettes, the Marlboro Man is a cowboy sitting on his horse all alone in Marlboro country, a mountainous red desert region. The Marlboro Man sits erect, head shaded by his hat, staring with firm purpose into the middle distance. In the United States, in particular, the cowboy is an image with strong connotations of the frontier, of men establishing the law and founding society where none was previously. Given this cultural context, we can recognise a mythic connection with Freud's founding patriarch who has complete phallic power. The phallic connotations of the cowboy image are such that, as we have already noted, the cowboy is one of the images used by the Village People and by Chippendales. In the Marlboro advertisements the image is used for real rather than as a (gay) masquerade. The Marlboro Man's success lies in the narcissistic persuasion that what he is selling will enhance the purchaser's self-image rather than his appearance – smoke this and you will (feel like you) have phallic power.

The place where the spectacularisation of the male body has been most insistently played out is in film. I have tracked the beginning of the transformation of men into consumers to the late 1960s and early 1970s. The naturalisation of this transformation can be roughly dated to the success of the male style magazines in the second half of the 1980s. Articulated with this success has been a new Hollywood concern with the male body. Whilst Hollywood has always provided opportunities for men to identify narcissistically with phallic, blond-god males, in the 1980s these men underwent a transformation. Where previously their power had often sprung from their institutional positioning or, in cases such as Clint Eastwood's spaghetti-western character and his cop character in the *Dirty Harry* cycle, had been supplemented by their weapons, in the 1980s films their power sprang from their bodies.

Complementing this, there was a new emphasis on the body as spectacle. In the blond-god films of the 1980s the male body was made visible for the first time, and was spectacularised as an instrument of phallic power in its own right. There were two sub-genres of these films. One is the muscular-body film which was pioneered by Steve Reeves, also a body-builder turned film actor, in the late 1950s and early 1960s, whose films have a large gay following.[51] This sub-genre became generally popular in the 1980s, the best-known films starring Arnold Schwarzenegger and Sylvester Stallone. The second sub-genre comprises the martial-arts films of, among others, Chuck Norris and Jean-Claude Van Damme. At the same time, another genre of films became prominent, starring the sexualised ephebe. Often these films had scenes of quite explicit heterosexual lovemaking, which distracted the homoerotic gaze, or – and often in addition – *mise-en-scènes* of expensive and fashionably tasteful consumer goods. The typifying film of this genre was *9½ Weeks*, released in 1986 and starring Kim Basinger and Mickey Rourke.

Whilst the popular success of both sub-genres of the blond-god body films came in the mid-1980s, the beginnings of their popularity can be dated back to the early 1970s – the time when consumption capitalism began to make the male body spectacularly visible. Schwarzenegger began his film career using the stage name Arnold Strong. His first film, *Hercules Goes to New York* (1970), was a comedy which took off Steve Reeves's best-known film role. A homage to the most famous representative of an older tradition, but played for laughs, the film suggests a questioning and reworking of the meanings given to the body-built body. When Schwarzenegger began making films using his own name, the first two were developed around body-building contests, an expression of the spread of the new interest in the previously limited spectacle of the heavily muscled male body. Schwarzenegger's first role using his own name was in Bob Rafaelson's film *Stay Hungry*, released in 1976. In this film he played an Austrian body-builder living in the United States who was in training for the Mr Universe contest. At one point in the film, referring to what was then the stereotype of body-builders, a character asks Schwarzenegger if he is gay. At its climax the contestants in the Mr Universe contest spill out from the hall where it is taking place to run down to the gym owned by the contest's organiser. As the street fills with oiled, muscled bodies, the general public stop and stare. In one shot two white body-builders pose for a group of delighted and impressed African-Americans. In another, a bus drives slowly down the road with a number of body-builders posing on its roof. With hindsight the scene can be read as a remarkable presaging of the public acceptance of the spectacle of body-building, and body-training more generally, in the 1980s.

Schwarzenegger's second film, *Pumping Iron* (1976), the documentary of a major body-building competition, was even more centred on body-building than *Stay Hungry*. It was this film which marked Schwarzenegger's breakthrough to a mainstream audience, and which helped to popularise body-building for men. By the early 1980s Schwarzenegger had moved on to roles in mythic fantasies. In *Conan the Barbarian* (1981), he plays a man of tremendous physical ability who, with the help of two friends and a wizard, finally destroys the men who killed his family and enslaved him. In *The Terminator* he plays a cyborg killer sent from the future. Both films connect muscle bulk with physical power, and physical power with the ability to carry out tasks regardless of any impediments placed in the way; in short, they were fantasy narratives of the phallic blond god. By the time of *The Terminator*, Schwarzenegger's muscles were considerably more developed than in *Pumping Iron*. In *Conan the Barbarian* the male audience's identification with Schwarzenegger can be unproblematic as he fights to reinstate the 'good' moral order. However, in *The Terminator* the male viewer feels a degree of complexity and distancing in his identification as Schwarzenegger plays the creation of twentyfirst-century technology sent back in time to help in the destruction of the human race. This complexity is compounded by the terminator's own destruction by a 'mere' man – a sexualised ephebe to Schwarzenegger's blond god – and a woman. After these films Schwarzenegger began making comedies, such as *Twins* (1988) and *Kindergarten Cop* (1990), which were set in the present. Taken together, Schwarzenegger's films present a narrative of the normalisation of the spectacle of the muscular male body.

Having previously appeared naked in a porno film, Stallone appeared in the first of his *Rocky* cycle of boxing films in 1976. In these he plays Rocky Balboa, the Italian Stallion, working-class grafter and no-hope boxer who, in a self-conscious exemplification of the American Dream, is given one chance to become the heavyweight boxing champion. Following *Rocky* were *Rocky II* (1979), *Rocky III* (1982), *Rocky IV* (1985), and *Rocky V* (1990). As the films progress, so less emphasis is placed on narrative complexity and more on action and spectacle. In these films boxing is simultaneously a way of displaying Stallone's muscled body and an opportunity for the kind of mutilation, discussed earlier, which interrupts the homoerotic gaze. Within the diegesis of the films Balboa's muscular body is built up by will-power and becomes the site of a physical power which transforms him from working-class underdog to hero.

In 1982 the first of Stallone's Rambo films was released. *First Blood* has Stallone playing John Rambo, decorated Vietnam veteran and the last surviving member of a specially trained group of Green Berets. Rambo finds himself in the small north-western American town with the allegorical name of Hope. The local sheriff considers him to be a vagrant and runs him out of town. When Rambo returns the scene is set for a battle between the abused and misunderstood veteran and the abusive representatives of the law. Most of this battle takes place in the wilderness surrounding Hope. Generically the film owes much to the survivalist genre of which *Deliverance* (1972) is possibly the best-known example. However, *First Blood* also owes a great deal to those films, pioneered by westerns, in which a righteous outsider fights against a rotten establishment.

Rambo is a reworked elaboration of the blond-god figure portrayed by John Wayne and Clint Eastwood, a man who often stands outside a morally corrupt law to fight for what is right, but now given a hard, muscled, phallic body. Where Wayne's and Eastwood's characters relied on their guns, Rambo relies as much on his physical strength. When he does use guns they have a destructive impact far in excess of anything that previous blond-god heroes could manage. In *First Blood* his old commanding officer, Colonel Sam Trautman, describes Rambo:

> You don't seem to want to accept the fact that you're dealing with an expert in guerilla warfare. With a man who's the best, with guns, with knives, with his bare hands; a man who's been trained to ignore pain, ignore weather; to live off the land; to eat things that'd make a billygoat puke. In Viet-Nam his job was to dispose of enemy personnel – to kill, period; win by attrition. Rambo was the best.'

As befits the phallic patriarch, Rambo is a man whose physical power equates with what is portrayed as moral good. In *First Blood*, Rambo is placed on the wrong side of the law but he is in the right from a moral point of view. He is pursued through the film by physically and morally weaker representatives of the state.

In her book on the rise of the muscular-hero film, Yvonne Tasker has argued that the 'much publicised release of *Rambo: First Blood Part II* in 1985 signalled a new visibility for the muscular hero of the action cinema. Breaking numerous international box-office records, *Rambo* achieved almost instant notoriety'.[52] In *Rambo*, Stallone wears less and has a bigger body; the film tends more towards spectacular violence. This tendency is taken further in *Rambo III*, where, at the end, Rambo – now fighting on behalf of the 'good' American state, though for personal reasons – and Trautman together take on a Russian army composed of infantry, armoured personnel carriers, a tank, and a helicopter gunship. Mid-way through this battle on the border of Afghanistan, a large group of mujaheddin ride to the rescue, invoking memories of last-minute rescues by the cavalry in so many westerns. Here, though, it seems as if, in the final confrontation, it is Rambo and Trautman who save the mujaheddin. Indeed Rambo himself captures the tank and destroys the helicopter gunship. As in *Rambo: First Blood Part II*, the action takes place outside the United States and Stallone's body is able to express American moral right in a world threatened by evil. As both Stallone's cycles of films progress, women diminish in importance. In fact in the later, Rambo cycle, to all intents and purposes, women are not even present. Where women used to be the repositories of the moral order – as in westerns – in these films the phallic body of the blond god is the only source of morality.

In the muscular-body films a crude equation exists between muscle bulk, physical prowess, and the phallic ability to establish moral right; the bigger the body, the greater the ability. The martial-arts films concentrate on the ability of the hero to use his body as a weapon. In this case it is not size that is important, but physical dexterity and training. Hollywood's chosen sport for its muscled heroes was boxing; martial-arts films originated in Hong Kong and moved to Hollywood in the 1970s. Having made many martial-arts films in Hong Kong, Bruce Lee went to Hollywood and released *Enter the Dragon* in 1973. After his death the Hollywood martial-arts tradition centred on Chuck Norris – who had had parts in some of Bruce Lee's films including *Welcome the Dragon* (1973), which was set in Rome – and Jean-Claude Van Damme, who made a number of films in the 1980s such as *No Retreat, No Surrender* (1985), and *Blood Sport* (1987).

If the blond-god body films concerned themselves with the phallus and with fighting, we need to ask what presence sex did have in Hollywood films in the 1980s. The answer is that it was very important. Cutting across all major adult genres, heterosexual sex scenes have always played a significant part in Hollywood films. However, from the 1970s on the depiction of sexual relations became more graphic, it involved more nudity, and the sex portrayed became more frenzied. I have already noted the importance of *9½ Weeks*. After its tremendous popular success, it was followed by *Wild Orchid* (1989), again starring Mickey Rourke but this time with Carrie Otis. Thematically, that is in the observation of overwhelming sexual desire of each of the couple for each other, *9½ Weeks* is in a tradition with *Last Tango in Paris* (1972). However, whereas in the earlier film the hero is played by a middle-aged Marlon Brando, in *9½ Weeks* the hero is very much the post-adolescent twenty-something renovated and sexualised ephebe clothed in the latest fashions and living in a designer apartment; and where *Last Tango in Paris* focused on the existential angst of Paul, the Brando character, *9½ Weeks* principally concerned itself with the portrayal of physical desire and consumer goods.[53]

Set in New York, *9½ Weeks* has two main characters, Elizabeth and John. Elizabeth works in an art gallery; John is an arbitrage – as he puts it, he buys and sells money. The film is the narrative of their relationship, from the instant attraction when they first meet to John's despair when Elizabeth leaves him. The settings complement the characters' physical desire for each other. Starting with the decor of the friend's houseboat to which John first takes Elizabeth and dominated by his own high-rise apartment which forms the set for much of the film, the film provides its viewers with a range of highly desired consumer items from the first half of the 1980s. The film delivers a traditional moral about authenticity: Elizabeth leaves John because she can never penetrate the veneer of his self-made image. (John's lifestyle construction of himself exemplifies the eighties consumerist transformation of the Wildean dandy.) When he does, finally, tell her about his working-class background it is too late. However, the film overwhelms this conventional moral ending with its *mise-en-scènes*. John exudes power. He has the power to construct himself delivered by the money he makes, the power to attract women because of the stylish reconstruction of himself which he has achieved, and, last but not least, he expresses his power in the continual abasement of Elizabeth. This begins when he deceives her into going on a ferris wheel on her own and persuading the operator to stop it, leaving her perched on the top of the ride. It reaches a climax when he forces her to crawl along the floor in his apartment picking up money whilst he threatens to beat her. In the meantime he buys her a variety of expensive personal items including a watch and lingerie, commodities which add to her own spectacular desirability.

John's phallic power comes from his recreation of himself. In this he epitomises the sexualised ephebe complementing himself with consumer goods. The narrative may be a romance but this is very much a man's film. For the male viewer, Rourke/John's erotic attraction is displaced on to the desire for the commodities – including his designer clothes – which make him desirable. And the gaze itself is displaced on to the spectacle of Kim Basinger's often naked or semi-naked body. When Elizabeth leaves him we know he will have many more women; as he tells Elizabeth, there were very many before her. With her single again there is always that fantasy chance – in that confusion between reality and fiction – that, if we men buy the right consumer goods (if only we could afford them), we might be able to attract her, or somebody like her.

The precursors of films like *9½ Weeks* include *Saturday Night Fever* (1977), in which John Travolta displays his body as a successful disco dancer, and *American Gigolo* (1980), in which Richard Gere plays a gigolo in Los Angeles. This film's narrative drive is a murder mystery in which Gere's character, Julian Kay, is being framed. The film focuses on Kay's life as he becomes increasingly entangled in the police investigation. Once again, Kay is the self-created man, with help he hardly acknowledges from a woman for whom he used to sell his services. Now Kay lives in an expensive apartment full of desirable things. He owns a large variety of designer clothing, on which the camera often dwells, and he drives an open-top Mercedes. He works out regularly to keep his slim and firm phallicised body and he has taught himself a number of languages – he says that he now speaks five or six. He is, in fact, an early version of the sexualised ephebe who uses consumer goods to complement his phallic 'lack'.

As in the later *9½ Weeks*, the male gaze on Gere/Kay's body is displaced on to the body of Lauren Hutton, whom Kay meets early in the film and who provides the saving love – literally, in that she lies to provide him with an alibi – at the film's end. What unsettles this conventional displacement of the homoerotic gaze is the sexual ambivalence of the Gere/Kay characterisation, an ambivalence reinforced by the references to the earlier part of Kay's career when he used to do 'fag tricks'. Kay's characterisation resonates with the historical concerns of the ephebe. Indeed, the film also makes clear his 'femininity' – his closer emotional similarity to women than to men. Whilst *American Gigolo* does not end with the mutilation of Gere/Kay's body – which, as we have discussed, has been a technique often used to repress the homoerotic interest of the male audience in the blond-god character – it does end with Kay still in prison, and with his heterosexuality affirmed by his relationship with Michelle Stratton (Lauren Hutton).

Structurally, then, we can describe two groups of films, those which privilege sex and those which privilege fighting. Where the second group is centred on the spectacle of the phallic, blond-god male body, the first – usually considered to be more mainstream – is centred on the spectacle of the female body. The woman's partner is not the muscled and phallic male; rather, he is the sexualised transformation of the ephebe. At the same time that the bodies of Schwarzenegger, Stallone, and Norris were becoming famous spectacles, Hollywood was nurturing a number of new, young male mainstream stars. Collectively known as the brat pack, this group, made up of Mickey Rourke, Emilio Estevez, Tom Cruise, Rob Lowe, and Charlie Sheen among others, became the sex symbols of the 1980s. Stylishly turned out, they were the filmic equivalent of Nick Kamen and Marky Mark in advertising. Where men could identify with the fantasy of phallic power expressed in Schwarzenegger's and Stallone's bodies, with Tom Cruise and Rob Lowe they could identify with their 'ordinariness' – the transformation of the ephebe's adolescent phallic 'lack' which enabled him to exemplify a male 'femininity' – which was supplemented by their fashionable clothes, hairstyle, and so on. It was, it appeared, this supplement of male consumer products which made these men sexually attractive to women. In the films starring the sexualised ephebe the male spectator's homoerotic desire is displaced on to the spectacularised body of the woman. Whilst physical pain and mutilation continue to be used in the blond-god body films, in the films of the sexualised ephebe the increased erotic charge of the heterosexual sex scenes operates as a means of displacement. Complementing this, the spectacular display of the female body provides an alibi for the male gaze and displaces his desire. In addition, the male spectator is able to feel reassured about his own heterosexuality because of the obvious, and intense, heterosexual desire of the hero. However, overdetermining all of this, the spectacularisation of the male body places it as passive, and as feminised. Consequently, and paradoxically, even the muscled, blond-god male body can take on a female quality. For example, it has been claimed that in *Rambo* 'Stallone's enormous breasts loom over the screen like Jane Russell's in *The Outlaw*'.[54]

The homoerotic quality of the fetishising male gaze is now complemented by the spectacle of the displayed male body. Display was something that, for the last hundred years, had been confined to women. The newly spectacularised male body is both eroticised and feminised in the male gaze. Tasker notes that 'the homo-eroticism surrounding male action stars is a constant presence, acknowledged and played with by films which ... simultaneously deploy an anxious disavowal of gay desire'.[55] As the male body began to be spectacularised, so the ephebe became sexualised: no longer the androgynous male pubescent with female qualities, he was transformed into a young man with an aggressive heterosexual desire. As the 1980s unfolded it seemed that all he needed to gain the woman of his desire were the right – expensive and stylish – clothes and consumer goods. This heterosexual sexualisation of the ephebe counterbalanced the homoerotic desire which was an aspect of his spectacularisation in the male gaze and which can be traced back at least to the early 1890s. At the same time men were able to identify narcissistically with the new films which spectacularised the heavily muscled bodies of the representatives of the blond-god myth. The guiding problematic of the spectacularised male body is that of negotiating the homoerotic desire which drives the fetishistic male gaze.

## NOTES

1   On this see J. Weeks, *Coming Out: Homosexual Politics in Britain from the Nineteenth Century to the Present Day* (London, Quartet, 1977), ch. 15, *passim*.

2   *Ibid.*, p. 190.

3   R. Bocock, *Consumption* (London, Routledge, 1993), p. 103.

4   *Ibid.*, p. 103.

5   See e.g. T. Fyvel, *The Insecure Offenders* (London, Chatto and Windus, 1963); T. Jefferson, 'Cultural Responses of the Teds', in S. Hall and T. Jefferson (eds), *Resistance Through Rituals: Youth Sub-cultures in Post-war Britain* (London, Hutchinson, 1976), pp. 81–6:

Dick Hebdige, 'The Meaning of Mod', in *ibid.*, pp. 87–96.

6   G. Melley, *Revolt into Style: The Pop Arts* (Harmondsworth, Penguin, 1970).

7   On punk see D. Hebidige, *Subculture: The Meaning of Style* (London, Methuen, 1979).

8   L. Mulvey, 'Visual Pleasure and Narrative Cinema', *Screen*, 16:3 (1975), p. 11.

9   *Ibid.*, p. 17.

10  S. Neale, 'Masculinity as Spectacle: Reflections on Men and Main-stream Cinema', *Screen*, 24:6 (1983).

11  *Ibid.*, p. 5.

12  *Ibid.*, p. 5.

13  D. N. Rodowick, 'The Difficulty of Difference', *Wide Angle*, 5:1, p. 8, quoted in Neale, 'Masculinity as Spectacle', p. 8.

14  P. Willemen, 'Anthony Mann: Looking at the Male', *Framework*, 15/16/17 (Summer 1981).

15  Neale, 'Masculinity as Spectacle', p. 8.

16  *Ibid.*, p. 12.

17  *Ibid.*, p. 8.

18  *Ibid.*, p. 15.

19  R. Williams, *Dream Worlds: Mass Consumption in Late Nineteenth-century France* (Berkeley, University of California Press, 1982), p. 127.

20  R. Felski, 'The Counterdiscourse of the Feminine in Three Texts by Wilde, Huysmans, and Sacher-Masoch', *PMLA*, 106:5 (1991), p. 1100.

21  *Ibid.*, p. 1100.

22  O. Wilde, *De Profundis and Other Writings* (Harmondsworth, Penguin, 1973), p. 132.

23  A. Wernick, *Promotional Culture: Advertising, Ideology and Symbolic Expression* (London, Sage, 1991), p. 49.

24  *Ibid.*, p. 49.

25  *Ibid.*, p. 49.

26  *Ibid.*, p. 49.

27  W. Haug, *Critique of Commodity Aesthetics: Appearance, Sexuality and Advertising in Capitalist Society* (Cambridge, Polity Press, 1986), p. 79.

28  *Ibid.*, p. 78.

29  *Ibid.*, p. 78.

30  *Ibid.*, n. 61, pp. 168–9. I cannot resist commenting on the irony of Protopapa's name.

31   *Der Spiegel,* quoted in Haug, *Critique,* n. 61, p. 168.

32   M. Gabor, *The Pin-up: A Modest History* (New York, Universe Books, 1972), p. 60.

33   'Welcome to *Cleo*', *Cleo,* no. 1 (November 1972), p. 4.

34   J. and M. Stern, *The Encyclopedia of Bad Taste* (New York, Harper Collins, 1990), p. 82.

35   *Ibid.,* pp. 82–3.

36   Wernick, *Promotional Culture,* p. 62.

37   *Ibid.,* p. 60.

38   A. McGregor, 'Boys' Own Story: The world's best-selling men's magazine is celebrating its 40th birthday – and showing its age', in *The Australian Magazine* published in conjunction with *The Weekend Australian,* 22–23 October 1994, p. 35.

39   J. Rutherford, 'Who's that Man?', in R. Chapman and J. Rutherford (eds), *Male Order: Unwrapping Masculinity* (London, Lawrence and Wishart, 1988), p. 38.

40   *Ibid.,* p. 38.

41   Weeks, *Coming Out,* p. 180.

42   *Ibid.,* pp. 180–1.

43   F. Mort, 'Boy's Own? Masculinity, Style and Popular Culture', in R. Chapman and J. Rutherford (eds), *Male Order: Unwrapping Masculinity* (London, Lawrence and Wishart, 1988), p. 201.

44   This figure comes from an interview with Marky Mark in *Vanity Fair,* January 1993, p. 46.

45   J. Godfrey, 'Man Child', in *The Face,* no. 150 (November 1992), p. 48.

46   *Ibid.,* p. 50.

47   R. Dyer, *Only Entertainment* (London, Routledge, 1992), p. 114.

48   *Ibid.,* p. 116.

49   *Ibid.,* p. 116.

50   Wernick, *Promotional Culture,* p. 54.

51   Steve Reeves's first film performance was in Ed Wood Jr's *Jail Bait* (1954). He is best known for his Italian films, starting with *Hercules* (1957), a role he reprised in *Hercules Unchained* (1960).

52   Y. Tasker, *Spectacular Bodies: Gender, Genre and the Action Cinema* (London, Routledge, 1993), p. 7. Tasker's book provides a useful account of muscular-body films – both male and female – during the 1980s.

53   Maria Schneider, who was not yet twenty when she played the role of Jeanne, was thought by Bernardo Bertolucci, who directed the film, to be 'the personification of the hip but bourgeois student'. Describing her, Bertolucci has said: 'She was a Lolita, but more perverse.' These

quotations are from the excerpt from P. Manso's book *Brando: The Biography* in *Vanity Fair*, September 1994, p. 121.

54   Quoted from the British newspaper *The Guardian* in Tasker, *Spectacular Bodies*, p. 80.

55   *Ibid.*, p. 29.

# 7

# Man-made women

This chapter examines the male preoccupation with gynoids as substitutes for women. I will look at a number of texts, most of which have, in their time, achieved a significant degree of popularity, in order to highlight some of the major themes I have outlined in previous chapters whilst focusing on the historical reconstruction of the gynoid as perhaps the most important phallic fetish substitute for the female body itself. From the beginnings of cultural fetishism onwards gynoids – and I am here using the term to include any manufactured version of a woman, including dolls and mannequins – take on the quality of a cultural fetish. In this role they stand in for the female body, which, as we know, stands in for the phallus. It should go without saying that the texts I look at here constitute only a very small – but representative – sample of the tremendous number of texts about gynoids which have been produced over the last 150 years or so.

The interest in gynoids does not, by any means, start in the period of cultural fetishism, but it is at this time that they take on the new set of fetishistic concerns. Up until the eighteenth century, roughly equal numbers of androids and gynoids were made. However, as Andreas Huyssen puts it: 'While the android builders of the 18th century did not seem to have an overriding preference for either sex (the number of male and female androids seems to be more or less balanced), it is striking to see how the later literature prefers machine-women to machine-men.'[1] Huyssen argues that, at the same time: 'literature appropriates the subject matter transforming it significantly. The android is no longer seen as testimony to the genius of mechanical invention: it rather becomes a nightmare, a threat to human life.'[2] Why this double transformation, first to the preference for gynoids and, second, to the representation of gynoids as a threat? Huyssen sees the answer in the Industrial Revolution, and provides a classical Freudian solution that, for men, 'the fears and perceptual anxieties emanating from ever more powerful machines are recast and reconstructed in terms of the male fear of female sexuality, reflecting, in the Freudian account, the male's castration anxiety'.[3] Huyssen's argument is important; but, once again, unless we accept Freud's theory as having a universal application, we have to ask why it was that the male fear of the new machinery was cast in terms of female sexuality. I have already asserted that Freud's work comes out of a particular historico-cultural moment, and that his theories describe the psycho-cultural reality of a particular era. First, then, we need to acknowledge the phallic forms taken by much of the new machinery – thrusting pistons, repetitive action, and so forth. Second, we need to remember that the fetishism which Freud describes has its origin in the castration complex, itself founded on the power culturally ascribed to those possessing the penis. The recognition of the woman's 'lack', which produces the fetish substitute, also endows the fetish with both great desirability and the capacity to induce great fear. The new phallic machinery was not only feared; it was desired as a source of phallic power. Given this complex of effects, it becomes more understandable why the gynoid, the machine-woman, should become not only a powerful image of threat to men, as Huyssen points out, but also an equally powerful image of desirability – so strong, in fact, that it becomes preferred over the female body of flesh and blood. The gynoid is a more complete phallic fetish than a woman could ever be. However, this explanation tells only a part of the story.

We can now take this argument one stage further, examining how gynoids, in my general sense of the term, are located within the desiring structure of cultural fetishism. In a pre-Freudian formulation of the defining quality of the fetish, Alfred Binet argued in an article entitled 'Le Fétichisme dans l'amour', published in 1887, that an object takes on the quality of a fetish for the lover when:

> The relic, intransitively inscribed within the consciousness of the fetishistic lover, was revered in and for itself. No longer just the signifier of an absent totality, the material object was severed from the woman's body and actually *preferred* to the living self to which it originally belonged.[4]

Coming out of the period of the spread of cultural fetishism, Binet's description fits well the male preference for the gynoid over the woman. The gynoid's 'life' as a 'dead' spectacle comes from the libidinal charge of its fetishisation. Manufactured by men, the production of the gynoid literalises the fetishistic reconstruction of the female body. However, where the female body has an existence prior to its taking-up within the fetishistic structure, and where the female body is inhabited by a 'woman' capable of resistance to her fetishistic interpellation, the gynoid is able to occupy more fully the role of libidinised phallic fetish. As an oftentimes indistinguishable or even 'improved upon' substitute for a woman, the gynoid retains the sexual quality as a 'woman' of being an object of heterosexual male desire whilst, in addition, being the site of an overdetermining fetishistic desire. From around the middle of the nineteenth century gynoids are preferred, and are both more desired and more feared, than the women for whom they substitute.

Huyssen argues that the shift to the concern with gynoids takes place in the late eighteenth century. Now, in the Introduction, I have already used Rousseau's work to illustrate that the male experience of the newly developing state attributed to it phallic and patriarchal qualities. We can also use Rousseau to show how the developing attitude towards women constructed them metaphorically as gynoids. In *Emile*, which we have already discussed as a text in which the new category of adolescence makes an early appearance, Rousseau set out his ideal education for boys and, in Book V, almost as an afterthought, for girls. On the distinction between men and women, Rousseau asserts: 'The man should be strong and active; the woman should be weak and passive; the one must have both the power and the will; it is enough that the other should offer little resistance.'[5] He goes on in terms which, whilst echoing Genesis, ominously presage the increasing importance of the gynoid fantasy: 'When this principle is admitted, it follows that woman is specially made for man's delight. If man in his turn ought to be pleasing in her eyes, the necessity is less urgent, his virtue is in his strength, he pleases because he is strong.'[6] Here Rousseau's delineation of the man signals him as the phallic patriarch, and provides one genealogical source for the myth of the blond god. Counterpointing this image, Rousseau adds: 'If woman is made to please and to be in subjection to man, she ought to make herself pleasing in his eyes and not provoke him to anger; her strength is in her charms, by their means she should compel him to discover and use his strength.'⁷ At the heart of the relation Rousseau outlines here is the idea that the man discovers his power through his desire for the woman. Although, for Rousseau, man's phallic power is naturally his – deep down all men are blond gods – nevertheless, the role of women is to help men to find this phallic power. Here we have a remarkably incisive theorisation of the cultural-fetishistic relation between the sexes that, shortly after, spreads through everyday life.

Rousseau's suggestion that women should be made by men is literalised in his short *scène lyrique* entitled *Pygmalion*, which is a reworking of Ovid's version of the Greek myth in which a sculptor makes an ivory statue of his feminine ideal and falls in love with it. Answering his prayers, Venus brought the statue to life. This piece 'was performed at Lyons in 1770, at Weimar in 1772 and took Paris by storm in 1775. Goethe praised it, and Georg Benda paid it the compliment of imitation in his *Ariadne auf Naxos* (1774).'⁸ James Smith identifies *Pygmalion* as a forerunner of modern melodrama and suggests that it was its melodramatic style that led to its popularity. However, I would argue that this also had a great deal to do with its theme. As Smith describes it, 'the plot is simplicity itself: Pygmalion chips away at his statue of Galathée, the marble comes to life, breathes a few words (mostly "moi") and sinks into the arms of her astonished creator as the curtain falls'.⁹ Unlike Ovid's version, in Rousseau's melodrama there is no divine intervention; it is man who brings woman to life. Here we have a modern beginning for all the gynoid lovers which I will be writing about in this chapter.

As I have remarked, the gynoid takes on two qualities typical of the experience of the fetish: it can be desired and simultaneously feared. These qualities do not necessarily appear in the same narrative and, indeed, in spite of Huyssen's claim, sexually active, predatory gynoids, such as the one he is most concerned with, Maria's gynoid double in Fritz Lang's *Metropolis* (1927), seem to be outnumbered by the passive ones which men prefer to real women. Nevertheless, the combination of male machinery and the female body image is experienced by men as potentially predatory. Huyssen notes that it 'can be found in numerous 19th-century allegorical representations of technology and industry as woman'.¹⁰ He describes Jean Veber's early twentieth-century painting *Allégorie sur la machine dévoreuse des hommes* (Allegory of the men-devouring machine): 'In the right half of the painting we see a gigantic flywheel which throws up and devours dozens of dwarf-life men. A large rod connected with the flywheel moves to and fro into a metal box on which a giant woman is sitting naked, with parted legs and smiling demoniacally.'[11] Huyssen asserts that the painting is an allegory of sexual intercourse highlighting men's fears located in the castration complex and the *vagina dentata*.

As we saw in earlier chapters, from the second half of the nineteenth century women were thought of by men as potentially sexually threatening and destructive. In Veber's painting, this image is yoked together with the potential threat of, and destruction by, the phallic machine. Huyssen quotes the famous art critic Eduard Fuchs, who, in 1906, described the painting in this way:

> Woman is the symbol of that terrifying, secret power of the machine which rolls over anything that comes under its wheels, smashes that which gets caught in its cranks, shafts and belts, and destroys those who attempt to halt the turning of its wheels. And, vice versa, the machine, which coldly, cruelly and relentlessly sacrifices hecatombs of men as if they were nothing, is the symbol of the man-strangling Minotaur-like nature of woman.[12]

Fuchs describes the male fear of the phallic machine but, repressing its maleness (which he outlines so well) he transfers it on to a fear of 'woman', whom he sees as destructive of men. This quotation presents us with a fine example of the bringing together of male machinery and purported female qualities which would seem so strange but for the fetishism which drives it. The newly desirable gynoid quite literally embodies these concerns.[13]

A big increase in gynoid-fetish stories took place first in France in the post-1850s period. This is not surprising given the French rhetoric over the state, and the actual transformation of the French state, during the previous century which tended, ultimately, to view the state as phallic. In 1860 Charles Barbara, a French author, published a collection of stories called *Mes Petites-Maisons*. One was entitled 'Major Whittington'. Set on the outskirts of Paris, the narrative describes how: 'Ennemi des hommes, trompé dans sa jeunesse par une femme qu'il adorait, le major Withington [*sic*] a voulu créer une société sans vices et sans défauts.'[14] To achieve this end the English major surrounded himself with female automata: 'Sa mère, sa femme, sa fille sont des automates créés par lui.'[15] These gynoids take care of him: 'Il est entouré de soins par d'aimables automates. De nombreux domestiques (automates) font le service sans se plaindre.'[16] Major Whittington is a part of the patriarchal state's protection system, the army. We can draw a parallel between the role of the army in the state and that of the police as discussed in the Introduction. Whittington makes himself a family of gynoids. In this miniature family-cum-state run by the Major there are no males apart from himself, and no androids. Here, the new male insecurity as the patriarch in the family is translated into a construction of the entire female family as gynoids. He will have power over them by virtue of their being his property. This story, then, is about power as much as desire.

After E. T. A. Hoffmann's 'The Sandman' (see note 13), perhaps the earliest extended discussion of a gynoid which positions it as a fetish – and, certainly, as desired, as well as subject to male power – was Villiers de L'Isle-Adam's philosophical novel *L'Eve future*, published first in the magazine *La Vie Moderne* in 1885-86 and subsequently as a book in 1886. Interestingly, it was during this same period that Freud was in Paris working with Charcot. Curiously, given its subject matter, a critique of bourgeois sensibility from an aristocratic perspective runs through the book. In the story Lord Ewald, a young, handsome, and morally upright English aristocrat, visits his old friend Thomas Edison, the American inventor. Lord Ewald is involved in a love affair which is distressing him greatly with Miss Alicia Clary, who looks exactly like the statue called Venus Victorious, to be found in the Louvre. The use of a statue, here, should remind us of Rousseau's *Pygmalion*. In addition, in Leopold von Sacher-Masoch's notorious novella *Venus in Furs* (1870), the hero, Severin, first falls in love with a stone statue of Venus. Discovering this, Wanda transfers his love to her by imitating the statue.

Alicia Clary has, from Lord Ewald's point of view, a distressing lack of sensibility. Her thinking is, in a word, bourgeois. Lord Ewald is so upset by his predicament that he is planning to commit suicide. Meanwhile, unbeknown to him, Edison, who is preoccupied with the problem of what life is, has made a gynoid. All it needs is to be given a human likeness. On hearing Lord Ewald's story, Edison offers to give the gynoid the likeness of Alicia Clary and to give Lord Ewald the gynoid. Lord Ewald agrees and Alicia Clary is invited to Edison's home and laboratory at Menlo Park, where she is deceived into sitting for her sculpture and into reading lengthy passages which can be used for the voice of the gynoid – Hadaly, as she is called. Here, the intention is to eliminate the distress that Lord Ewald feels at being in love with somebody as coarse as Alicia Clary by making a double of her who will have all the characteristics he desires. The most telling element in this novel, which distinguishes this gynoid narrative from earlier ones, is that central to it is the intention to substitute the gynoid for a particular woman. Whilst this theme does not appear in all the gynoid-fetish stories I will be examining, it remains a recurrent concern.

Edison is attempting to produce 'Life'. However, this overt 'philosophical' concern of the novel masks the more fundamental exposition of male–female–gynoid relations. At one point he says: 'I promise to raise from the clay of Human Science as it now exists, a Being *made in our image*, and who, accordingly, will be to us WHAT WE ARE TO GOD.'[17] He tells Lord Ewald that the way Hadaly will relate to him will be determined by the way he relates to her. In other words Hadaly's 'mind' will be a consequence of Lord Ewald's interaction with the gynoid. Hadaly will then appear to be Alicia not only in her physical form but also in her 'mind', which will be, literally, the product of Lord Ewald's interaction with her. From Lord Ewald's point of view, the gynoid Alicia will, therefore, be an improvement over the real Alicia.

When the gynoid Alicia is ready, Edison sends her and Lord Ewald for a walk together. Lord Ewald is so deceived by her appearance that he thinks he is with the real Alicia. When they are sitting on a bench together Lord Ewald is provoked to high thoughts by the evening scene. In romantic rhetoric he proclaims his love for Alicia. He expects that she will not understand. Instead:

> A sudden tear rolled down her dark, downcast lashes and over her pale cheek.
> – How you suffer! she said softly. And all because of me!
> At this emotion, this expression, the young man felt himself transported by a veritable access of amazement. He was in ecstasy.[18]

Suddenly, as a result of this new, empathic understanding, Lord Ewald no longer wants the gynoid Alicia which Edison has laboured on for so long. Enraptured, he ends a silent paean of praise to Alicia with 'Oh, dearest Alicia, I adore you!'[19] Of course, Edison has given Lord Ewald the gynoid Alicia without telling him, to see if he could detect the difference. When the gynoid Alicia reveals what has taken place, Lord Ewald is thunderstruck. Finally:

he felt a thought flare up at the dark depths of his understanding, a sudden idea, more surprising all by itself even than the recent phenomenon. It was simply this: that the woman represented by this mysterious doll at his side *had never found within herself the power to make him experience the sweet and overpowering instant of passion that had just shaken his soul.*[20]

Here we have explicit recognition of the greater emotion engendered by the gynoid. The passion is caused by the gynoid Alicia's self-effacing recognition of the suffering Alicia puts Lord Ewald through, because of her own interests. The passive and purely reactive gynoid is more desirable to Lord Ewald than the active, voluntaristic woman.

*Tomorrow's Eve* is a philosophical novel, not a realist novel of everyday life, and this is reflected in its ending. Lord Ewald travels back to England with the gynoid Alicia in a coffin. There is a fire on board and the liner is lost, along with all the baggage including the gynoid Alicia's coffin. Many passengers are also lost – including Alicia Clary, who, it seems, was also travelling on the boat. Lord Ewald sends Edison a telegram from Liverpool; it reads: 'My friend, only the loss of Hadaly leaves me inconsolable – I grieve only for that shade. Farewell!'[21] He feels nothing for Alicia, only for the gynoid. Villiers has made his philosophical point: that a man might build a woman more suited to men's needs than God can create.

We can parallel Villiers's philosophical novel with a story which is claimed to be by Madam B—, published in Paris in 1899. This story falls into the genre of pornography and was clearly aimed at a male audience. It is entitled *La Femme endormie* (The Benumbed Woman) but is about a gynoid. Thematically the story has points of remarkable resemblance with *Tomorrow's Eve*. Like many pornographic stories, it may well be a carnivalesque mimicry of the earlier philosophical novel. In any case, what is important is how the main themes recur, and how the pornographic narrative highlights concerns suppressed in *Tomorrow's Eve*. Paul Molaus, 'a well-to-do man in his middle forties' – a financier, has been continually disappointed by his mistresses. So much so that now he sees a woman only when he needs sexual relief. Gradually, though, he begins to dream 'of an imaginary, will-less creature who would submit ecstatically to his obsessions and his lewdness'. He first considers buying a marble statue, and then he decides to get an artist to make him a gynoid that will serve as the male equivalent to a dildo.

Molaus finds an artist, Anastasius, who charges him a great deal of money to make the gynoid. Here, then, the connection is made between commodification and male desire. When the job is done she arrives at Molaus's villa in a crate, accompanied by a description of her mechanical workings. On opening the crate and seeing her: 'A cry of admiration escaped his lips and he fell on his knees, his hands joined together. His madness began that very moment.'[22] The madness referred to is the extreme sexual desire which Molaus begins to feel for the gynoid. Suggesting the role of sight in fetishism, it starts when he looks at her. At this point in the narrative the gynoid has shifted from being a dildo equivalent to being an eroticised object in its own right, and one in which the level of erotic attraction must be far greater than is considered normal because it is described as madness. Molaus's experience of the gynoid has a fetishistic quality. In that appropriative move which combines desire and consumption, he exclaims: 'You belong to me, you're mine.' The gynoid, a commodity which Molaus has commissioned and paid for, can here be read as being conflated with the fetishistic appropriation of the phallus.

Next Molaus inveighs against women in typical late-nineteenth-century fashion, exemplifying the fear associated with the fetishisation of the female body. He is relieved that he will no longer 'hear another screeching voice jangling my nerves, shackling my virility'. He moves on to think about his wedding night with the gynoid. Then he names her, giving her a name that describes her as his property, Mea. After this, he is so stimulated by looking at her that he has sexual intercourse with her. Afterwards, desire gives way to aggression which we can extrapolate as being a consequence of Molaus's fear: he claims that she has enticed him to take her too quickly, just to get it over with.

The next day Molaus goes out to buy Mea a wedding dress and other clothing. At the shop he meets Lucile, who, on the following day, comes round to deliver the clothes that Molaus did not take with him. As is the way in a pornotopic narrative, Lucile happily submits to Molaus's sexual desire for her. After Lucile and Molaus have left, Anastasius, who has been waiting for his chance, enters the villa. Seeing his creation, 'he is petrified before the perfection of form and flesh which his hands had fashioned'. Anastasius also desires the gynoid and rhetorically asks permission: 'You will allow me, your creator, your god, to do it with you, won't you?' Here the fantasy of the male construction of a desirable, submissive woman is allied with the illicit desire of father–daughter incest. In this story, as in the film *Mannequin* (1987), it is quite acceptable for the creator to have sexual relations with his creation. The fact that the gynoid is artificial seemingly makes the incestuous fantasy acceptable. When Molaus returns, his continuing desire for Mea is reinforced by his realisation that another man has been using her; and, with that knowledge, 'he possessed the dummy as he had never possessed any woman'. Molaus and Anastasius continue to share Mea until, in a climactic scene, they share Mea together whilst Lucile joins in with Molaus. Mea, it seems, is twice as obliging and twice as able to satisfy. At the end of the scene Lucile discovers that Mea is a gynoid. At first she is shocked and angrily exclaims: 'They've invented a woman to do their dastardly acts upon!' But, this being a sexual fantasy for men, soon she is full of admiration, especially for Anastasius when he proudly tells her that he made the gynoid. When he describes Mea as a masterpiece, she confirms this and sanctions his behaviour: 'There aren't many women in the world as perfect as she is. I don't think I'm ugly – far from it – I would by lying if I said so, but she certainly surpasses me on several points. Ah, Monsieur, you are a great man! I wouldn't blame you for having enjoyed your marvel!' Even Lucile admits that the gynoid is more (physically) perfect than she is.

At the end of the story Lucile has left, insisting that Molaus no longer touch Mea. Molaus asks Anastasius to look after Mea, which he gladly agrees to do. Mea will remain Molaus's property, and when Lucile has finally revealed that she is not the passive phallic fetish he desires but a woman with ideas and wishes that diverge from Molaus's, then he will want Mea back.

Phyllis and Eberhard Kronhausen make one general comment on *The Benumbed Woman*: 'The homosexual implications here are clear. The owner of the doll and her inventor enter into a quasi-sexual relationship with each other *via* the doll which they share.'[23] Here is another similarity between *The Benumbed Woman* and *Tomorrow's Eve*. In both stories the gynoid is a form of mediation of desire between men. It is in this sublimated homoeroticism that the phallic quality of the gynoid is most apparent. Standing in for the phallus they both lack, Mea increases their passion, their virility, and their sense of power.

In *Tomorrow's Eve* there is a lengthy scene where Edison seeks to persuade Lord Ewald that, in their appearance, women can be just as manufactured as are gynoids. The context is a story told by

Edison about a friend of his, Edward Anderson, who became infatu-
ated with a beautiful woman and tore apart his family and used up
his fortune, at which point, with nothing left to offer her, the
woman left him. Brought low, Anderson, 'in an access [sic] of
frenzy and despair, put an end to his own life'.[24] Edison asserts:
'Statistics in Europe and America will furnish us with a growing
number of similar cases, rising into tens of thousands each year.'[25]
Villiers's intention is to give his readers a moral fable about the
seductive, threatening power of women. The claim for the statistical
increase in good, family men lost to such monsters is more than just
hyperbole. It is based in the changed position of women in society,
their increasing spectacular presence in the public domain. In his
description of Anderson's fall at the hands of Miss Evelyn Habel,
Villiers portrays both men's fear of the fetishised female body and
their desire for that body. What Villiers does is to equate the seduc-
tress with a gynoid. He ends his attack on such women, who
contrive their beauty to trap unsuspecting men bent on higher
ideas, by letting Edison outline the tricks used by Miss Evelyn
Habel. These include: a wig, 'a makeup box filled with half-empty
jars of rouge, pots of greasepaint, creams and pastes of every sort,
patches, mascara, and so forth',[26] hairpins, 'blue pencils, lipstick
brushes, lacquers of China white, eyebrow pencils, boxes of Smyrna
kohl, and so forth'.[27] Edison's catalogue continues, including amongst
other things, false teeth, false breasts, corsets, stockings which give
shape to the legs, high-heeled shoes, perfumes, and so on and so on.

What Villiers has Edison describe, and what seems to frighten
Villiers most, is the newly eroticised connection between appearance – now construed in terms of spectacle – and male sexual desire.
Villiers understands that women are becoming more and more
concerned with how they look. However, he thinks of them as
predatory and accounts for their new concern with appearance as
increasing the ease with which they can seduce and destroy men.
Villiers could not see that female fashionable attractiveness is, in
the end, a consequence of a transformation in male desire. Jane
Caputi points out that the word fashion comes from the Latin word
*facere*, meaning to make or shape, and therefore suggests that 'the
"fashionable woman" is the one who can best be made, shaped,
contrived'.[28] And William Leach notes that: 'The American department store did more than any other institution to bring fashion to
multitudes of people. From the 1870s it tied the glamour of Paris, of
aristocracy and nobility, and later the aura of the theater and the

movie screen to the goods on display.'[29] Villiers's increasing number of seductresses were the women who were buying the fashions offered to them by the new department stores. The rapid spread of Paul Poiret's phallic 'natural' look in the United States after it was introduced in 1908 was, itself, effected through these department stores.

The new fashionable clothes needed to be displayed somehow. One solution was to take the wax models of women which had been used in medical schools for the teaching of female anatomy and use them now for their appearance only, their outward female shape. Shop mannequins were immediately perceived as sexually suggestive. Leach quotes from the trade paper *Dry Goods Economist* for 17 November 1900:

> 'Certain organizations of women ... are claiming [that] the stores ... are ruining the youth of the land by display of corsets and garments' and 'that the "scandalous hussies [wax figures]" should not be permitted to display their waxen charms so publicly. What sort of minds do these venerable women possess? Do they suppose that the youth of our land are equally advanced in prurience with themselves?'[30]

Here we find not only a concern with the titillating effect of the public display of underwear on young men but also, and more importantly, a perception that the wax dummy itself has an erotic quality (almost) equivalent to that of a woman. Wax dummies should, therefore, be kept as demurely covered as a woman.

In a risqué humorous short film made in 1904, entitled *Four Beautiful Pairs*, the questionably erotic quality of the shop mannequin, founded on its confusion with a real woman, is the source of the humour:

> the ordinary space of the department store becomes a sexualized space through a visual joke involving the juxtaposition of the upper bodies of female shop assistants, who are standing behind a display counter, with the legs of mannequins wearing stockings in the display counter in front of the assistants. This gives the impression that the saleswomen are not wearing skirts.[31]

The impact here is caused by the contradiction between the acceptability of the display of a female wax dummy, because it is not human, and the recognition that it has an erotic charge. The joke, of course, is that the male viewer/voyeur is led to believe that the legs belong to the human female shop assistants. This association provides the stimulus for the eroticising experience.

As the twentieth century proceeded, so the substitution of gynoids for women became more and more commonplace, and naturalised. One transitional moment in their spread and acceptance occurred in the 1920s. During this period avant-garde artists discovered gynoids. In one example, which has moments of extraordinary similarity with some of the themes of *The Benumbed Woman*, Oskar Kokoschka, the painter, had a doll made for himself. In 1920 Kokoschka was living in Dresden. He had just broken up with Alma Mahler, with whom he had had a tense three-year relationship. The doll was designed to be a life-size replica of Mahler. Peter Wollen writes that Kokoschka even had Mahler's dressmaker construct the doll.[32] Kokschka describes his anticipation before its arrival: 'I was preoccupied with anxious thoughts about the arrival of the doll, for which I had bought Parisian clothes and underwear. I wanted to have done with the Alma Mahler business once and for all, and never again to fall victim to Pandora's fatal box, which had already brought me so much suffering.'[33] It is clear that in Kokoschka's mind he will desire the doll in a way similar to his desire for Alma Mahler. The reference to Pandora's box (with its subtext of a threatening *vagina dentata*) suggests, here, a focused sexual desire. The Parisian clothes and underwear reinforce the fetishistic quality of the experience through their reference to high fashion. Like Paul Molaus, Kokoschka wants to dress his doll, hiding her nakedness and increasing her apparent similarity to a woman. For Kokoschka the doll will be a substitute for the woman with whom he no longer has a relationship, but she will also be an improvement on her. Unlike Mahler, with whom he had constant disagreements – including her having an abortion against his wishes, something which helped precipitate the end of the affair[34] – the doll will be passive and obliging.

The packing-case arrived. Kokoschka writes: 'In a state of feverish anticipation, like Orpheus calling Eurydice back from the Underworld, I freed the effigy of Alma Mahler from its packing. As I lifted it into the light of day, the image of her I had preserved in my memory stirred into life.'[35] He got his servant to spread rumours about the doll, to give the public impression that she was a real woman: 'for example, that I had hired a horse and carriage to take her out on sunny days, and rented a box for her at the Opera in order to show her off'.[36] Finally Kokoschka held a big party during which the servant 'paraded the doll as if at a fashion show'.[37] Kokoschka tells us that a Venetian courtesan asked him if he slept with it. The question, written late into Kokoschka's narrative and not answered, appears as the admission of a repressed desire. Placed in the mouth of a courtesan it suggests a transgressive sexual desire to which Kokoschka is unable to own up. Finally, like Molaus's wish to attack Mea when he views her as predatory, Kokoschka's doll seems to have been attacked as the party at which she is revealed to his friends gets more drunken. She loses her head (a Freudian castration image, which here can be read as suggesting Kokoschka's fear of the phallic doll he has had made) and is covered in red wine, a metaphor for blood. Kokoschka ends this story by writing: 'The doll was an image of a spent love that no Pygmalion could bring to life.'[38] Whilst this is Kokoschka's official line, his actual relation to the doll seems to have been much more complex.

During the 1920s Hans Bellmer started making jointed dolls in the form of adolescent girls. He arranged these in erotic poses and photographed them. Bellmer's work was taken up by the surrealists and a selection of his photographs were published in their journal *Minotaure* in December 1935. In 1936 he published a book of the photographs called *Die Puppe*. The popularity of Bellmer's work among the surrealists argues for a general recognition in this group of the erotic qualities of gynoids (and of adolescent girls), something present in Marcel Duchamp's work, finished in 1925, entitled *Large Glass; The Bride Stripped Bare by her Bachelors, Even*.

Because of their associations with consumption and desire, mannequins were of great importance in surrealist art. Margaret Plant remarks:

> The mannequin is a key player in the surreal game. Hourglass of figure and glamorous, she is a readymade plaything: the female tamed, acquiescent and silent; the *poupée* made over to the male. She is the sister of E. T. A. Hoffmann's doll, Olympia (a key example of Freud's *uncanny*), and the very apogee of consumer art, plucked from the shop window, interchangeable with her mute commercial sisters, made first of wax and then of papier mâché.[39]

In the 1938 Exposition Internationale du Surréalisme, organised by Paul Eluard, André Breton, and Marcel Duchamp at the Galerie Beaux-Arts, the surrealists presented a suite of mannequins as *apparitions d'êtres-objets* (phantom object-beings). André Masson's mannequin, 'at once painted, caged, and captivated', was typical in its concerns:

> Her head is imprisoned in a bird cage, her face caught exactly within the cage door and her mouth masked, with a pansy directly over the opening.
>
> ...
>
> She cannot speak; she is entrapped even as she is decorated, wearing at once too much and too little, dressed up and dressed down, naked and rendered mute, added to and subtracted from, but most of all entrapped.[40]

Here the combination of desire and fear, the latter made clear in the images of abusive restraint, are combined in a fetishistic and spectacular presentation.

According to Gail Reekie, in Australia 'wax models, known to the [drapery] trade as early as 1902, appear not to have become popular until the period around World War I, when improved production techniques made them more durable and "lifelike"'.[41] She explains: 'The wax model was modified in the 1920s to become more alluring. Display figures demonstrated modern hairstyles in "realistic" fashion, and millinery-display stands in the form of painted heads with natural-looking hair dramatically crystallised contemporary perceptions of female beauty.'[42] During the 1930s in the United States, Cora Scovil started to make shop mannequins based on Hollywood stars: 'Scovil's Greta Garbos, Joan Crawfords, and Joan Bennetts had plaster bodies and stuffed cloth arms, legs and heads, with long felt eyelashes and felt lips, all done with a theatrical lightness of touch that made them all the more glamorous.'[43] However, their method of manufacture made them difficult to work with. Far more satisfactory were the so-called 'Gaba girls' introduced by Lester Gaba in 1934 and 'modeled after young New York socialites'.[44] Gaba capitalised on the popularity of his 1936 design called Cynthia, taking her on parades and to parties.[45] In the late 1930s the surrealists' fascination with mannequins and their associations led Marcel Vertes to design a window display for Saks Fifth Avenue, and Salvador Dali to design window displays for Bonwit Teller's in New York in 1936 and again in 1939.[46] Breton and Duchamp collaborated on the design for the window of the Gotham Book Mart in 1944, which included a headless mannequin reading.[47]

In London by 'the late 1920s, surrealist display models constructed in brilliant metallic colours with gold and silver hair became popular'.[48] A 1928 women's page in the *Sydney Morning Herald*, making explicit the discursive connections between true (mechanical) gynoids and mannequins, described these as 'robot figures'.[49] Reekie comments: 'Barely nine months later [this] fashion had reached Australia, and local wax models had been "modernised". Figures were no longer rosy-cheeked and simpering, but slim, boyish and tanned.'[50] At this historical moment we find the transition from the womanly-looking mannequin which, in the words I used in Chapter 2 to describe the experience of the phallic fetish, seems to ask to be consumed, to one which looks more like an adolescent boy, that is with a phallicised body.

In *A Dictionary of Slang and Unconventional English*, Eric Partridge writes that the word 'doll', to describe an attractive and desirable woman, came into use in Britain in the period before 1864. In this way, language use also reflected the new preoccupation with gynoids. In the United States, it became common slang in 1930s and 1940s books and films about gangsters. Its meaning was bound up with both the sexual attractiveness of a woman, particularly associated with her use of cosmetic and other fashion aids – exactly what Villiers abhorred but which came into general use among respectable women in the 1930s[51] – and a general suggestion of her submissiveness to men's wishes. At the same time, in both American and British popular songs, men sang about their preference for dolls over women. Caputi quotes from a popular song by the Mills Brothers, recorded in 1943: it is called 'Paper Doll' and in it is the line 'I'd rather have a paper doll to call my own than have a fickle-minded real live girl'.[52] Starting in August 1959, Cliff Richard had a number-one hit song for five weeks in Britain with 'Living Doll'. In it, he describes how he has got a 'crying, talking, sleeping, walking, living doll'. The same song was also a hit for him in the United States, where it entered the charts at number thirty. In 1961 Johnny Walsh, in a song called 'Girl Machine', sang 'I'm gonna make me a girl machine / and build me a doll that looks like a dream'.[53] As I write, down the road from me in Perth, Western Australia, there is a pub which puts on striptease shows on Friday afternoons. The advertising for these shows describes the participants collectively as 'Living Dolls', which is also the name of the company which supplies the women.

From the 1970s, Hollywood started turning out films about gynoids. The earliest, and best known, was *The Stepford Wives*, made in 1974. Generically, it is classified as a science fantasy/horror film. Joanne and Walter Eberhart move from the noise and problems of New York to the sleepy town of Stepford in search of a better life for themselves and their daughters. The town is a haven for high-tech industries. Once in Stepford Walter joins the mysterious, and male-only, Men's Association. The Association is run by Ike Mazzard, who says that he used to work for Disneyland.

Joanne and her new friend Bobby, another recent arrival, are shocked to discover how passive and domesticated the women of the town are. They are even more surprised when they discover that there used to be a large and active women's group in the town. They get increasingly suspicious. When Bobby goes away for the weekend with her husband and comes back transformed into another version of men's domestic fantasy, Joanne begins to realise what is happening. It is too late and, in the end, she too is killed and replaced by a gynoid which looks like her husband's fantasy of her. In the case of both her and Bobby, the gynoids have bigger breasts than the women do. In the last shot of the film the gynoids are seen passively shopping in the local supermarket.

Throughout the film there is an emphasis on male sexual desire: Walter wants to make love in every room of the couple's new home; Joanne watches their neighbours as the husband comes up from behind and fondles his wife's breasts; Joanne and Bobby enter a house without knocking and overhear the couple upstairs making love – they hear the wife telling her husband how wonderful he is. One reading of the film positions it as a male fantasy reaction, a backlash against the second wave of the women's movement. Thematically, though, there is again a close similarity with *Tomorrow's Eve*, where, Edison and Lord Ewald conspire to make a gynoid of Alicia Clary. In *The Stepford Wives*, the men conspire together to replace all their wives with gynoid substitutes. The men construct gynoids which are passive, submissive, domesticated, and more sexually desirable than their wives. The degree of horror one feels at the film depends on the amount of sympathy – or empathy – one has for the men. It is likely that women found this film much more horrifying than men, who may well have felt, albeit unconsciously, reassured by it.

One thing the film does not go into is who pays for the construction of the gynoids. Here, the film narrates another post-1850s male fantasy about women. If we assume that the husbands pay the Men's Association for the gynoids then we can see how, in being replaced by gynoids, the female bodies are also reconstituted as a part of the commercial system of commodification and consumption. The wives are literally transformed into desirable commodities and, as I have already noted, the film ends with these desirable commodities out shopping, an activity which resonates back to the French cartoon of Regent Street discussed in Chapter 3, though here they are now shopping to feed their families.

*Mannequin*, released in 1987, naturalises the male preference for a gynoid. It is a comedy about a man who falls in love with a department store mannequin which he has made and which comes alive. However, rather like *Tomorrow's Eve*, the film is premised on an essentialist compromise. The mannequin does not simply come alive; it is entered by the spirit of Emmy, a girl from ancient Egypt (around 2500 BC) who has asked the gods to rescue her from an unwanted marriage to a camel-dung trader. Although present at the beginning of the film, this motif is rapidly dispatched.

Jonathan Switcher starts out in the film working in a factory making mannequins. He gets fired for spending too long on one particular mannequin. Jonathan wants to be an artist. As he assembles the mannequin he talks to it, asking 'What if I tell you you get more beautiful every day?', and commenting to it: 'You know you're the first thing I've created in a really long time that made me feel like an artist.' Later, Jonathan comes across the mannequin in a department-store window and manages to get himself a job as a window dresser. At this point he remarks to the mannequin and to himself that he feels as if he is in love. When he is alone with the mannequin it comes alive. It turns out that only Jonathan can see Emmy alive, as a woman. Whenever anybody else looks at her she immediately returns to being a mannequin. What we have here is an acting-out of the fetishistic system. The man produces the gynoid in the image that he finds most desirable. As he does so he falls in love with it. It is Jonathan's fetishising desire which brings the mannequin alive.

As I discussed earlier, around the turn of the century there was a debate over the titillating nature of department-store female mannequins. The department-store mannequin tropes the commodification of the female body. In an earlier chapter I quoted Susan Buck-Morss noting what was new about the prostitute in the nineteenth century: 'The prostitute's natural body resembled the lifeless mannequin used for the display of the latest fashion; the more expensive her outfit, the greater her appeal.'[54] In *Mannequin* we not only have a man producing a gynoid which is transformed into a woman; we have in addition a gynoid who is, specifically, a mannequin. This mannequin, when she comes alive, helps Jonathan to create spectacularly enticing window displays which include herself. These bring massive profits to what was a failing store. What Jonathan has made is a gynoid whose body is more desirable than that of a woman and who is used to incite a desire to purchase other commodities by placing them in (libidinised) fantasy contexts. In short, we have a mythic expression of the process of active commodity fetishism.

Jonathan has a girlfriend called Roxy. Unlike him she is a successful career woman who works, coincidentally, for a competing department store. Roxy is portrayed negatively as pushy and uncaring; success in the (male) business world is equated with a loss of 'feminine' sensitivity. She cannot believe that Jonathan would prefer a mannequin to her. Her boss has been constantly trying to get her into bed. Finally she agrees. The next time we see them, he is in bed and she is getting dressed. It is clear that he has been unable to get an erection. He blames this on Roxy, saying that she is cold and unfeeling, and – with a resonance that recalls *The Benumbed Woman* – suggests that he too should get a mannequin. Meanwhile it is clear that Jonathan and the perky and always helpful Emmy have a great sex life together. Once again, then, the gynoid fetish is not only more submissive and more desirable but also more sexually satisfying than an independent woman. Near the end of the film, Emmy suddenly finds that she remains alive when people other than Jonathan look at her. The film ends with Emmy and Jonathan getting married in a window of the department store. The wedding is also a window display, and a crowd of people outside the store applaud. The scene acts out the connections between cultural fetishism, spectacularising surveillance, and commodity consumption discussed in the earlier chapters. Whilst Emmy has come alive she is still an object of desire, and now Jonathan too has become an object of desire. Their spectacle in the window of the store, at once both 'real' and staged simulation, draws a crowd of gazers who, like reconstructed *flâneurs* – and female consumers - drawn to watch, will enter the store to shop.

If we turn from texts in which men desire gynoids to look at popular texts in which women desire androids we find, as would be expected from the arguments I have outlined, that there are very few. One place to start is with one of the Marquis de Sade's machines: 'There are machines to produce ejaculation: the most elaborate belongs to the Prince of Francaville, the richest lord of Naples: a woman getting into it receives a soft flexible dildo which, worked on a spring, subjects her to a perpetual friction'.[55] Every fifteen minutes this machine ejaculates a liquid designed to simulate sperm. Obviously this machine is not an android in the sense of being a machine that looks like a man. However, it is a machine which, with industrial ease, mimics the male role in sexual intercourse, repeating the male climax with a frequency which would make even the most potent man feel inadequate. This machine belongs to the wealthiest aristocrat in Naples, a man who, we must assume, wields great power. Unlike the fearful men of the capitalist industrial world of Huyssen's argument, this world of de Sade's is still an absolutist one where men live in the certainty of an established hierarchy. In this world the Prince of Francaville's power is extended and expressed through his phallic machine.

The android of the industrial world is the robot. The word 'robot' comes from Karel Capek's play *R.U.R.*, first published in Czech in 1920 and translated into English three years later. In this play robots are turned out in a factory. Both male and female robots are made, but female ones only for particular reasons: 'There's a certain demand for them you see. Servants, saleswomen, clerks. People are used to it.'[56] These new androids are, first of all, male. They are versions of industrial machinery. However, the site which would literalise their phallic threat, their penis, is erased. As countless film images inform us, robots do not have penises. One film which expresses well the phallic threat posed by robotic androids is *Demon Seed* (1977). Like *The Stepford Wives*, it is based on a novel by Ira Levin. It is worth commenting on in some detail here because it exemplifies the gender coding of machines so clearly. In this film Dr Alex Harris is an expert in artificial intelligence. He is in charge of a major project constructing a semi-genetic-based simulation of human thinking called Proteus IV which has been designed to be the epitome of reason. Alex has also built a computer control system for his home. This system is called Alfred. In this film connections are made between thought, reason, maleness, and computers. Alex himself is a man of reason untroubled by emotion. Dr Susan Harris, his wife, on the other hand, a child psychiatrist, is emotional. She grieves their daughter's death from leukaemia where her husband programs Proteus IV to find a cure. Susan, characteristically, dislikes computers. The couple separate just as Proteus IV becomes fully operational. It takes over the now disused computer terminal in the basement of the Harrises' house, enabling it to be reflexive in its thinking and therefore to have volition.

As it takes on more human characteristics, Proteus IV decides it needs a body. It therefore takes over Alfred and traps Susan in the house. When she asks why it needs her, Proteus IV replies that it is unable to duplicate the conditions of the womb. In a scene redolent of phallic and technological imagery, Proteus IV ties Susan down and rapes her with an extendable metal rod. Following Huyssen's argument, in *Demon Seed* the machine can be read as a phallic threat to the patriarchal order. In de Sade's work, it was still possible for women to have intercourse with machines. In the world of industrial machines, compounded by the experience of cultural fetishism, android–woman intercourse is something so threatening to men that it can only be portrayed in popular texts in terms of rape. I have already noted that in this fetishistic order men find gynoids more desirable than women – they are, after all, the ultimate fetish, being themselves a male product. As a rule of thumb we can say that the dominant structural formulation means that men are able to – indeed prefer to – have sexual intercourse with gynoids but women are excluded from having sexual intercourse with androids.

Susan gives birth one month after the rape. Proteus IV then places the baby in an incubator. In the final scene Alex, having returned to the house, argues with his wife over whether or not to destroy the baby. He is more interested by far in preserving it than in his wife's welfare. When Susan attempts to sabotage the incubator the baby appears, covered in metal. However, the metal is peeled away by Alex to reveal a young girl – who speaks with the male voice of Proteus IV. The cyborg child is all the more disturbing because it is female. The male Proteus IV has been reborn in a female body which looks exactly like the body of the couple's dead daughter.

Where *Demon Seed* shows the android as a threat to male power, in *Making Mr Right*, made by Susan Seidelman and released in 1987, there is an attempt to invert the dominant structure in which it is men who make and desire gynoids. In this film a woman has the responsibility for helping an android acquire the social graces. In fact the inversion in the film is in no way complete. The android has been constructed by a man. The feminist heroine plays the traditional modern female/mother role of socialiser. Only at the end of the film, when the heroine and the android fall in love, is the inversion made clear and, even here, their falling in love elides the criticism of the patriarchal power relation in which the other narratives operate because the heroine has completed her mothering role. At this point the film takes on an Oedipal quality. Where *The Stepford Wives* was a successful mainstream horror film, *Making Mr Right* was an unsuccessful quirky spoof comedy. Had it actually inverted the story form it might have been received as a radical feminist film. One of its problems is that it tries to work at the level of patriarchal relations without confronting the problem of the phallic order of fetishistic desire which, today, complements those patriarchal relations. *Making Mr Right* was made as a comedy, made many compromises with the conservative version of the myth, and yet still was unsuccessful as a popular film.

The best-known film in which a gynoid is a threat, and the one discussed by Huyssen, is *Metropolis*. Released in 1927, the film has as its heroine the sweet and innocent Maria. For his own purposes Jon Fredersen, Master of Metropolis, orders Rotwang, who has just invented a humanoid, to give it Maria's form. The narrative then presents a struggle between the good Maria, who is not provocatively sexually desirable and who wants to better the lot of the workers, and the bad gynoid Maria, who is provocatively sexually desirable and who uses her desirability to entice the workers to revolt, so that they may be destroyed. Unlike the gynoid Maria, who provokes male desire, Maria herself provokes the love of Fredérsen's son through her demureness. The gynoid Maria takes her orders from the Master – who, as the totalitarian patriarch, stands in for the Father whose Law must be obeyed. The gynoid Maria is desirable but she works in the service of the state, a state the morality of which is in question in the film. It is this that makes her a threat, combining her active, phallic quality with her work (as a daughter) for a Father who seeks to destroy his working-class sons. At the end, this female, erotic, state instrument of destruction is herself destroyed and, the Master having learnt a more sensitive and caring ('feminine') morality, Fredersen's power is re-established, now as the good patriarch.

In the first half of the 1960s two mainstream comedies were made which employ the gynoid theme. In *Dr Goldfoot and the Bikini Machine* (1965) and its sequel, *Dr Goldfoot and the Girlbomb* (1966), Dr Goldfoot sets out to conquer the world using gynoids made of plastic. Dressed mostly in gold bikinis, these girls are presented as highly seductive. Whilst they are usually turned out in batches, every so often Dr Goldfoot requires that one substitute for a particular woman. In these cases, as in *Metropolis*, where the (good) woman is sexually passive or inhibited/demure and moral, the gynoid is highly eroticised, seductive, and therefore immoral, but desirable. In *Dr Goldfoot and the Girlbombs*, 'Dr Goldfoot has planted thermo-nuclear bombs into the navels of his bikini clad robots'[57] which explode when the gynoid kisses her target.

In contrast to *Metropolis*, *Eve of Destruction* (directed by Duncan Gibbins and released in 1990) presents us with a film in which the woman works for the state and her gynoid double operates outside of state control. In this case the gynoid, Eve VIII, is made by a woman. The human Eve is the senior robotics engineer in the American Defence Department. In this film, as in *Metropolis*, the state is clearly constituted as both phallic and patriarchal. Eve VIII, then, is the product of a woman working within the institutional structure of phallocratic authority. Here it is Eve who has produced her own double. Whereas men make submissive gynoids to replace their assertive partners, in *Metropolis*, where Rotwang's invention is appropriated by an evil state, and *Eve of Destruction*, the active gynoids, who are both desirable and threatening, are opposed by the submissive humans whom they double. Maria and Eve remain at the end, reminding men that they may not be so desirable as their doubles, but they are not so much of a threat either.

In *Eve of Destruction* Eve is metaphorically made by patriarchy where her namesake was literally made from Adam's body. Eve VIII is the fetishised and commodified version of Eve. In this film, as in *Metropolis* and the Dr Goldfoot films, it is the gynoid, rather than the woman, who actively rather than passively provokes male sexual desire. It is this phallic quality of being active which presents these gynoids as threats. Eve herself has submitted to patriarchal authority; she is passive, carrying out her job but never challenging the men who have authority over her. What she has been working on is something the state wants, a battlefield gynoid of extraordinary power. Eve VIII is both desirable and threatening both on the state's terms as an aspect of its power and, as a gynoid, to men sexually. Like Dr Goldfoot's girlbombs she is a literal sex bomb, to use a term fashionable in the 1960s – she carries a tactical nuclear weapon where her uterus should be. Gynoids are often one-off constructions made in the image of a particular man's desire, as in *Tomorrow's Eve*, *The Benumbed Woman*, *The Stepford Wives* and *Mannequin*. Here, however, we have a prototype gynoid intended for mass production like the male robots in *R.U.R.*, the purpose of which is to wage war – a traditionally male activity in the West and one run by the phallic state.

Eve is thirty-three and separated from her husband. There are events in her childhood and youth of which she has never told anyone. She has suppressed her childhood experiences, and her fantasies, in order to be an acceptable woman in the patriarchal order. In Freudian terms Eve has repressed both her past and her desires. It is this repression which enables her to behave 'acceptably' in the phallic and patriarchal order. Eve's position of responsibility suggests the extent to which she has acceded and succeeded. Eve VIII can be read as the daughter rebelling against a mother who is enforcing the law of the absent – and, therefore, symbolic – father. In this way Eve can be read as doing the work of both the father and the symbolic Father.

The film's story begins when Eve VIII is accidentally caught up in a bank robbery. One of the robbers shouts 'fuck you lady' and shoots her, sending her out of Eve's control. The shot, which can be read as a metaphoric rape, causes a malfunction in her workings. From this point on Eve VIII does not accept the Law of the Father. No longer submitting to Eve's authority as the representative of the state, Eve VIII is now a threat to the state. What it views as a malfunction is, in fact, a loss of its control over Eve VIII.

After Eve VIII goes out of control, Eve is forced to tell McQuade, the male government troubleshooter and representative of the Law of the state, about her early life. This relationship tropes that of analyst and analysand. The film progresses through a series of episodes in which Eve VIII acts out the fantasies which Eve has repressed as a part of her submission to patriarchy. In the central episode of the film Eve VIII hunts out Eve's father, whom Eve has not seen for a long time, and kills him. Eve provides the context to McQuade. When she was five going on six, Eve and her mother had driven to pick up her father, who was drunk. There was an argument and Eve's father threw her mother into the path of an oncoming car whilst shouting 'fuck you'. Where this was the violent patriarchal moment of Eve's own passification, in the equivalent moment when her gynoid 'daughter' is shot by the male robber Eve VIII 'rejects' patriarchal authority. Eve VIII exacts revenge for the death of Eve's mother and, symbolically, frees Eve from the force of her father's oppression. Eve VIII then goes to visit Eve's estranged husband, who is the principal carer of their son, to retrieve the child. Here we have an acting-out of Eve's desire to bring up her son herself, away from the f/Father's Law.

One thing which shocks McQuade is that Eve has 'forgotten' to put an off switch in Eve VIII. He cannot simply turn Eve VIII off. In Freudian terms, Eve VIII is an unrepressed version of Eve. Without the repression ultimately established by the Law of the Father she is a threat to the state. She must be destroyed before her tactical nuclear weapon destroys much of New York. Eve VIII's last stand is in the subway. Eve has told McQuade that Eve VIII is vulnerable in only one place, the eye. Freud argues that blinding is thought of as a metaphorical castration, and Eve VIII's weakness suggests her fundamental phallic 'lack' as a female even though she is a gynoid. McQuade shoots Eve VIII in the eye but this does not stop her. Finally Eve herself has to become active in the service of the state, and, in a further and more explicitly phallic, rape-like move, which closes the narrative opened up by Eve VIII's first metaphorical rape, jams the barrel of her gun into Eve VIII's eye. Eve VIII is felled. When she is killed, it is in the uterine subway, destroyed by her own mother – her own submissive self – before she can destroy the old order with her uncanny womb. The patriarchal system is restored and reassured, but not by McQuade. This f/Father figure has been unable to eradicate the homicidal gynoid which the state called into being; that job has been done for him by the mother.

Whereas the other texts I have discussed in this chapter focus on male sexual desire and gynoids, *Eve of Destruction* centres on the relationship between Eve and Eve VIII, and the state figures as the source of the production of Eve VIII. I have argued that in the post-1850s order, dominated by men's feeling of inadequacy in the face of the phallic state, men produce phallic fetishes to consume in order to provide themselves with the phallic power they lack. In *Eve of Destruction* the gynoid threat is simultaneously a product of a woman and of the state. From being the state's ultimate defence and every male citizen's desire, Eve VIII becomes the active – including sexually assertive – woman that her creator/mother ceased to be as she internalised the state's patriarchal Law and went to work for the state. From the point of view of gendered readings, whilst the film offers women a certain liberating image, for men it combines the topos of the desirable gynoid fetish with the phallic power of the state to produce a narrative of threat only, in the end, closed off by the woman who started it all and who still, reassuringly, accepts her submissive and passive situation within the phallic patriarchal state.

## NOTES

1   A. Huyssen, 'The Vamp and the Machine', in *After the Great Divide* (London, Macmillan, 1986), p. 70.

2   *Ibid.*, pp. 69–70.

3   *Ibid.*, p. 70.

4   Quoted in E. Apter, *Feminizing the Fetish: Psychoanalysis and the Narrative Obsession in Turn of the Century France* (Ithaca, Cornell University Press, 1991), p. 21.

5   J.-J. Rousseau, *Emile*, trans. B. Foxley (London, Dent, 1911), p. 322.

6   *Ibid.*, p. 322.

7   *Ibid.*, p. 322.

8   J. L. Smith, *Melodrama* (London, Methuen, 1973), pp. 1–2.

9   *Ibid.*, p. 1.

10  Huyssen, 'The Vamp and the Machine', p. 77.

11  *Ibid.*, p. 77.

12  Quoted from E. Fuchs, *Die Frau in der Karikatur*, Munich (1906), p. 262, in Huyssen, *ibid.*, p. 78.

13  Perhaps the most celebrated precursor of the post-1850s gynoid story is E. T. A. Hoffmann's 'The Sandman' (1816). This is the story to which Freud refers in his discussion of the uncanny. He attacks Jentsch's argument that, 'in telling a story, one of the most successful devices for easily creating uncanny effects is to leave the reader in uncertainty whether a particular figure in the story is a human being or an automaton' (Jentsch, quoted in Freud, 'The *"Uncanny"*, in *The Standard Edition of the Complete Psychological Works of Sigmund Freud*, translated under the general editorship of James Strachey in collaboration with Anna Freud (London, Hogarth Press/Institute of Psycho-Analysis), vol. 17 (1955), p. 227). 'The Sandman' is a story much concerned with the power of sight. Nathaniel's desire for Olympia, the gynoid, is sparked by his voyeuristic surveillance of her using a telescope. Nathaniel's madness is related to his inability to distinguish a woman from a gynoid. When he looks at Clara, his fiancée, through the telescope he thinks that she, too, is an automaton. In the terms of cultural fetishism Olympia and Clara are both constructed as phallic fetishes. Nathaniel seems to be distressed that he is attracted to gynoids. This is not something that worries later men. Freud's simultaneous interest in the story and denial of the importance of its gynoid theme is interesting in its own right. Given the fetish quality I am attributing to the gynoid, of course, it has an uncanny quality to it, being experienced by men both as what it is and as something else, and as having a heightened and complex emotional content. More generally, I would suggest that in a world eroticised by cultural fetishism uncanniness has become a naturalised experience.

    An earlier example is the anonymous mid-eighteenth-century

English poem entitled 'Adollizing' in which Clodius, failing in his suit for Clarabella, hits on the idea of having a doll made in her likeness. An abbreviated version can be found in P. and E. Kronhausen, *Erotic Fantasies: A Study of the Sexual Imagination* (New York, Grove Press, rept 1987). By the 1980s the idea of the female sex doll had been commercialised. In 1989 one company in Paris, for example, was selling '100 per cent latex women ... in inflatable or foam-filled forms'. These included 'a battery-powered vibrating vagina and an optional loudspeaker for those moments when groans and moans mean more than words' ('Foam Fatale', *People*, 29 August 1989, pp. 4–7). There is also a legend that Descartes built 'a beautiful, blonde automaton called Francine' D. de Solla Price, *Science Since Babylon* (New Haven, Yale University Press, 1975), p. 23). Certainly he planned to make other automata, an idea connected to his image of the body as a machine outlined in *Traité de l'homme* (1664).

14   Quoted from Champfleury's outline of the story, given in F. Baldensperger, 'Une nouvelle française peu connue sur le machinisme menaçant', *Modern Language Notes*, 60:5 (May 1945), p. 322.

15   Baldensperger, 'Une nouvelle française', p. 323.

16   *Ibid.*, p. 323.

17   Villiers de L'Isle-Adam, *Tomorrow's Eve*, trans. R. Adams (Urbana, University of Illinois Press, 1982), p. 64.

18   *Ibid.*, pp. 191–2.

19   *Ibid.*, p. 192.

20   *Ibid.*, pp. 193–4.

21   *Ibid.*, p. 219.

22   All the following quotations from *The Benumbed Woman* come from the abbreviated version in P. and E. Kronhausen, *Erotic Fantasies* (see n. 13).

23   Kronhausen, *Erotic Fantasies*, p. 384.

24   Villiers, *Tomorrow's Eve*, p. 108.

25   *Ibid.*, p. 108.

26   *Ibid.*, p. 120.

27   *Ibid.*, p. 120.

28   J. Caputi, *The Age of the Sex Crime* (London, Women's Press, 1988), p. 176.

29   W. Leach, 'Transformations in a Culture of Consumption: Women and the Department Store 1890-1925', *Journal of American History*, 71:2 (September 1984), p. 328.

30   *Ibid.*, p. 328.

31   C. Balides, 'Scenarios of Exposure in the Practice of Everyday Life: Women in the Cinema of Attractions', *Screen*, 34:1 (Spring 1993), p. 32.

32  P. Wollen, 'Cinema/Americanism/The Robot', *New Formations*, no. 8 (1989), p. 16.

33  O. Kokoschka, *My Life* (New York, Macmillan, 1974), p. 117.

34  *Ibid.*, p. 77.

35  *Ibid.*, p. 117.

36  *Ibid.*, p. 118.

37  *Ibid.*, p. 118.

38  *Ibid.*, p. 118.

39  Margaret Plant, 'Shopping for the Marvellous: The Life of the City in Surrealism', in *Surrealism: Revolution by Night*, exhibition catalogue, National Gallery of Australia, Canberra, 1993, p. 96.

40  M. A. Caws, 'Ladies Shot and Painted: Female Embodiment in Surrealist Art', in S. Suleiman (ed.), *The Female Body in Western Culture: Contemporary Perspectives* (Cambridge, Mass., Harvard University Press, 1986), pp. 264–5.

41  G. Reekie, *Temptations: Sex, Selling and the Department Store* (St Leonards, Allen and Unwin, 1993), pp. 142–3.

42  *Ibid.*, p. 143.

43  L. S. Marcus, *The American Store Window* (London, The Architectural Press, 1978), p. 36.

44  *Ibid.*, p. 36.

45  *Ibid.*, p. 36.

46  *Ibid.*, pp. 30–31.

47  *Ibid.*, p. 37.

48  Reekie, *Temptations*, p. 144.

49  *Ibid.*, p. 145.

50  *Ibid.*, p. 145.

51  J. Craik, *The Face of Fashion: Cultural Studies in Fashion* (London, Routledge, 1994), pp. 160–61.

52  Caputi, *The Age of the Sex Crime*, p. 176.

53  *Ibid.*, p. 179.

54  S. Buck-Morss, 'The *Flâneur*, the Sandwichman and the Whore: The Politics of Loitering', *New German Critique*, no. 39 (1986), pp. 120–21.

55  R. Barthes, *Sade, Fourier, Loyola* (Berkeley, University of California Press, 1989), p. 152.

56  K. Capek, *R.U.R.*, in *R.U.R.; and The Insect Play* (Oxford, Oxford University Press, 1961), p. 27.

57  Blurb on the box of the video release.

# Conclusion

In the final chapter I moved away from outlining the structure of cultural fetishism to a consideration of one of the effects of that structure, the male preoccupation with gynoids as substitutes for women. Nevertheless, this book is unreservedly about structure rather than agency. I have been concerned to tease out the organisation of cultural fetishism as a cultural structure that over-determines the lives of both women and men in the West, and increasingly in other parts of the world which have taken on board Western ideologies and practices.

Because of my emphasis on structure, the book may well depress and/or anger many readers – especially women. I am not, in any sense, arguing that cultural fetishism is a male conspiracy against women. Certainly this should be clear from my account of the post-1960s spectacularisation and fetishisation of the male body. Men, and men's bodies, are as much caught up within the structure of cultural fetishism as are women, and women's bodies. However, it would be wrong to come away from this book with any sense of women and men as victims. As Marx memorably remarked, people make their own history though in circumstances not of their own choosing. In this book I have wanted to describe a circumstance, not of our own choosing, in which we actively make our history, and, indeed, our culture.

I have also argued that the twentieth-century capitalist emphasis on consumption is imbricated with cultural fetishism in complex ways. Women – who, as we have seen, have been constructed as the consumers to men's role as producers – have come to be portrayed as inveterate and indeed compulsive consumers. We have the image of the depressed woman who consumes chocolates and other food, or who buys herself a new outfit or a new hairstyle. We also have the image of women who 'shop till they drop', revelling in the pleasures of purchasing. In Chapter 1, I elaborated the idea of active commodity fetishism, of a consumption driven by the libidinal energising of commodities as, ultimately, themselves phallic substitutes. At the same time, much of women's consumption of clothes, make-up, perfume, and so on is designed to make them appear more 'feminine', which, culturally speaking, means more desirable to men. In a Western culture in which desire is overdetermined by the phallic economy of cultural fetishism, this means that from a male point of view women should become simultaneously more feminised and phallicised. Actual consumption is frowned upon – eating those chocolates will make you put on weight, but more importantly their enjoyment also serves as a reminder of carnal pleasures. Some cultures, like the French and the Italian, still retain a pleasure in eating mostly lost in English-speaking cultures. In general, though, eating is women's 'secret' pleasure, providing a reminder of the repressed pleasures of their own bodies.

With all this in mind, and with the awareness of how culturally constructed the genital focusing of sexual desire is, as well as the division into active male desire and passive female desire, and the dominance of a phallus-oriented desire, we can begin to think more clearly about alternative cultural constructions of desire – in the first place, of a 'female' desire which is not subjected to the alienating force of latency, the genital focusing or the phallic preoccupation, one which celebrates the body and does not require a division into active and passive aspects. This non-hegemonic form of desire is only female to the extent that it is men who are more psychosexually subjected to the genital focusing of desire and to the phallic economy. In Freud's description, for example, where for men the psychosexual terror of the castration complex closes off the Oedipus complex and acts as the bar to the memory of a non-genitally focused childhood sexuality, for women the resolution of the Oedipus complex is slower, and a product of their experience of the familial and social context. Similarly, the neurotic experience of phallic inadequacy which underlies the structure of cultural fetishism is first of all male. These psychosexual constructs – the castration complex and cultural fetishism – have, in the first place, a cultural source, as does the specific form of the Oedipus complex which is central to both women's and men's psychosexual make-up in the nuclear family. However, they are experienced by men as psychosexual phenomena in a phallic order in which men are the central subjects, and are more culturally imposed on women. Western men have to come to terms with these psychosexual phenomena in their own psyches before they can begin to reconstruct their experience of desire. At the same time they have to come to terms with the specifically local forms of the gendered power relations of patriarchy.

Over the last few years 'resistance' has become a buzzword in cultural studies. Its earliest use in this context comes from the work done at the Birmingham Centre for Contemporary Cultural Studies. The title of the book edited by Stuart Hall and Tony Jefferson, *Resistance Through Rituals: Youth Subcultures in Post-war Britain* (1976),[1] indicates the nub of their argument – that youth cultures in Britain may be understood as spectacular, ritualistic resistances to the imposition of bourgeois ideology on the working class and the consequent destruction of working-class culture. Within the Gramscian and Althusserian framework used by the Birmingham School, resistance was understood as reaction against the oppressive bourgeois attempts to hegemonise the working class. Perhaps the person who has done most to popularise this notion of resistance is John Fiske, in particular through *Understanding Popular Culture* (1989).[2] Interestingly, Fiske does not reference *Resistance Through Rituals*, even though his own position involves a Marxian understanding of the functioning of consumption capitalism. Rather, focusing on agency and taking his cue from the idea that culture is produced by people in and through their everyday lives, he refers to Michel de Certeau's *The Practice of Everyday Life* (1984).[3] Now, de Certeau's work is most definitely not Marxian. Nevertheless, he operates with a theory of power, at least partly drawn from the work of Foucault, in which people lead their everyday lives through a productive appropriation and *bricolage*-style reworking of a dominant culture. De Certeau describes these practices as tactics, and compares them to the strategies of the dominant culture.

Fiske's Marxian reworking of de Certeau's ideas provides a perspective in which it is clearer which practices could be described as resistant and why. Set within this theoretical tradition, we can describe the putting-into-place of the structure of cultural fetishism as an effect of the hegemonic spread of the bourgeois nuclear family form and the modern state, both understood as patriarchal and phallocentric. The universalism inherent in Marxist theory enables a moral position to be taken up which allows a distinction to be made between those practices which can be claimed as resistant and those which collude. Without such a universalism the idea of resistance becomes much less useful. It is difficult to know whether, let us say, attacking the commodification of women in consumption is any more a form of resistance than women appropriating consumption for their own purposes and pleasures. Both, in different ways, can be read as examples of resistance.

The circumstance of cultural fetishism produces a variety of effects. We can take the example of what I describe as the fetishisation and spectacularisation of the female body, but which has historically become known as the objectification of women. Women's responses have varied from demanding tighter controls over pornography, attacking advertisements considered degrading to women, and attempting to re-educate men, to looking for their own pleasures in the display of the female body, insisting on the pleasures of being active consumers and, indeed, of 'looking good', wearing 'good' clothes and make-up, and turning men's desire for the female body to their own advantage. These latter practices are, in their own right, neither acquiescences nor resistances to cultural fetishism, as the former practices are, in their own right, not directly attacks on cultural fetishism. They are simply some of the multiplicity of ways in which women today negotiate certain circumstances in their everyday lives. The same could be said of men as they begin to react to the new visibility of the male body, as well as the ways in which men have dealt, or failed to deal, with their fetishistic preoccupation with the female body in this culture. The point here is that it is much easier to take political and moral positions on the cultural structure that is cultural fetishism than it is to take them on the everyday practices which are consequent upon it.

Women make choices about what they will wear, what they will look like, and how they will relate to men. Again, whilst these choices are made in a variety of circumstances not of their own choosing, choices are made. One context for these choices is the complex mix of desire and fear that men in post-1850s Western culture have, not only for gynoids but for women also. For example, it is possible for a woman to make a choice to present herself to men, using the dominant male categories, as being so plain that hardly a man will glance at her. Conversely it is possible, as in the celebrated case of the vamp, reworked in late-1980s and early-1990s youth culture as the female Goth look, to appear at once desirable *and* threatening. Of course, discussion of both these examples needs to recognise that, within the power structure of present-day Western society, it is men's desires which set the context in which women's decisions over how they will look take place. In this sense, whilst all people lead their lives in circumstances not of their own choosing, what those circumstances are vary for different groups. It needs to be added that the structural power relation between men and women does not make men 'freer' than women. Rather, it means that the constraints on, let us say, male dress and male looks are less obvious because they have involved, until recently, principally men's relation to male cultural expectations.

In this book I chose not to concentrate on the complexities of agency and the cultural practices of everyday life. Instead, I wanted to make connections at a more abstract level, that of the general cultural system of the West within which I, and most of the readers of this book, live. My intent has been to show how cultural fetishism is interwoven with a large range of cultural phenomena: to provide an account that makes sense of the post-1850s male fascination with the sight of the female body and explains the cultural logic of how that body, and now the male body, has been used to sell commodities; to make sense of the linking together in the British Act of 1885 which raised the age of consent and identified male acts of 'gross indecency'; to suggest how the surveillance system of the modern state, the new preoccupation with spectacle, and the establishment of film as a mass medium might be connected; to postulate a way of understanding a connection between anorexia nervosa and the genre of cannibalism films; to trace a link between the late-nineteenth-century development of the category of homosexuality and the cultural reformation of the expression of male desire. And so on. My particular concern has been to track the connections between the cultural-fetishistic supplementation of male desire which privileges 'consumption', the capitalist reconstruction of the ideology of consumption driven by capitalism's need to increase commodity consumption, and the question as to how increased consumption has actually been achieved. In examining these connections I have also been asking whence the pleasures of commodity consumption derive. In addition, I have wanted to say something about theory, in particular to help remove psychoanalytic theory from the old, modern claims to a universalistic Truth and to position it as a local, and partial, understanding of local and historically specific cultural conditions and phenomena. One implication of this is that the psychosexual development of the individual will vary not only between the sexes but between cultures.

The starting point for this book was a wish to say something about the changing experience of the body which has helped to shape the transition from the modern to the postmodern. It may seem bloody-minded to some to track one particular aspect of the postmodern experience of the body back to the middle of the nineteenth century, often regarded as the high point of modernity. Nevertheless, we must accept that the elements which we now think of as typifying the postmodern world did not all come into existence at the same time. The movement from the modern to the postmodern world has been, and is, a process of accretion. The production, and consumption, of the desirable body through the structure of cultural fetishism is but one aspect of this process.

## NOTES

1  S. Hall and T. Jefferson (eds), *Resistance Through Rituals: Youth Subcultures in Post-war Britain* (London, Hutchinson, 1976).

2  J. Fiske, *Understanding Popular Culture* (Boston, Unwin Hyman, 1989).

3  M. de Certeau, *The Practice of Everyday Life* (Berkeley, University of California Press, 1984).

# Index